# LYING IN STATE

# LYING
# IN
# STATE

*By STANTON GRIFFIS*

*DOUBLEDAY & COMPANY, INC., Garden City, N.Y., 1952*

*Library of Congress Catalog Card Number: 52-11622*

COPYRIGHT, 1952, BY DOUBLEDAY & COMPANY, INC.
ALL RIGHTS RESERVED
PRINTED IN THE UNITED STATES
AT
THE COUNTRY LIFE PRESS, GARDEN CITY, N.Y.

*To the staff of*

MEMORIAL CENTER FOR CANCER AND ALLIED DISEASES

*doctors, scientists and nurses alike*

*particularly to*

DR. C. P. (Dusty) RHOADS, DR. HAYES MARTIN

*and* DR. HENRY T. RANDALL

*who give their lives that other men may live*

*and in loving memory of*

DR. JULES ABELS

*who laid down his life for his patients.*

# FOREWORD

A long time ago, when I cracked many a bottle of *vin ordinaire* with Donn Byrne in the pubs of the French Riviera, just before his untimely death, he was writing a series of pieces called *The Changeling and Other Stories,* and as a preface to his dedication he wrote, "I could as little think of sending a story friendless into the world as I would of sending a child or horse or dog." So I have dedicated this story to some of my friends of Memorial Center for Cancer and Allied Diseases, which I have watched grow from a tiny, dreary, and almost hopeless institution to the magnificent congeries of hopes and buildings and laboratories which it is today. Perhaps they will befriend this writing, for it is theirs.

It may be that the American reading public will enjoy the story of a plain American businessman in government service and take it to their hearts. But if they do not, I shall weep no bitter tears, for the writing of it has been a labor of love, and I have set it on paper particularly for my children and my children's children.

My deep thanks and appreciation are due to Bennett Cerf, who has permitted me to reprint herein a large part of his inimitable "Story of Brentano's," which appeared in the *Saturday Review of Literature;* to Mrs. Helen Reid of the New York *Herald Tribune,* who granted me permission to use parts of an article entitled "Whirlwind in Warsaw," written by Jack Iams, which was published in the New York *Herald Tribune's This Week* magazine. My thanks go also to Miss Edna Ferber who suggested that the book be called "The Rover Boy," and who graciously permitted me to use a series of letters which passed between us at a time when the German-American Bund occupied Madison Square Garden for an evening. I acknowledge with appreciation the permission of Irving Berlin and the Irving Berlin Music Corporation to use the lines of Mr. Berlin's song "Lazy." Certainly my thanks are due to my faithful and hard-working secretaries: Mrs. Gertrude Lee Stearns, who for many years maintained scrapbooks of the newspaper clippings and speeches and other trivia of my life, and Miss Anne Erskine, who struggled with my dictation, my involved corrections, and the final typing.

It's been a lot of fun.

**STANTON GRIFFIS**

*San Sebastian, Spain*
*The Florida Keys*
*Bimini, Bahamas*
*The Surf Club, Miami Beach*
*1952*

# HOW IT ALL STARTED

*Madrid, Spain, November 6, 1951*

*Mr. Douglas Black*
*Doubleday and Company*
*9 Rockefeller Plaza*
*New York, New York*


*Dear Doug:*
    *This is to give you the startling news of an event which is due to astound and excite the publishing world in about a year and a half; the birth of a semi-whimsical, semi-serious book, being the life story of the son of a country minister and traveler who got into Wall Street by mistake and then found himself, to his great surprise, in the amusement business and later, to greater surprise, in the service of the Government—a sort of laughing autobiography.*
    *I have never kept a diary; I have no important State Department documents to reveal, but I have had a great life, a far-flung life, and I am always reminded of a conversation with the King of Egypt who said that he had been reading about me and I had covered a lot of waterfront. I quoted the remark of an old friend of mine from Texas who told me once that he had done every-*

9

*thing in his life "except preach the gospel and be a whore." The king looked at me thoughtfully and said: "I have never preached the gospel myself."*

*The story should cover briefly early days in college when I ran the college paper, traded advertising space for trousers, and did about everything else except go to classes; a short period as a farmer in Oregon; a dive into Wall Street, interrupted by service in the First World War. Then a few years of money grubbing, specializing in industrial reorganizations, and later the show business period covering the organization of the Katharine Cornell Productions, purchase of control of Madison Square Garden, and finally some years as Chairman of Paramount Pictures. There was a concurrent job of about ten years as Chairman of the Finance Committee of Cornell University, following that, beginning in 1942, ten almost uninterrupted years of Government service. The story might tell for the first time my part in the secret work under the aegis of OSS (covering Sweden, Finland, Portugal, and Spain), the operation of the far-flung OWI propaganda motion-picture series, which I directed; the "now it can be told" adventure which ended the shipment of Swedish ball bearings into the heart of the German war machine; then the last year of the war as head of the American Red Cross in the Pacific Islands. Finally five years of what is known as diplomacy, covering service in Poland, Egypt, Argentina, and then the finish—the Spanish adventure, all trouble-shooting jobs. It might even include by that time the really astounding story of through whom and how Mikolajczyk escaped from Poland. It is a far cry from his own published account.*

*The book when, as and if written will contain a good many kindly jibes at the State Department and a good many that will not be very kindly at all, for I shall never enter public life again and I can breathe the free air of anti-bureaucracy. It will contain, of course, a deep and friendly tribute to all publishers, who by the time the book is written will no doubt have ceased their perennial habit of eating their young.*

*Now I am writing to you and to one or two other old friends in the business to ask some questions and perhaps get some advice at this strange time of life when a bookseller who has sworn never to add to the general chaos by bringing another book into the world, violates his oath.*

*On account of the fabulous Irish income which I have obtained from bookselling, which accordingly, puts me in an intellectual atmosphere far above ordinary mortals, I do not wish to soil my hands further with any of the filthy lucre for which so many authors and publishers so avidly strive. However, if there are any such things as royalties to be found through this book, I should like them to go to what has become one of my main interests in life, the development of Memorial Center and Memorial Hospital. So I would plan to give this brain child of mine to Memorial, and being now allergic to such things as business relationships, you would have to make your contract with them. I would propose, upon my resignation here next year, to go to Florida to write and return the fruit and flowers of my work to you in New York for research and comment.*

*Altogether is the whole idea any good?*

*In all this adventure I would appreciate your advice even though it turns out to be only a shot in the dark and a kindly hand to your long-time grocer boy of Brentano's. Perhaps you will want to turn this letter over to Ken McCormick or whoever is your chief obstetrician for trade books.*

*With every good wish,*

*Sincerely yours,*
STANTON GRIFFIS

# CONTENTS

# CONTENTS

# ILLUSTRATIONS

# ILLUSTRATIONS

# LYING IN STATE

# CHAPTER ONE

## ABOUT TITLES

I was raised in an atmosphere of books. The parsonage of the Shawmut Congregational Church on Tremont Street in Boston, where I was born and spent my baby years, was lined with them. A few years after my birth we moved to Ithaca, New York, where my father felt it was far cheaper and easier to educate his tribe; and I can still remember the sanctity of father's great library there, with every inch of wall space covered with bookcases filled with volumes of every kind. Even the spaces above and below the windows did not escape, and I remember well the old-fashioned ladder which ran on rollers around the room to locate the books on the shelves above the reaching space of humans.

I can remember the constant clicking of the typewriter as my father walked up and down the room dictating to his secretary, my much loved and faithful stepmother, one of his voluminous output of volumes: Japanese and Dutch history, fairy tales, and biographies of Americans associated with the two countries of his dreams. First always was Japan, where around 1870 he was the first American to penetrate the interior and, as a teacher, to see the nation at the end of its feudal system. He was a minister of sorts, but his real interests lay in travel and writing, and despite his publication of thirty books during his lifetime, I doubt if he ever much more than kept the wolf from the door of his household by his tremendous work and high erudition.

From this constant contact with books and talk of books, I came to realize that they, together with children and paintings and dogs and boats, indeed plays and motion pictures, were never to be sent out into the unfriendly world without a name or title. In later years when I became a bookseller myself, and spent many years as an executive of Paramount Pictures, I often wondered at the ingenuity of the human mind which could create such a variety, and a fantastic variety at that, of titles. I remember once when Alexander Woollcott, who had spent some week ends with me on my boat on Long Island Sound, called me up one day at my downtown office and asked to borrow *Lloyd's Register of Yachts*, for from his apartment at the end of 52nd Street he was constantly watching the ebb and flow of yachts at the River Club across the way, and was impressed with the utter stupidity of most of their titles. His pleasure was contempt and his *New Yorker* article on boat names particularly ferocious.

In the motion picture game I have frequently watched a meeting of super-minds spending hours to decide on the title of a picture. Had it been used before? was it too long or too short? did it mean anything? and—above all—would it bring them into the box office? The mountain of minds would heave and bring forth such titles as *Chartreuse Love, Walk a Crooked Mile*, or some other strange concoction having nothing at all to do with the contents of the film. In the many thousands of books through which I have plodded in my life, I have thought many times that the author should properly explain his title in advance, placing the explanation perhaps with his dedication and his copyright notices. He should not depend on the family cat to bring in a line from Shakespeare or the Bible, shattering the context on page 398 in some extraneous and always labored fashion.

So for this writing I am going to follow my own dictum and

explain at the beginning why I wanted to call this book *The Descent of Horatio Alger*. Probably it isn't box office, but it is truth.

I have referred before to the bookishness of my life in the family of a father who was one of the last of the old encyclopedic minds. My mother, one of the early graduates of Vassar College, was the daughter of a professor of Greek in Union College. Legend says that she often used to teach his classes when the professor was indisposed. On both sides of my family there were generations of preachers, of professors, and of savants; Americans all, back through the scholarly age of that vanished type, so rare in the bustle and roar of the atomic days.

Certainly I do not think that father ever earned more than three thousand dollars a year as a minister. But somehow he managed by writing and by lecturing. My childhood household memories are of the combination cook and maid of all work in the house, but also frequent trips to Europe given us free by the Holland-America Line because of father's books; of being dragged through all of the cathedrals and museums of Europe after long study periods in the evenings, and this whether or not we were properly clothed or fed. Yet I remember no starvation in the household, and I can always remember my mother saying that ours was "plain living and high thinking." I can remember Sunday mornings in my father's library, when I was required to read the New Testament in the original Greek, and I suppose that I could still read it today, yet I hope no one really tries me out on this.

So from the intellectual cathedral of my home in a small university city, and with definitely compulsory church life, I grew up in the Horatio Alger environment. As the son of a country minister, I had all the makings of Horatio's well-known hero. I carried newspapers and sold them, and devised every possible means to add to the microscopic allowances which my brother Elliot, my sister Lillian, and I were given, wangled my way through Cornell, and started out in the wicked world.

The rise of this Horatio Alger, so famous in song and story, lasted only a few years, while my intellectual road led me into the great fetish of the day—"back to the land," and I was for four years a fruit grower in Southern Oregon. But the cancer in my soul was there, a desire to accumulate a small fortune. And it grew apace. The realization that it was probably just as easy to starve to death in New York as in Oregon, and probably more pleasant, started my descent. It has been continuing ever since. Before I fell, I tried hard to hold tight to my intellectual heritage by serving a few months as professor of English in the Oregon Agriculture College, but ambition grew and temptation prevailed.

My first misstep, comparable to the first drink, the first cigarette behind the barn, was a grave one. I found myself in New York with a small job in Wall Street, and that has remained my home base until now when I sadly write these lines. But this was only the beginning of my descent. It was not many years before I found myself in the amusement business, dabbling with the theater, and becoming chairman of the board of Madison Square Garden, and finally chairman of Paramount Pictures. I was on the toboggan, and finally after service in two world wars, I took the last horrible step, going into the Diplomatic Service, where I found myself in rapid succession, United States Ambassador to Poland, Egypt, Argentina, and but recently to Spain. As I write these confessions, I am a beachcomber on a sleek white yacht in Florida. I can see no further ignominy ahead except perhaps the Bowery or daily luncheon at the Colony Restaurant.

So in brief, the story of my descent—"*Facilis descensus Averno.*"

Of this wayward and strange life I shall tell you more, but I shall try to call the shots as I have seen them, whether in business, in the world of masques and silver screens, or of that strange organized chaos known as the State Department and the Diplomatic Service.

I should add one final note about the title.

I was unable when the showdown came to call the shot. When it comes to naming a baby or a book, all friends of parents or authors share a morbid desire, as Jimmy Durante expresses it, to "get into de act." From the unconscionable numbers of titles suggested by me, or to me by willing friends, mine was the sole vote cast for *The Descent of Horatio Alger*, and in despair I asked my publishers to submit the whole horrid brew to their sales force and let them select their own title. I told these gentry salesmen in whose hands the fate of the book lay that they might call it anything except *The Death of a Salesman*. Without primaries or a struggle for delegates, *Lying in State* was nominated on the first ballot. I don't know what it means, but it sounds all right. The salesmen have named the baby, and I hope they feed it.

## CHAPTER TWO

## CHILDHOOD DAYS ENCHANTED

Ithaca, the home of Cornell University, nestling in the Finger Lakes district of central New York, is one of the beauty spots of the world. Just north of the little city is Lake Cayuga; three hills, east, south, and west, half-moon the lower end of the lake, and far above Cayuga's waters the Cornell campus rises in towering dignity. Here, more than a hundred years ago, came Ezra Cornell, the pioneer of the telegraph industry, to found "an institution where any person can find instruction in any study." Here was the home of Andrew Dixon White, of Goldwin Smith, and of many other intellectuals who came to aid the early development of the university. It was here in Ithaca that I grew up in the peace and security of the closing days of the last century, an idyllic atmosphere which, in the international storm and strain of today, we sometimes feel will never be seen again.

In retrospect, after a stormy life, and despite the little alarums and excursions of those days, it all seems like the end of one of my father's benedictions: the peace that passeth all understanding. The life of the household flowed with the calm regularity of Ithaca's Six Mile Brook, for father was the essence of careful habit. We were aroused from our beds promptly at 7:30, and after breakfast we assembled in his study for a short reading of the Bible, after which we knelt by our chairs while father prayed and we said the Lord's Prayer in unison. Never did we sit down to breakfast or midday or evening meal without a blessing in which we were all required to join. The day started, and we scattered to our respective schools, while father took his regular walk to the post office and returned to work in his study on his sermons or books until the noon dinner of those days. The master of the household then slept for exactly fifteen minutes, no more, no less, and again retired to his study until supper; he made a second pilgrimage for the mail at 7:00; again he worked, in his study, and at exactly 11:00, carrying his old-fashioned student lamp in one hand, he descended to the kitchen for his bottle of beer with cheese and crackers, inevitably toasting the cheese over the flame of the student lamp, much to the disgust of the family slavey.

Father eschewed electricity. He maintained that electric lamps were ruinous to the eyes, and while the household was at long last permitted this newfangled development, his working light remained a student lamp until the end. He especially hated the telephone. We could always tell when he had been forced to use it for he inevitably left the receiver dangling from the hook as though he had fled in disgust. His method of household accounting was a modern miracle. When he received bills he placed them carefully in the right-hand top drawer of his desk, and when some manna in the form of a check came in, he paid the top bills and left the older ones below in gentle oblivion. Walking up and down in the library dictating, or standing at work at an old-fashioned shelf desk correcting manuscripts with a stub pen, a gaunt figure with white mustachios, he will always remain in my memory as the picture of a contented, philosophical Christian man, not far separated from the spiritual world.

No child born since the turn of the century can understand much of those days. It was the end of the Victorian era. England and its empire guarded our world. Russia seemed a mystic land, interpreted to us only by its gloomy sagas. Japan was only beginning its great industrial expansion; and China was a great sleepy giant far away, of which we heard little except through the Christian missionaries to whom our churches regularly sent contributions of money or discarded clothes. For the child of those days, Mexico and the lands below its borders seemed largely settings for Richard Harding Davis revolutions, and there wasn't any neighbor policy either good or bad.

To be sure, there were little wars and rumors of wars. The sinking of the *Maine* in Havana Harbor in 1898, the year my mother died, brought a frenzy of patriotism and flag waving. We declared war on Spain, and troops marched off for Cuba. We were excited by the race of the battleship *Oregon* around South America to join the fleet in Santiago. We cheered at the thrilling news that Dewey had taken Manila, that the Rough-riders had charged up San Juan Hill, and that the final destruction of Cervera's fleet was accomplished as it dashed out of bottled-up Santiago. But it all seemed to the children of those days pretty much a musical-comedy war, as did the last imperialistic war of the British, against the Boers in South Africa. We did not even hear of a young subaltern, Winston Churchill, who served there.

Conservatives all, we feared the doctrine of William Jennings Bryan, running for the Presidency against McKinley, on a platform of "free silver" and the declaration that "You shall not crucify mankind upon a cross of gold." He was the shadow of the New Deal, but young and old in staunchly Republican Ithaca were relieved when McKinley was safely returned to the White House. It fell to my lot, while visiting the Pan-American Exposition in Buffalo during a late afternoon in September 1901 to see McKinley drive in to the grounds; only to hear later that he had been assassinated by an anarchist and was dying in the Milburn House in Buffalo. We followed the medical bulletins with bated breath, and sorrowfully learned of his death and the ascension of the great Theodore Roosevelt to the Presidency.

As exciting as all this must have been, it seems now a dress rehearsal in low-toned technicolor. As the son of the local Congregational minister, I pursued the usual course through grammar school and the Ithaca high school, doing all the usual things of usual children, excited by high school clubs and dances (these were the days of "The Merry Widow Waltz") and by cliquish friendships. Ithaca was dominated by the Treman family, prominent in its banks and its fabric of stores and enterprises, and to a poor boy, the Tremans seemed one and inextricable with the Morgans, the Rockefellers, and the other financial tycoons of whom we knew and read. But Bob Treman, the oldest son of the family, was about my age, and we became boon high school companions, forming a friendship which has never halted though I have chased unceasingly around the world and Bob has loyally and brilliantly carried out the traditions of his family, serving as a trustee of Cornell and one of its most faithful workers.

High school days came and went. I graduated when I was fifteen, took an extra year, and by that time was rolling in the luxury of an income. I was delivering the Cornell *Daily Sun* in the early morning to its local subscribers, my first and last time in the employ of a dramatic critic, for its editor was George Jean Nathan. I reveled in the job of high school reporter on the Ithaca *Daily News*, for which I was hired at $3.00 a week by my lifetime friend Frank Gannett, who during his lifetime has accumulated one of the largest chains of newspapers in the country, never ceasing to claim that in my first employment I was grossly overpaid by him. After I left high school our paths diverged, and it was twenty years later before I heard from him again, when he called me from Rochester to say that he wanted my banking assistance in raising some $20,000,000 to purchase the Chicago *News*, which had then come on the market.

After high school graduation, it still seemed early for me to go to college. My eyes had been troubling me through constant application to Greek script and I departed on a year of hoboing it around the country; during the first few months I had a job on a cattle ranch just south of Yuma, Arizona, and later, munificent employment with what was then known as the United States Reclamation Service. The Colorado River had just broken its banks and was rapidly forming the great Salton Sea, flowing to what is now a garden spot across the California border, the below-sea-level Imperial Valley. The Reclamation Service was building a great levee along the river, and as a brush cutter, rod carrier, and man of all work, I enjoyed the exciting times we occasionally had when the river went on a rampage and threatened all our lives. This was in 1906, when Yuma was almost the last of the old frontier towns. Nearly every building on its main street was a gambling house or a saloon, with the hospitality of women of all nations offered in the rooms above. Every Saturday night at our camp a few miles down the river, we would harness the six-mule team and pile into town for a shave and a bath, dinner at the Chinaman's, and a night of revelry and gambling at such high stakes as our respective incomes would permit. There would always come the dawn, and we struggled back to camp sadder and wiser. We did not know that we were seeing the end of an era.

In the springtime came the news of the San Francisco fire. The far-famed Yuma heat had become unbearable, and most of us promptly quit our jobs and left for the new scene of excitement at the Golden Gate.

I came into San Francisco on a train empty except for doctors and nurses. The city was still burning, but I finally acquired a room across the bay in Oakland, in which a gentleman of the local police force slept during the day and rented to me at night. The scene was incredible. It was almost impossible to get food, and I left quickly for Portland, Oregon, to sustain life by serving as a waiter in a restaurant, which I remember served a full meal, and a pretty good one at that, for 15¢. I was completely out of money, and too proud to write to my family for help, so by one means or another, and finally from the sale of my last pieces of high school finery, I got as far east as Iowa. There I remember a gruesome month of planting corn on an Iowa farm owned by a distant great-uncle of mine, who rewarded me with the wage of fifty cents a day, and board. But what board it was. I think it is the memory of those meals that has always made me covetous to own Grant Wood's great painting, The Threshers. However, the joyous memories of a magnificent farm supper were slightly dimmed when I heard my uncle stamping up the stairs at four o'clock in the morning to remind us that another day had come and that the cows must be milked before breakfast. By some means that I ill remember, the prodigal son returned to Ithaca in the summer of 1906.

For many years I had thought seriously of going to Princeton, urged in this academic direction by an uncle, a Presbyterian minister, somewhat of an eccentric, who had offered to lend me part of the money for my college education. I had thought much, too, of entering my father's college, Rutgers. However, I was home again. Ithaca was very beautiful, and the financial obstacles of board and room in another city seemed insurmountable. The opening of Cornell in the autumn found me, a townie, registered in the college of arts and sciences. Horatio Alger was going forward hopefully toward a college degree.

*CHAPTER THREE*

## BRIGHT COLLEGE YEARS

I never cared either in college or in the long days since about the marks a student made or the extent of his scholarship. If he learned to think, if he acquired intelligent reading habits and mastered the classic art of getting along with his fellow men (an art now grossly distorted under the name "public relations"), if he managed to avoid either excessive shyness or overconfidence, if he learned a *soupçon* of sportsmanship, and of give and take, he has been, for my money, a success in college; even though he may have got his diploma by a hairline.

Scientific students are, I suppose, an exception to this rule, but even so I have seen mediocre scientists become the heads of great companies, though I have seldom seen a brilliant scientist who could successfully manage the manufacturing and selling complexities of a major corporation. He usually had to leave these aspects of the work to men more exactly trained for the job.

Certainly none of these ideas was very clear in my mind in the autumn of 1906, but they were my subconscious guides.

Cornell was then a sleepy, central New York university, with something over three thousand students. It was coeducational, but its contingent of women was largely confined to a dormitory known as Sage College. There were no other dormitories for either men or women, and most of the students who did not live in the fraternity houses stayed in private homes and rooming houses in the city or on the broad hillside leading to the campus.

The campus social arbiters were extremely snobbish about the coeds, and although biological urges frequently caused the ranks to break, coeds were seldom acceptable visitors at fraternity dances. I can well remember the lengths to which this determination was carried when later I became the editor of the Cornell *Daily Sun* and refused to print a speech of Andrew Dixon White's on the educational therapeutics of coeducation. I made some silly statement in the editorial columns to the effect that as long as I was the togaed editor the *Sun* would not recognize the existence of coeducation at Cornell. I sent a copy of this world-shaking editorial to Mrs. White, and can remember distinctly the whiplash of her answer—"the view of the Cornell *Daily Sun* must always depend upon the wit, or the lack of it, of its editor."

The Greek-letter fraternity system ruled Cornell in those days, and I assume it still does; though the dormitories have grown apace, and today the women students are housed at least as well as the men. The fraternities did not think much of Townies, and I still remember my anguish during the first few months when I was not invited to join. All at once my hopes of success were dashed. However, my adolescent faith, uncrushed by the social system, reasserted itself, and sometime later I was the happy wearer of a Theta Delta Chi pin.

My desperate financial situation was an additional prod to glory, for I had heard of the fat profits being made by the editors of the Cornell daily, and since I had an embryonic knowledge of journalism through my work on the Ithaca papers, I entered the competition for freshman editor of the Cornell *Daily Sun*, and won.

It was at that time that I formed a friendship which has lasted for forty-five years, and will surely go on until one of us is gathered to our fathers. It was in a class of freshman English, I think, that I first met a rotund, "Quaker Oats baby-faced" boy from Dansville, New York, who rejoiced in the name of Jansen Noyes, but who somewhere in his youthful career had picked up the nickname Polly. To his great disgust, Polly he was for years thereafter, although he was about as feminine as Gargantua. We found out later that our mothers had been students in Vassar at the same time, and, indeed, that our grandfathers were college mates at Union. Furthermore our joint resources were not to be counted in more than three figures, and we were both determined to finish college under our own financial power.

Our friendship has always been a strange one. Noyes was an extrovert, and I an introvert. He was a hail-fellow-well-met, I was a bit suspicious of all mankind; he was an athlete of sorts, while I was puny and scholastic. If he ever read a book, it was probably Chamberlain's *Principles of Bond Investment*; whereas throughout my life I have been given to poring over books of every kind far into the night. He was the complete optimist and I the complete pessimist. The partnership was a natural and normal combination of action and reaction. The history of it is very much the history of my life.

Noyes carried off with great gusto and success the competition for business manager of the *Sun*. I finally defeated Max Elser, Jr., another lifetime friend, in the competition for managing editor, and again for editor in chief, and with Noyes' drive and my brakes, we developed the *Sun* into the first college paper with Associated Press news, and it became the leading morning paper in Ithaca, and what seemed to us in those days the original of all the gold mines of the world.

And so it came about that my college life was inextricably mixed with the operation and destinies of the Cornell *Daily Sun*. It was a man-sized job getting out a newspaper six days a week and carrying on college work in addition. During our stewardship, Noyes with his usual energy persuaded the Associated Press to give us a summary of its morning news at a nominal price. We increased the paper from its normal size of four pages to eight. Assisted though we were, both in the business and the editorial end by countless competitors (for all editorships and business managerships were filled by competition), we still had the responsibility of chief executives, and during the afternoons and usually from seven o'clock onward in the evening, we were in the *Sun* offices.

The town was a long way down the hill from our respective fraternity houses. There were no buses and taxis, and not more than one or two automobiles among the entire student body. The last trolley from the Ithaca Hotel to the university, popularly known as the jag car, left at 11:45 P.M. Noyes and I were its most regular passengers; we caught it after a quick run from Mitchell's printing office, where we had put the paper to bed, via Brownie's Dog Wagon (the Twenty One of Ithaca), where we had an egg sandwich and a glass of milk.

The editorial content of the *Sun* ranged from comments on the events of the day to attacks on university policy. Besides my attack on coeducation, I remember distinctly one editorial which bore the violent title "The Diabolical Idiocy of Final Examinations," which I wrote following the nervous breakdown of a fraternity brother who had too often looked upon the wine when it was red, and who because of this took to the infirmary rather than face "block week."

We also were the social reformers of those days, objecting to what we felt was the snobbery of one or two clubs whose members wore strange Arabic insignia on their hats. In order to counteract this movement we decided to form so many hat clubs of our own that democracy could not help but prevail, but I suspect that our reform was motivated by a slight dash of envy since neither Noyes nor I had been asked to become members of the elect. However, it was a fruitful crusade whatever the motive, for shortly thereafter the faculty itself abolished the famous Mummy Club and its sister, Nalanda.

While I was carrying on my editorial campaigns, the business end, managed by Noyes, soared to financial heights never since equaled or approached, aided by scores of hungry competitors. Merchants and manufacturers not only in Ithaca but throughout the country were hounded for advertisements, and we developed a remarkable system of payment among the local merchants. If it was not convenient for them to pay cash, we were glad to accept due bills for goods in their stores, and I recall distinctly that I was completely outfitted for years by the Ithaca tailors, and my supply of what college funny papers described as "trade pants" was not exhausted for years after graduation. We spent many pleasant days and nights in New York hotels which had advertised in the *Sun*. These were halcyon days of prosperity. My income during my senior year amounted to more than $3,000 in cash or "trade," and I am frank to say that it was many years after my graduation before I again reached this figure.

Yet there were other rewards from the *Sun*, for those were the days of the theatrical road companies, and Ithaca was one of the favorite and most prosperous one-night stands. On Cayuga Street was the famous Lyceum Theatre, now gone forever, operated by the brilliant Max Gudstadt, with whom we made a colossal and never-to-be-forgotten deal of four seats in the third row for every performance, to be allotted without charge to *Sun* executives in return for the Lyceum's advertising bill. It was in these seats that the juniors and seniors sat much to the disgust of the younger group, and here I developed my first love for the Great American Theatre, which eventually led me into interests in a great many Broadway productions, and finally into the motion picture industry. Every star of those days played Ithaca. Sothern and Marlowe, Maude Adams, William Gillette, and even the great Mansfield visited us. Anna Held and Fritzi Scheff were at the height of their glory, Montgomery and Stone sang *The Red Mill*, Mrs. Leslie Carter brought us the latest Belasco production. Viola Allen, Marie Doro, James K. Hackett, and a host of other stars stopped at the Lyceum, and we were always there to welcome them. Musical comedies with such favorites as Anna Laughlin, James T. Powers, Raymond Hitchcock, and Richard Carle, always filled the old theatre from the orchestra to the peanut gallery, and immediately after the performance there was always a long line of students at the stage entrance on Green Street hoping that some fair damsel of the chorus would consent to a few beers at the Dutch Kitchen, the pride of the Ithaca Hotel.

It was backstage at the Lyceum Theatre that I first met Cecil B. De Mille, later to become my distinguished associate in Paramount Pictures. Hollywood was nothing in those days, and C.B. was acting as business manager for his brother, William C. De Mille, who was starring in a play, the name of which I have long since forgotten.

These were also the days of Cornell's great athletic teams. When we annually journeyed to Poughkeepsie for the intercollegiate regatta in June, it was always even money that Cornell would win all three races, varsity, junior varsity, and freshman. These were tough odds, but we took them and usually won. Jack Moakley's track team swept the intercollegiates with the help of such athletes as John Paul Jones, Eddie Cook, and Walter Carpenter (later to become the distinguished president of the Du Pont Company), and we were able to win in practically everything else except football. We always returned "broke" from the annual Thanksgiving trek to Franklin Field in Philadelphia and the Penn games.

No doubt there were other highlights in my college life besides the Cornell *Daily Sun*, the Lyceum Theatre, and the athletic games, but they are difficult to recall. The high school songs about monkey love and the ones glorifying darkest Africa, particularly the Congo, gave way to the melodies of *The Red Mill*, and there was every possible variation of songs about the moon. Moreover, we were always in the shade of the old apple tree, and we never stopped singing "I'm

33

Afraid to Come Home in the Dark" and "Down in the Sub-way." Dick Rodgers was an infant, and no one had heard of Irving Berlin. Adolescent hearts broke and healed rapidly at fraternity house parties, and the married student of today was unknown. It was the pre-diaper days of universities.

With constant attention to the *Sun* and evenings at the Lyceum, and with a few extraneous interests, my college scholastic record suffered disastrously, until by the end of my sophomore year, it was obvious that, unless I acted quickly, Cornell would no longer cherish me to its bosom. I had seen my marks for all the year-end examinations except the one in French, and I knew that my French was execrable. But if I passed French I could slide through. In the dead of night I called on my French professor and explained my predica-ment, blaming his favorite paper, the Cornell *Daily Sun*. He sadly read my examination paper, told me what I already knew, that my mark should be approximately forty, and graded me up to passing with the wreckage of his conscience and my solemn promise that I would do better the next year. His name was Guerlac, and I shall bless him to my dying day.

My summer vacations were surprisingly varied. The first one was an astonishing experience as a sort of secretary to Elbert Hubbard, famous in those days as the writer of *Little Journeys to the Homes of Famous Men,* and as the head of the Roycrofters of East Aurora, New York. It was an experi-ence never to be forgotten; I greatly loved this charming charlatan, and deeply regretted his death on the *Lusitania.* I spent my second summer on a cattle ranch in the Big Horns of Wyoming, and I returned as far east as Chicago, in the caboose of a fifty-car train of cattle. The next year I was at the home of a great college friend, Sam Nixon, in Westfield, New York, near Chautauqua, the original of all the Chau-tauquas.

The end of senior year, the great hours of college, found me determined to prove that I was something of a scholar rather than simply a dilettante, and having become a deep admirer of Woodrow Wilson, I entered the senior oratorical contest with an impassioned speech called "The Side Show and the Main Tent," inspired by one of President Wilson's magazine articles bewailing the fact that so-called college activities were overshadowing scholastic endeavor. Though I had been a fervent pursuer of so-called college honors from college activities, and had completely eschewed scholarly activity, I nevertheless agreed with the distinguished president of Princeton, and won a prize of $100. It was reliably reported by my fraternity brothers that half of the Ithaca merchants, having heard this news, gathered on the fraternity veranda on the following morning, determined to obtain a small payment on their various bills.

The inevitable time had arrived when I could no longer bask in the affluence of the income of the *Sun*. College was over. I wrote a poem for the college magazine about the famous Cornell chimes playing the blues. Eddie Goodwillie sang the Cornell "Evening Song" on the steps of Goldwin Smith Hall. Jack Johnson destroyed the idol that was Jim Jeffries in Reno, and I was out in the cold, cold world.

## CHAPTER FOUR

### INTERMEZZO

The long and troubled years between 1910 and the end of World War I seem somehow more blurred and distant than the days of childhood and college. The death of Edward VII, the last bit of scenery of the Victorian age, seemed to bring a shadow on the land, which I suppose was heightened in my own mind by the natural fears of the young college graduate suddenly thrown into the outside world, and upon his own resources.

About this time in the United States there was a great hue and cry of "back to the land," toward which philosophy I had been influenced by a great Cornell friend, Roger Hitchcock, who now sleeps peacefully in France; one of the early fliers of the first war to be shot down by German planes. It was his talk of the glories of fruit-growing on the Pacific Coast that led me to take a course in agriculture during my senior year in college, and after graduation to turn toward the beautiful Rogue River Valley in southern Oregon. The little city of Medford and all the surrounding country was in the midst of a fruit boom, promising fabulous profits in pears and apples; and almost before I knew what had happened to me, I had borrowed enough from friends and relatives to make a down payment on a showy orchard a few miles from the metropolis in the foothills.

No more picturesque community has ever existed in the United States than Medford, Oregon, in 1910 and 1911. Countless young college graduates and older men disillusioned with life in the great cities followed the boom to invest their all in orchards and ranches; and they were followed by many, like myself, who had nothing to invest except their own work, their dreams, and their future. The community was teeming with young and hopeful life, and before long we had organized a university club, which dominated the social life of the community; followed by a country club, under Chandler Egan, a former national golf champion, which boasted the first course laid out between San Francisco and Portland. Most of us were very young; all of us very hopeful, and as the frost and the blight and the drought began to teach us something of the hazards of wringing a living from the earth, we drowned our sorrows at parties, and the majestic flow of scotch in the University Club increased.

Not all of us were orchardists. There were aspiring lawyers and engineers, and young and old collegians of every kind. Robert Ruhl, young and Harvardish, came out to organize a daily paper; and poets gave us such songs as "One Rubber Plant Will Never Make a Home" and "No Fruit Tonight."

Sitting on my hillside ranch one day a few months after I had mortgaged my soul to buy it, I received the astonishing news that there was a telegram for me at the Medford telegraph office, and my faithful mules promptly carried me in to the bustling city. The telegram, from Corvallis, Oregon, read something like this: "Cornell man here suggests that you might be interested in accepting chair of English and public speaking Oregon Agriculture College wire promptly." The years have long since obliterated my memory of the signer, but I remember perfectly the return wire that I instantly dispatched, a strange beginning for someone who became a Wall Street trader. It was as follows: "When do I come and how much do I get?"

The answer brought me the prompt offer of a salary of $100 a month and immediate employment; so sadly leaving my ranch to the dolorous tune of apples and pears falling to the ground with the torrential rains that had just hit the valley, I departed for my first and last academic winter in the university town of Corvallis.

All I can recollect of the place is a winter of unending rain, covering the roof tops with moss, and my own brilliant efforts to teach the young students of the college the elements of English literature and what every young orator ought to know.

When the year was up I returned to Medford to find that fortunately a young hopeful gentleman from Chicago was willing to pay me a profit for my ranch. I was a free lance again. Yet the lure of the life in the Oregon mountains was too much to pass up, and I made what I thought was a fabulous contract with two Chicago capitalists, Arnold Scudder and Corning Kenly, who had bought orchards at the height of the boom, and who were willing to pay me the magnificent salary of $150 a month and a third of the profits in return for my services. The $150 per month seemed flattering. The profits were rosy to start and turned a deeper red.

My young wife and I had been showered with wedding presents, and in those good old days the proper gift for the bride and groom was a mass of cut glass. These monstrosities were all carefully stored in the tiny bungalow that we had built at the ranch, and when, in my bride's absence in the East, I received the shocking news from a near-by orchard that the house had burned down and that the cut glass and other munificent wedding presents were fused, I probably became the first capitalist who obtained his beginning stake from the insurance avails of melted glassware and wedding loot.

We built another house, but it became increasingly apparent to me that the weather, the soil, and I were all too temperamental for life together, despite the beauty and the mountains of southern Oregon. My old friend Noyes, who had immediately made a beeline for Wall Street after his graduation, wrote me that he was making $6,000 a year as the manager of a bond department of a banking house. I did not believe there was that much money in the world, and felt that I should return to look into his declining veracity.

So ended my career as a fruit-grower. I returned to New York in the autumn of 1914 to take up residence in the tiny Judson Hotel on South Washington Square and to seek my fortune in fresh fields and pastures new.

The fates which led my nervous and uncertain feet to Wall Street in the autumn of 1914 were kindly over the years but in the beginning they were capricious indeed. No doubt because it was apprehensive of my arrival but perhaps, too, because of the outbreak of World War I, the Stock Exchange had closed down completely, the security business was at its lowest level in years, and banking houses throughout Wall Street were discharging employees right and left. Noyes was worried, but finally I heard the thrilling news that I was to start work—without a salary—in the statistical department of Hallgarten and Company, the great international banking firm by which Noyes was employed.

Worried but excited, I plunged in, and for several months I had a desk next to a son of one of the Hallgarten partners, Maurice Newton, who is now the head of the firm and with whom I have since been associated in many other businesses. There came a day, however, in the spring of 1915 when Noyes departed for a new job with the firm of Imbrie and Company, and I joined him as the first head of its statistical department at a salary of $10 a week. Maurice Newton was very much disappointed when I told him that I was leaving Hallgarten and told me that he had been considering seriously a plan to put me on the payroll.

But I had not been very long with Imbrie when I was confronted with one of those decisions involving divided loyalties, which come to everyone in the course of his life. Noyes had left Imbrie and Company to form his own firm of Hemphill, White and Chamberlain. Jim Imbrie, who had been very kind to me during my months with his firm, told me that he was extremely disappointed at Noyes' departure but that he did not want me to go under any circumstances. He told me to go to the cashier and set my own salary, that he was interested only in building a great banking house, and that he knew I could be of help to him. Yet unfortunately I had promised Noyes to come with his new firm as the first employee, at the highest salary that I had ever received, $50 a week. I was in a quandary that kept me awake through a long night. I decided to go to Mr. Imbrie and put so fabulous a price on my services that it would be utterly impossible for him to afford me. I asked for $5,000 a year; when I broke the news to him the next morning I received only a curt "I told you I did not want to hear what it was. Go ahead. I am delighted." Thus began a period of more sleepless nights, but finally I decided that my financial fate lay with Noyes.

Imbrie was disgusted, and properly so. I started in December 1915 as the first employee and later the first new partner, in addition to the original partners, in the firm Hemphill, White and Chamberlain; later to become Hemphill, Noyes and Company. Imbrie and Company went into receivership some few years later.

Alexander J. Hemphill, then head of the Guaranty Trust Company, and J. G. White, fathers of two of our partners had lent the original small capital of $250,000. Lawrence Chamberlain was a distinguished author in the field of bonds and finance, and Noyes, whose name did not appear in the firm, nevertheless had the largest interest in it. And so it started with one employee and grew during its first year to an almost respectably sized banking house, which succeeded in paying off its borrowed capital through one lucky venture, the purchase and prompt resale of two Oklahoma oil refineries.

Chamberlain had been giving a series of lectures at this time at New York University's Wall Street branch. His subject was railroad bonds, and when the business of the new firm began to take up all of his time, he turned the job over to me. I proceeded to give what must have been one of the weirdest courses in academic history. Four nights a week in my suburban house in Montclair I studied railroad bonds and histories of American railroads. Two nights a week I delivered the lectures to a group of young and hopeful financiers, and the seventh night, as the Old Testament has willed, I rested, taking a wild fling into Montclair society. But that $20 a lecture which I received tided me over the lowest period of my financial history, coinciding as it did with the advent of my two children, Theodora and Nixon.

But the war mounted, business became worse, and at times in 1916 and 1917 it seemed doubtful that the infant venture could survive. Our first coup, the purchase and sale of the two refineries, encouraged me to go to the oil country in the latter part of 1916 in quest of another venture which might, we hoped, duplicate the success of the first. But it did not, and to make matters worse I was struck down with a vicious attack of typhoid fever that laid me low for many months in 1917. When I finally became conscious again of the world around me, I found that we were at last in the war ourselves. Most of our organization had enlisted or been called in the service, and the really desperate days were upon us.

When I got back to Montclair I found that I had been drafted, but when I turned up for my medical examination I was promptly dismissed because of bad eyesight, which has dogged me all of my life. However, the war spirit was upon us all. I could not resist the lure of the uniform. I went to Washington and wangled myself a commission as Captain in the General Staff, and with the help of a large crew of statisticians my job was to determine how much raw material such as copper, steel, sulphur, camphor, leather, wool, and so on would be required by an army of five to six million men. It was a colossal assignment, but the war was over in the fall of 1918, long before the job was completed.

So ended the battle of Washington. I never saw a ship, never fired a gun, but I had an interesting training and watched the military machine in action. I was mustered out before you could say "Black Jack Pershing," and I returned to New York to put my uniform, of which I had been very proud, in moth balls. I was back in Wall Street and I was promptly made a partner to save my salary. Broke but hopeful, we all started again.

## CHAPTER FIVE

## WALL STREET IN THE
## FANTASTIC TWENTIES

There is an old-time rule of the New York City Police Department, for the protection of the great Wall Street banks and security boxes, that a known crook is never allowed south of Fulton Street. It certainly prevailed in the twenties and I think that it still does, but all my partners and nearly all my friends in Wall Street doubted its effectiveness when they began to understand that I believed strongly in the philosophies of the Democratic Party. If there were any other Democrats in Wall Street in the Roaring Twenties, I never met them. Not until Franklin Roosevelt's days in Washington did a few begin to appear, but, needless to say, they have remained a microscopic minority. Frequently I had to control my temper when my partners criticized the New Deal, and even now serious political discussions are taboo in our partners' dining room when I am around.

From my college days, I had been a violent hero-worshiper of Woodrow Wilson. I had fought and bled intellectually for the League of Nations, and I sadly watched Wilson's decline as the shadows closed about him. Almost a quarter of a century later, with the dead counted in millions, and Europe in rubble, we helped to create and lead the United Nations. Experience is a grim teacher. I certainly had no stomach for Mr. Harding, who defeated Cox in 1920, but probably by the time Mr. Coolidge came along and I began to savor the profits which poured into my firm like a Mississippi flood, I was not crusading as violently as I had once done, though certainly I was unhappy with the defeat of my beloved Al Smith. Later, when I joined Paramount Pictures, I never needed a calendar to tell me when the month began, for Al, who had apparently become one of our stockholders, called me up on the first of each month with the invariable inquiry, "Stan, how're we doin'?" I have great respect for Mr. Hoover today, but Hoover's stature has increased geometrically since he was President, and I am afraid that I cannot go along with the statement in his recent autobiography—that he could have worked the nation out of its deep depression with the same facility that Mr. Roosevelt did. I believed when Hoover was defeated, and I believe now, that Franklin D. Roosevelt was not so much an individual expressing his own ideas, as a symbol of the rising tide of world liberalism, of the earth's cry for improvement of the lot of the ordinary man, of the necessity for far greater national social consciousness, resulting in a paternalistic attitude of government toward its unemployed, its aged, and enfeebled. My partners of course never received these views with enthusiasm and I was generally regarded as a queer combination, a capitalistic yet socialistic type who was slightly touched. Yet I stuck to my belief in Roosevelt, as I have in his successor, Harry Truman. But I must confess that I strayed from the fold under the hypnotic personal influence of Wendell Willkie and cast my vote for him.

Reflecting on my early years in Wall Street, I wonder sometimes if there is anyone today who can diagnose the hysteria that emanated from the financial columns and swept over the nation in the twenties. Probably no one can diagnose the passion for money and more money, profits and more profits, higher prices and astronomical prices, which shook sensible men of all sorts, and which deprived economists and bankers

44

alike of their reason. Ours was not to reason why, ours was but to do and buy, and the market swept ever upward. Everyone told us that this was a new era, that we must never sell the United States short, that world conditions had completely changed, and that common stocks were the thing. The great speculators' paradise would last forever. And the very men who should have sounded great trumpets of warning were quietly purchasing more and more securities, and telling us more about the new era.

At the risk of being called an old fogy, or at the even greater risk of being confounded, let me observe that we are now undergoing one of those great booms—like the one that ended in 1929—that could, conceivably, lead to disaster. Everyone tells us that inflation is here and here to stay. We cannot help noticing the terrifying spectacle of great educational institutions, hospitals, and philanthropic funds, increasing their common stock portfolios as they shy away from high-grade bonds on the assumption that the latter will not be worth more than a few pennies when they fall due. Lawmakers in many states are letting down the safety bars on investments for the trust funds of the well-known widows and orphans and even for savings banks. But meanwhile there is no assurance whatever that common stocks, depending as they do upon the earning power of the corporations that issue them, will retain their value or that the national income, on which that earning power is based, will continue to rise.

We are told that great corporations, obliged to purchase vast amounts of securities in order to provide income for their workers' pension funds, threaten to break the dike of stock prices. The cry persists that common stocks are the only safe investments, that inflation will continue to mount, and that prices and wages will grow daily, weekly, monthly, and yearly.

The theories on which this hypothesis is based may be correct, but they have a familiar ring. And though the govern-

45

ment is doing its best to avoid a financial disaster, I cannot believe that the economy of a country as large as the United States can be regulated by law. Prices and wages are not subject to bureaucratic fiat. They rise and fall according to factors over which Washington, despite its best efforts, has no real control, and though I remain a Democrat in most important aspects, I must disagree with my party when it undertakes to make water run uphill.

Today's overwhelming prosperity is bound to have its aftermath. Galileo and Newton were right in insisting that whatever goes up must eventually come down. During the twenties the stocks of great banks sold for a price that included not only their capital and surplus but their customers' deposits as well. Today, of course, bank stocks barely include the bank's capital and surplus, which is somewhat reassuring, as is the fact that bellboys and bootblacks are no longer the prime source of financial information.

However, we may be close to such a situation. Great markets have a way of vanishing overnight. I remember the sardonic philosophy of my old banking friend James Speyer. I remarked to him one day as we were crossing the English Channel that the stock market had taken a terrific bang. Mr. Speyer expressed himself in three laconic words, "There's always somethin'."

So, as I utter these warnings from my ancient fireside, let me make a confession. I have underwritten and sold securities of every sort for thirty-five years, but it is my firm belief that a consistent, carefully worked out policy of life insurance purchases, from great companies whose staffs wisely select the best and most varied investments, should always be included in any program of security purchases and sales. If the life insurance companies want this free advertisement from an investment banker, it is theirs.

Perhaps I am influenced by an event that occurred shortly after the great crash of 1929, when I was at my lowest financial ebb, and had to go to the Fifth Avenue Hospital for a major operation. The insurance examiners had always told me that I would be a better risk if I had my physical difficulties surgically corrected, so I thought it would be fun to go back at them with the impossible proposition that they issue me a million dollars' worth of life insurance before I climbed on the operating table. Most of the large companies looked out of the window, but the proposition so intrigued one great company, and only one—the New York Life—that it summoned all of its doctors together, described the operation, and had them vote their opinions on my chances to stay alive following the operation. The answers were pooled and apparently the doctors reached a verdict. The going rates for my survival were 98½ per cent. Accordingly, the company put me through every conceivable physical test and, to a nervous patient through a nervous agent, announced that they would not give me a million, but would give me three hundred thousand if I would pay the additional estimated risk of 1½ per cent. This I did, and the policies were delivered to me as I left my apartment for the hospital. I have always been grateful to the company for its extreme solicitude for my recovery, which immediately followed. Every day one of its representatives called on me in the hospital to inquire hopefully about my welfare. They won the game temporarily. The policies now rest quietly in a trust, aged in the wood for twenty years.

As Wall Street and all its inmates, accompanied by nearly all of the American population, rushed into the Roaring Twenties, they might have taken a warning of things to come during the decade, from the mighty bomb explosion that shook its favorite corner on the morning of September 16, 1920. The offices of my firm were then on the fifteenth floor of the late Equitable Trust Company Building at 37 Wall Street, next to the House of Morgan. My desk was directly under a window on the Wall Street side. That morning I was driving from Westhampton, where we had a house for the summer, and was due at my office before the time of the explosion, but I was delayed by the frequent requirements of a non-car-broken Sealyham terrier that I was bringing to New York. As the result of his frolics I arrived in the financial district a few minutes after the explosion, and found the corner of Broad and Wall a shambles of dead and dying, fear and hysteria. In my office I found that a piece of one of the iron window weights used in making the bomb had ricocheted from the granite top of my window, going down through the ancient roll-top desk itself, taking with it a large piece of mahogany, and burying itself in the monthly directors' statement book of the Thatcher Manufacturing Company. This piece of iron is my favorite paperweight, a reminder that had I been more prompt in reaching my office, it would no doubt have passed directly through my brain.

The decade began its dizzy dance, punctuated only by occasional frightening market breaks, reminding certain cautious investors that securities could not go up forever. In the houses of issue everything had to be done with great haste. Bond issues, debenture issues, and issues of preferred and common shares were whipped together and passed on to the public with bewildering speed. In retrospect, it is obvious that every Wall Street firm, large or small, old or young, sinned gravely, but both bankers and investors were under the spell of the new era, the great never-never land of Coolidge prosperity. The hypnosis was complete.

Soon there developed a tremendous vogue among the Wall Street houses for buying issues of industrial companies and receiving, in addition to their normal banking underwriting fees, a substantial bonus of common stock, for these were the merry days before the creation of the Securities and Exchange Commission. It was not necessary to tell the public of these little gifts of roses, which were to be put away in the bankers' boxes and sold later when the occasion presented itself. Many of these bonus stock deals were the real foundation of the great Wall Street fortunes made in those Alice in Wonderland years. It became fashionable, as well as profitable, for banking houses to buy entire properties and refinance them in such a way that when the new securities were resold to the public the bankers remained the proud owners of a very substantial portion of the common shares. One of the master deals along this line was the purchase and partial resale of the Dodge Motor Car Company by Dillon, Read and Company. I can remember another when I stood on the sweltering steps of the courthouse in Toledo, Ohio, bidding $5,500,000 for the Electric Auto Light Company when it was sold at public auction. My firm purchased the great White Sewing Machine Company, and we received many blocks of bonus common shares of companies that have lived through the years with prosperity and now remain some of the standard issues on the New York Stock Exchange.

With Merrill, Lynch and Company and others, we purchased nearly all of the United States Pathé company, the American subsidiary of the great French concern, and attempted to finance it through an issue of 8 per cent bonds, repayable at 120 per cent of par, and convertible into a common stock at a very low price. We owned so much Pathé common stock that Charlie Merrill, his partner Ed Lynch, my partner Noyes, and I used to play bridge with Pathé shares as the stake. But even dressed up like a Christmas tree, the bonds were unsalable for a long time. Then, without warning, the company developed a small motion-picture camera for home use, the first of the many that later came on the market. The common stock rose to ninety-eight dollars a share, and the bonds to four thousand dollars for each one-thousand-dollar bond because of their convertibility. It was that kind of market.

Toward the end of the twenties, there developed a great era of so-called construction bonds, which were issued and sold to raise money for projects that had progressed no farther than the engineers' drawing boards. These included toll bridges, the financing of which has a flavor strangely similar to the countless so-called revenue bonds that are being sold today to finance bridges, turnpikes, throughways, and every other conceivable form of municipal adventure designed to keep a municipality within its reasonable debt limit, and yet find for investors that happy haven of tax-exempt securities. The toll-bridge issues, including those for the great International Bridge at Detroit and the Mount Hope Bridge in Rhode Island, which we financed, were not without merit as contributions to civic improvements. But the profits went only to those who stuck through the calamitous decline in traffic that occurred in the early thirties, and who patiently awaited the developments that brought the properties back to a reasonable earning power as the nation worked out of its depression. This was also the era of newspaper financing, during which my firm raised many millions for the Gannett papers; among other things, it purchased outright the Hartford *Times*, but was out-generaled by the local firemen in its attempts to buy the Chicago *News* and the Kansas City *Star*.

Then, at last, came the magic era of investment trusts, which meant that under the management of the great Goldman Sachs and Company or Lehman Brothers, or Dillon, Read and Company or J. and W. Seligman or others, a company with only money and a charter could suddenly achieve a value far above its estimated assets and find miraculous heights of value a few days after its shares had been purchased by an eager public.

Floyd Odlum, a sound, able, and adventurous financier was the only one to recognize the mathematical certainty of the opportunities of this sort of investing, and, as a result, when the inevitable crash came he proceeded to make his fortune simply by buying investment trusts at lower than liquidating prices, seeing them through to liquidation and using the cash to buy still other securities of the same type.

Odlum's plan was unique, but there were, of course, other investors who could sit out the horrid decline and come through the years in good shape. But no one will ever know how many billions of dollars worth of really worthless securities were unloaded on the American public during the twenties. The real punishment came to those investors who had become over-extended and were unable to withstand the depression.

There was also a wave of purchases and sales of the so-called alien properties, which brought me at least one amusing experience. It was usually necessary for the potential investor to post a large certified check before going through a German property to be sold, and when we heard that Dow, of the Dow Chemical Company, might be interested in purchasing an alien firm that was about to come on the market, we cheerily put up the check and took him on a tour of the plant. It was operated by an alert Irishman, who, as I remember, was slightly deaf and whose name, I think, was Jimmy Brantigan. He learned my name, because I had the written approval of the government to inspect the plant, but he did not catch the name of his famous visitor. As we proceeded through the department in which bromides were manufactured, Dow shouted at his guide, "Do you make any money out of your bromide business?"; the reply was, "No, that son of a bitch Dow has ruined the bromide business." Brantigan was, I believe, also the man who, after he had been in the plant for a few weeks, called the German chemists together and told them to sit down at a table and write out their formulas, saying that he was going to write down his ideas of what the formulas were, based on his studies in the different departments. His closing comment was: "If I make a mistake, I'll apologize. If you make a mistake, you'll go to the penitentiary."

During these lurid years I took a good deal of pleasure in developing my estate in Connecticut, rebuilding the place from top to bottom. I bred dogs, kept a small stable, and undertook to raise chickens, turkeys, pheasants, and rabbits. The tinkling profits of the twenties enabled me to carry on these enterprises apparently only for the welfare of the livestock itself, but I later found that even Wall Street in a depression did not yield quite such losses as the chicken business. After 1929 the dogs and the horses vanished forever, and the later purchasers of the place found that, as part of their acquisition, they possessed kennels decorated with thousands of dog show ribbons, ancient silver-plated cups, and stuffed sailfish, which had been refused by the country club and all my friends, but which still adorned my main kennel house.

Toward the end of the boom times, a number of the citizens of New Canaan, in an excess of civic pride, subscribed to the formation of a village-improvement company. The whole operation blew down in the great wind, but urged on by my old friend and partner John Brotherhood, several of us bought up the fragments of the operation and the various claims against it and have had the thrill of all but rebuilding the main street of the village in a way that has certainly increased its look of New England cleanliness and beauty. Incidentally, the development has, over a period of twenty years, substantially divested itself of its circus tent of mortgages. It is now owned by the stockholders and not by the insurance companies. We also built and resold countless dwelling houses, for I am a glutton for building houses and watching their development. But no matter how frequently I plan them for my own use I have no joy in living in them when they are finished, and promptly rush to build another.

Another of our pleasures in those years was angeling Broadway plays, in whose financing I usually hooked my hopeful downtown partners. But it was all in the spirit of the game. Except for the theatre owners, only a rare and small percentage of American theatrical productions end with any profit, and my adventures contributed to the proof of this rule. However, we always had high hopes and always gave a large party after the curtain fell on the opening night. I can still remember coming back early to my apartment in the Carlton House one night with my chief co-backer, Conger Goodyear, and Miss Margalo Gillmore, hoping to arrive before the flock of guests. Margalo remained in the living room as Conger and I stepped out into the dining room, where both of us opened bottles of champagne and popped the corks. Miss Gillmore, who is not unknown for her wit, said, "My God, the backers are killing themselves." We should have.

Throughout the hilarity of these times, the sounds of the approaching cyclone were no louder than an alarm clock in the desert. We heard only the cry "This is a new era" as it echoed and re-echoed through the land. But with the business of continually forging security issues and the inevitable nervous strain of the period, I had become weary and felt that the business of money making had lost its savor for a while. I decided to take a long vacation in France, and in order to pay my expenses I purchased a thousand shares of Standard Oil of New Jersey on the morning of my departure. To protect myself, I put in what is known as a stop-loss order, at two points below my purchase price, which is to say that if the stock declined two points it was to be sold immediately at the market price. As I was packing in my apartment on the afternoon of my departure, I heard the news from the office that I had been stopped out, but I assumed that it was only a temporary reaction and I sailed at midnight October 25, 1929 on the *Mauretania*. The next day, when I was far out at sea, the storm broke. And though I realized from the ship's bulletin and from frantic radios from my office that it was really a cataclysm, I could hardly alight and walk back home. When I reached Paris, I spent hideous hours in my apartment at the Crillon, trying to telephone my partners, but with no success. There was no immediate return boat, except the ancient, lumbering *Homeric*, a ten-day ship, but I took it anyway, not knowing whether I was solvent or not.

53

When I arrived in New York, Noyes met me at the boat with the day's sheet of stock market quotations in his hand. I asked him if we were still solvent. He said we might be. At the office, late in the afternoon, I found my own private room filled with cots for the clerical staff, which was working literally day and night. I reached my uptown apartment at five o'clock the next morning without knowing whether or not I was solvent.

Finally the tumult and the shouting died. Many a great national financier went back to the ribbon counter, which he never should have left, and we gazed around at the ruins. The profit sheets which I assiduously kept for the firm had, on October 1, shown a gain for the year of close to three and a half million dollars. The December 31 statement showed a loss of almost as much. It was quite a swing for a young firm, but Wall Street had given and Wall Street had taken away.

As the depression deepened in the very young thirties, we reached the ultimate low with the closing of the banks. Sadly I decided to take what assets I had besides what was tied up in Hemphill, Noyes, and invest half of it in life insurance and half in sound common stocks selling under five dollars a share. It was a good decision and it kept the family ship afloat until I reached the amusement business and regained what had been swept away with the debacles of 1929 and 1932.

Can it be that we learned nothing from the heartbreaking financial hurricane of the late twenties? The same old new era is upon us again, this time with the grave fears of inflation and the theory of regulated economy. We do, of course, have the Securities and Exchange Commission, and I believe that under its present laws and regulations any investor who will really go to the trouble of reading the prospectus of a proposed new issue of securities can know exactly what he is buying. With real, honest, and complete facts at his disposal he can make his own decision, which will be right or wrong depending on his financial acumen and judgment. It is true that the operations of the SEC have taken the great profits out of the investment banking business, but they have also thrown a great protective mantle over both the individual investor and the banking house itself. This, combined with the careful provisions for high margin requirements, and the system of competitive bidding preventing private negotiation which has developed in recent years, has changed the color and quality, indeed the profits, of Wall Street.

While I am a faithful Democrat and these trends have developed entirely under the Democratic administration, I do not regard these arguments as special pleading. It would be difficult to find any sound, active investment banker in Wall Street today who would like to go back to the old buccaneering system, even with all its easy profits. I have had my own share of personal difficulties with the SEC, but, properly administered, it is the greatest protection for both the investor and investment banker afforded by any institution in the history of our economic system. It cannot, however, be expected to control the hypnotic effects of new investment theories, and the very natural temperament of the American investor.

While there were giants in the old days, they were no greater than some of our present financiers. Many of the idols of the twenties have gone back to the obscurity from which they sprang. But there are some who did not. I am not sure what constitutes a great financier. Probably he is a dead banker. But Clarence Dillon, the head of Dillon, Read and Company, is not dead, and certainly he is the greatest financier of our times. Trained under him, or in friendly association with him, were James Forrestal, later to become Under-Secretary and then Secretary of the Navy, and finally the first Secretary of Defense; Ferdinand Eberstadt, who contributed so much to the sound thinking of government and the production drive during the second world war, and who is now head of his own firm of F. Eberstadt and Company; and Paul Shields, who has for many years moved the pieces on the Democratic chessboard, though usually from behind the scenes. There were other trainees in the Dillon school, including Dean Mathey, now chairman of the board of the Empire Trust Company, and Dillon's own son, Douglas. It is not, of course, strange that Douglas should be cast after his father's mold, but why Forrestal, Eberstadt, and Shields have been so similar to Dillon is beyond me.

Dillon himself is a remarkable man. He was born with a psychic, Oriental mind adapted to the business of buying and selling securities. He had a great athlete's sense of timing. When securities were stagnant, Dillon, Read would become strangely quiescent, while other firms exhausted themselves trying to buck a dead market. But when things improved, Dillon, Read and Company was right there with an important deal, which, as we used to say in the investment business, "went out the window" at exactly the proper moment.

Clarence Dillon's financial brains are smooth ball bearings running in clean oil, and the younger men he has trained have been of enormous value both in finance and in the government. But though he gave Forrestal to the government— and though Forrestal leaned heavily on the advice of both Eberstadt and Shields—Dillon himself, except for his work as director of the Navy Relief campaign and his service on the National Rubber Commission and some other advisory boards, has never accepted high government office. Forrestal constituted a deviation from the Dillon pattern in the continuity of his devotion to the government. Eberstadt is perhaps less of a diplomat and a bit more quixotic, and Shields perhaps most closely duplicates Dillon's reserve. Yet while each was strong, quiet, scholarly, and at the same time hard working and hard driving, as well as ice-cold in financial decisions, they were all nevertheless sensitive and sentimental. But they were too strong to stay together in one room. They used up all the oxygen and it was only normal that each should finally go his own way—Forrestal to the government, Eberstadt and Shields to form their own firms, and Dillon to stay with the firm he founded.

Part of their business success, I suppose, lay in their ability neither to over-trade nor under-trade, but as good as they were, I once saw Dillon himself make the mistake of trying to over-trade. I remember bringing to his office the head of a large American corporation who was anxious to negotiate a loan of something like ten million dollars. I watched Mr. Dillon, relaxed in his chair, swinging his eyeglasses on their black ribbon, as he advanced all the current arguments about why the company should be willing to give up a large block of its common stock as a bonus in order to obtain the financing. The visiting tycoon listened to Dillon explain how important it was to an industrial concern that a great and powerful banking house should come to its aid in time of trouble; then my friend got up and reached for his hat as he said, "Thank you, Mr. Dillon, good-by. I cannot at the moment think of any good reason why I should spend all my life building up this company, and at the end give it to you." Even Dillon smiled as we went out into the darkness of Nassau Street.

Charlie Merrill was another of the really great financiers whom I knew well from the day that I first tramped that cavern of hope from Church to River. Fresh out of Amherst, he started his own small firm to sell the preferred stock issues of what was then a small chain of stores, and later he and Edmund Lynch formed the partnership that brought them both great fortunes. Two more widely varying types of human animal had never before come together in the common barrel of a business partnership. Eddie worked like a great bull elephant charging through a primeval jungle, while Charlie was suave and diplomatic regardless of how troubled the waters became.

I shall never forget a day in the thirties when Eddie Lynch

57

and I were in Paris and he invited me to join him in a visit to the Salon d'Automne, the great semi-annual exhibit of modern French paintings. He told me that he wished to buy two or three canvases for his new office in New York, and we strolled from room to room in the great palace, looking for some likely purchases. After studying the prices in the catalogue, Eddie asked me if I thought it would do any good to enter under-price bids for the pictures. I did not know, so we consulted the morning-coated French manager, who told us that this was an unusual request but that he would be glad to present any of our bids to the respective artists. Eddie said to me, "I think I will put in very, very low bids for about fifty of these pictures. I may be able to get two or three."

Two mornings later the telephone awakened me in my room at the Crillon, where Eddie had an apartment in the adjoining corridor. His anguished voice said, "Stan, come over here right away, will you. Something terrible has happened." In my bathrobe and pajamas, I rushed to his room, expecting to find him in great pain, but in his shaking hand was a letter from the salon. "My God," he said, "I've bought forty-six pictures."

After Ed's untimely death, Charlie went on, for no good financial reason that I know, to develop one of the largest stock exchange houses on Wall Street, where he rules like a smiling potentate and dispenses new ideas on how to develop the investment business.

Another of my good friends from Wall Street is Sidney Weinberg of Goldman, Sachs and Company, who delights in his Phi Beta Kappa key, which he says he bought in a Brooklyn pawnshop, and who at the drop of a cigarette ash will tell you of his humble origin in Brooklyn, although everyone knows that he is the pampered son of a Flatbush bank president. Undisturbed by the adversities that beset him during the depression, and though he has often been called to Washington to serve his country in one important capacity or another, Sidney is probably a director of more great American corporations than any other businessman. His success is the measure not only of his natural acumen but of his uncanny ability to make and keep friends. He is a charming person though politically he is a chameleon—one year a Democrat, the next a Republican.

Wall Street, despite its reputation to the contrary, has given the government some of its ablest men. Averell Harriman and Bob Lovett, two of the most important figures in Washington, are both Wall Streeters. Harriman has been a sturdy man of all work under two Democratic Presidents. He has served in so many capacities that it is literally impossible to enumerate them. He has been a general trouble shooter, from ambassador to cabinet officer, always with high distinction. His associate Bob Lovett was a key member of General Marshall's team, as Under-Secretary of State, during my tours of duty in Poland and Egypt. It was a joyous thing to see the fighting team of Marshall and Lovett go into the Department of Defense, with Lovett fully qualified to step into the great Secretary's shoes when the latter retired.

Most of the Wall Streeters of whom I have written have been saddled at one time or another with the financial responsibilities of their respective colleges and universities, or with those of the great philanthropic institutions of New York. For hard and nerve-racking job number one, I recommend the position of chairman or member of such a finance committee, especially during a depression. I am sure that nearly everything that has happened to Cornell University in the last decades has happened to other institutions with great funds. I can still recall how I felt in 1932 when I became a member of the Cornell committee and learned that while the endowment funds were carried on the books at twenty-six million, they were selling at something under sixteen, or about 60 per cent of their book value. The old idols, in which Cornell placed its faith—railroad stocks and bonds and guaranteed mortgages—had toppled in the general crash. And so, I assume, had the financial structures of other properly managed institutions. But luckily Cornell was able to survive until it reached the better markets of the late thirties and regained a semblance of stability. It was just after we passed parity that I handed the fund to Joe Ripley and entered government service. Ripley had come out of Cornell a few months after Noyes and I did, and he went to work with J. G. White and Company before becoming head of the National City Company and later the active head of Harriman Ripley and Company. Today the figures make happy reading for the University, which has a book value of endowment funds of more than sixty million dollars, and an unrealized profit appreciation of over seven million, as well as a reserve of another five million dollars in the investment account of profits already taken. Allowing for inflation, a rapid calculation indicates that more than seventy million dollars today is far better than sixteen million dollars in 1932.

As I finish this chapter, the advertisements in this morning's New York papers tell me that Charlie Merrill's firm, sometimes known as "We, the People," or "Merrill and the Telephone Directory," is trying to augment the enthusiasm for common stocks by showing that a number of the great universities and funds have increased their common stock percentages to figures that would have been frightening a few years ago. I know that Cornell has done so, and I can only pray that we are right and that we are indeed entering a new era.

The normal American is always very something—either very optimistic or very pessimistic. Fortunately the optimist usually prevails despite the apostles of doom, who are currently pointing to our ever-increasing debt and to the billions of dollars that we pour into Western Europe in order to check Stalinism. But there remains only one clear-cut financial problem for the American people today and that is to find a method whereby we can protect ourselves from Communism and at the same time keep the nation sound financially. To assume the burdens of empire without accepting its rewards is, of course, an enormous undertaking even for a country as rich as ours. But if we are to survive, we must accept the responsibilities of survival. We must contribute heavily to the reorganization of Western Europe, but we can continue to do so only as long as our domestic economy retains its strength. Let us hope that our enormous investment in civilization remains sound and that our faith in America's current prosperity will be rewarded.

## CHAPTER SIX

## BOOKSELLING AND KINDRED
## EVILS—BRENTANO'S

Perhaps the first hundred years in the retail book business are the hardest. I hope so, for Brentano's Booksellers to the World, is now entering its hundredth year of operation; and for the last twenty years, since about 1933, when I purchased the business at receiver's sale, I have had the glory and taken the punishment of operating this fine old institution and of being its controlling stockholder. But it has had to be all fun and glory and no cash, for despite its twenty to thirty stores, I have never had the good fortune to take a dollar out of it since I started with it.

However, as I have already written, I spent my childhood in a bookish atmosphere, and even Wall Street could not dislodge my literary tastes. It was only natural, therefore, that I should form a close friendship with Arthur Brentano, Sr., in his old store near Madison Square early in the twenties, where I would drop in occasionally and talk to him about his favorite department—the "Old and Rare." He was at that time planning a large expansion to the north, with a great store in the Fifth Avenue district. I reasoned with him against it, only to find that I myself made the same mistakes of expansion many years later when the business came into my hands. No more lovable man than Arthur Brentano ever lived. No one had more friends throughout the country, and his love for and delight in old

books and early editions was something like the love of a
mother for her child. He did not change even when the business came on evil days, and he stayed with his beloved old
books after my control started, until the day of his death at
the age of eighty-nine.

The story of Brentano's, and that of its founder, is long and
colorful. Perhaps the best version of it is the one that Bennett
Cerf wrote for the *Saturday Review of Literature* some years
ago, and with his generous permission I should like to quote
parts of it here.

August Brentano came to New York from Austria with no
money and no friends, but he had energy and he had imagination.
His first venture was a single table of books and periodicals in
the hallway of the old Revere House at Broadway and Houston
Street, but he called it "Brentano's Literary Emporium"—and
he prospered. By 1865 he occupied half a building at 708 Broadway, sharing the premises with a tobacco business owned by
the fathers of Charles and Daniel Frohman, of theatrical fame.
The store was opposite the New York Hotel, patronized largely
by wealthy Southerners and the most distinguished visitors from
abroad. The visitors demanded books and periodicals hitherto
unknown in America, and Mr. Brentano's stock became unique
in this country. At the same time the Southern gentlemen—and
their ladies—brought into the shop an atmosphere of gentility
and class on which the proprietor was quick to capitalize. When
the business moved to 33 Union Square in 1870 it was already
the most flourishing and successful bookstore in America.

Union Square was then the residential section of New York.
The Goelet mansion was next door to the new store. Tiffany's
was down the block and that wily reprobate Dan'l Drew lived
on the Seventeenth Street corner. Visitors to New York were
cautioned not to miss a trip to Brentano's, where they might
catch a glimpse of Charles Dickens or Ralph Waldo Emerson
or William Cullen Bryant or even of Ulysses S. Grant.

In 1873 August Brentano's staff was enlarged by one. His
nephew Arthur, fifteen years old, arrived from Evansville and
was promptly put to work delivering newspapers to customers

south of Sixteenth Street. He learned his job so quickly that his appreciative uncle soon promoted him by adding Seventeenth and Eighteenth Streets to his route. His brother Simon also came into the shop and it wasn't many years—nine, to be exact—before the enterprising pair bought out their uncle entirely.

This was in 1882. Two years later the Washington branch was opened. And in 1887 Arthur went to Europe and established a Brentano branch in Paris. He was also married there in 1890, with Whitelaw Reid arranging the formalities for him and Robert Chambers acting as best man.

One day in 1898 a fire burned down the house next door to Brentano's New York store and every book in stock was destroyed. The water in the basement was six feet deep. There wasn't such a magnificent clean-out of old stock in the book business again until twenty-six years later when the Boni & Liveright stockroom went up in flames. Even that occasion fell short, for the New York Fire Department arrived just in time to save for posterity 11,000 copies of Hendrik Van Loon's *Story of the Bible* despite the barbed wire and sandbags loyal employees put up to impede the intrepid fire fighters' progress.

Brentano's rebuilt—bigger and better than ever—and Admiral Dewey unwittingly assisted in the opening ceremonies of the new store. The hero of Manila was virtually the Clark Gable of his day and his arrival at Brentano's was attended by the autograph hunters of 1901 en masse. Arthur Brentano spirited the Admiral out through a back alley. "It was the nearest thing to a riot in our store," he recalled years later, "until the day we gave an autographing party for Gertrude Stein."

In 1907 Brentano's moved to Fifth Avenue and Twenty-seventh Street. I can remember the wonderful store they had down there, with the originals of all the magazine covers in the side-street windows and the huge pile of periodicals from all over the world in the basement! This was when Arthur Brentano began the fine and rare book department that is still a feature of the main store today, when George Bernard Shaw signed to have all his plays published in America by Brentano's, and when Theodore Roosevelt came in one day and ordered the pigskin library that he took with him to Africa. . . .

Retail trade was heading northward in those carefree days of bull markets, flaming youth, and pocket flasks—and Brentano's followed the trend. The present store at Forty-seventh Street was opened in 1925, and three New York branches were established soon after. The chain spread to Pittsburgh, Cleveland, and Philadelphia. Business boomed but so did expenses. The crash in 1929 left Brentano's, like so many of the country's best bookstores, with a huge inventory of expensive books and a top-heavy overhead. In the spring of 1930 a group of publishers formed what I believe they called a protective committee and in three years of unique mismanagement threw the entire corporation into bankruptcy. In March, 1933, Brentano's found itself in the tender hands of that well-known and experienced retail bookselling organization, The Irving Trust Company.

A pretty pass. And what to do? "Save Brentano's" was the rallying cry of all the generous publishers (who were also the creditors). Expenses were pared to the bone. The publishing department was disposed of to Coward-McCann. All but the main store in New York and the branches in Washington, Chicago, and Paris were discontinued. But most important of all, frantic beaters flushed Stanton Griffis from the Wall Street bushes and cajoled him into buying control of the Brentano business. It was the dawn of a new day in the history of a fine old firm.

When Brentano's finally came into my hands, I believed that it could be expanded along the lines of many of the great chain-store businesses that had spread throughout the country. I saw no real difference between it and the great food stores—Safeway, Atlantic and Pacific, National Tea, and others, or the clothing stores, the hat shops, and the great novelty chains such as McCrory, Grant, and even Woolworth. In my ignorance of the business I felt that there was no reason why this expansion could not be undertaken and undertaken profitably, and I spent a great deal of time and money during my early days with Brentano's, trying to prove this theory. I opened branches in San Francisco, Los Angeles, San Mateo, Beverly Hills, Honolulu, and Hartford, Connecticut. And though we managed to survive the thirties and benefit from the World War II boom, we never really prospered, for the retail book business was not really susceptible to such expansion.

Indeed I have never known of a really successful chain of bookstores that expanded regularly and with profit. The Womrath chain went into receivership long ago, and while the Doubleday book chain insists that it is successful, I, myself, feel that it is probably only because of its records and such novelties as Silly Putty and other little operations that it has carried on.

An honest-to-God bookstore, as distinguished from book departments in department stores and novelty stores that call themselves bookstores, has only one source of supply for its merchandise—the book publishers. Through my years in the book business, I have had many close friendships with publishers, including the eccentric and brilliant Nelson Doubleday, Cass Canfield of Harper's, Alfred Knopf, Frank Dodd of Dodd, Mead and Company, George Brett of Macmillan, Bennett Cerf, Donald Klopfer of Random House, and Harold Guinzburg of Viking, whom I almost seduced into a merger in 1946.

I have had more or less the same sort of relationships with these distinguished gentlemen that I have had in recent years with the rulers of the various autocratic countries to which I have been accredited. In private we are great and charming friends. But whenever I have had a chance to speak about these men publicly, it has always been with great distaste, for I am convinced that publishers are the bookseller's natural enemies. In no other industry does the manufacturer go to such lengths and use such vicious means to destroy his outlets. First, there are the great book clubs which have been fostered for years by the publishers, and through which the reader—if he is willing to have his literature selected for him and mailed to him in a can, if he is willing to buy books one at a time or four at a time, and if he believes the advertisements—can usually purchase books at a lower price than I, through my firm, which does the largest retail book business in the world, can afford to sell them. Brentano's must have at the customer's disposal many, many thousands of books so that he can come in, browse around, and pick out what he likes. From its operational gross, it must pay rent, light, salaries, and all the thousand and one overheads of a retail store, and it should be able to make a fair profit for doing so. But the book-club member can, unfortunately, buy most of the current books at a lower price than I can buy them—and all this with the publisher's smiling consent.

There is also that unhappy bane of the retail bookseller, the department store "loss leader," the theory of which is very simple. It is based on the assumption that the buyer will be so influenced by high-pressure advertising that tells him that he can buy a nationally advertised article for well below the usual retail price, that he will be lured into the store, and while there will buy a piano, a Ford car, a hide-a-bed, a poodle dog, and a basket of groceries. Someday the great publishers will see the iniquity of permitting these practices and will stop them by legal means. Someday perhaps the booksellers will rise in their might and insist on some semblance of fair play and fair trade in the book business; but not yet.

A few months ago when the price war was on between a number of the great New York department stores, I wandered through the book department of one of these shops with the proprietor himself, a man whom "nobody but nobody" undersells. At that time a book called *From Here to Eternity* was the great rage. It cost Brentano's $4.50 less 40 per cent from the publishers, or a net cost of $2.70, in large lots. I asked the manager of my host's book department what he could sell me a copy for, and with great delight he produced a copy at $1.29.

I can even at my advanced age remember the happy days of the book business when a man was able to employ bright young intellectuals, to whom the satisfaction of working among books was payment enough in itself. They were willing to work for a great bookstore for little or nothing. Perhaps this was slavery in the name of culture, but those days are gone forever, and now we are unionized through our chain from top to bottom. It is the unions, not the intellectuals, that tell us what we should pay everyone in the business from the shipping clerk to the buyer. Yet the retail book business still has great vitality, and I suppose it will continue to live indefinitely.

Something of its vitality is proven in the history of Brentano's, which over a period of a hundred years has gone through two receiverships, good and bad managements, periods of depression and prosperity, and yet somehow continues to do business at the same old stand and under the same old name, though its profit now yields to glory.

I have had a friendly warning from my publisher, who is also my chief competitor in the book business, that no buyer really gives a hoot about the troubles of any given business, whether it is bookselling or the corner grocery, so long as he can buy his merchandise cheaply. I sympathize somewhat with this theory, so I shall speak no more of the troubles of bookselling, but I would spend sleepless nights of horror if I heard that any customer of Brentano's felt that we had made a profit on his purchase. We are in trade only for dignity, atmosphere, and service.

In the old days, of course, things were different. When August Brentano, the founder of the firm, opened Brentano's Literary Emporium at Broadway and Houston Street, he found that many of his clientele were devotees of horse racing. But there weren't many horse races in the United States then, and most wagers were on the great English races, such as the Derby, the St. Leger, and the Grand National. Clipper ships carried the results, and cables were fragmentary and uncertain. So it came about that the bets were decided by the columns of the London *Times,* which arrived in New York many weeks after the great races had taken place. The wily August, who saw great profits in this situation, was able to arrange large shipments of the London *Times* at, say, five cents a copy, which he promptly sold to his racing clientele at a dollar a copy.

But if there are no longer such profits in Brentano's, there are other rewards, and one of them is the Paris store, on the Avenue de l'Opéra, which remains Paris's leading American bookstore and which was founded in the year I was born. We are a little proud, too, that it was the first American store to be opened after the liberation of France, and as Arthur Brentano, Jr., tells the story, it was on the morning of April 19, 1945, that our first postwar customer arrived, an American sergeant, who purchased two Penguin books, *Walden* and *The City of Beautiful Nonsense.* During the war years the Germans had treated us with some kindness, for though they confiscated nearly all of the stock of fountain pens and small novelties, they moved most of the books to the very back of the store, and the front became a photography shop for the sale of films and for the development of snapshots that Nazi soldiers took with their complacent French girls walking along the banks of the Seine. A few thousand of these still remain there to be called for, but the store is once again doing business, and someday we shall get a dividend from it instead of simply taxes and francs.

Booksellers as well as publishers are always held responsible for books which may be thought scurrilous, indecent, or offensive to public taste. There is no question, I think, that publishing has, since the war, taken an unsavory turn. But Brentano's believes that the condemnation of any given book should be determined by the courts and by the publishers themselves, and not by the booksellers. If we refuse to sell a book because of its attacks on individuals in public life, we are likely to get a blast such as the following from Drew Pearson when I once made the mistake of refusing to sell a book for personal reasons. "Brentano's bookstore is playing down Bob Allen's new book *The Truman Merry-go-round*. The book is critical of Ambassador Stanton Griffis, and the Ambassador just happens to own Brentano's." This was correct and we did refuse to sell the book, thus probably giving it much more publicity than it would otherwise have received.

Recently we have been in the throes of the controversy over an unpleasant book known as *U.S.A. Confidential*, and we have received a good many complaints about it from distinguished citizens. One from a United States Senator read as follows: "Please close out my account with you at once. I do not remember when I have *ever* before severed my business connections with any institution because of such an incident. I do not normally believe in such action, but it is shocking to me that an institution of your heritage can bring itself to the selling of such a book as *U.S.A. Confidential*." Probably the whole matter is best summed up by the recent pronouncement of the American Booksellers' Association that "A bookseller can be dishonored not by any single book he sells, but only by reacting to pressures not to sell any book that people wished to buy, because it offends, insults or exposes any individual or group.

"Bookselling is an old and dignified vocation, and it came to be that way because it has always accepted the responsibility of offering for sale *Macbeth* or *Mein Kampf*; truth and fiction, exposé, and muck-raking history and prognostication, side by side on its shelves for the reader to choose at his discretion. If the bookseller is to retain a free place where free men select reading matter each to his taste, then he must contribute to expose to the light all books of all publishers for public examination."

Some books, of course, should not be placed on sale for reasons other than the quality of their contents, and in this con-

nection I recall an incident that illustrates still another evil that
the bookseller falls heir to. Some years ago Arthur Brentano,
Jr., called me downtown and told me that he had an opportunity to buy an Audubon book for $5,000. I did not quite
know what an Audubon book was, but he explained that it
was one of the massive volumes of bird drawings and paintings
that were becoming increasingly rare in this country. He told
me that he thought he could cut up the book and sell it in individual pages with a considerable profit; taking his judgment
at face value, I told him to go ahead. I completely forgot the
incident, but about two years later, the book having long since
been cut up and resold, we received a visit from the attorney
of one of New York's old families, famous for its great library
of "old and rare." The family counselor told us that the book
had been sold to us without permission and without accounting by the son of the family. In other words it had been stolen.
The lawyer called upon us to return the volume. But the book
no longer existed. It could not be recreated and we were unable to meet their demands, whereupon they threatened to sue
us for many thousand dollars. Arthur asked my advice and I
said to him, "Tell them to go ahead and sue if they wish to
bring out in court that their son, unknown to us and without
authority, stole the book and sold it to us. Tell them to go
ahead and we will take the consequences." That was the end
of the story of the Audubon book.

We", I am happy to have had the experience of high hopes
and failure in the retail bookselling business, but I am happier
to turn it over to the younger generation, with the hope that
they will have greater pleasure and success out of it than I
have had. I still hope that the publishers will come to deal
reasonably with their clients, and realize what would happen
if General Motors or any other great manufacturer deliber-
ately created a separate organization through which they could
undersell their own dealers. Great changes might come and
fair play might yet prevail, but in the meantime I, like most

other booksellers, agree with the lines in "Ol' Man River"— "I'm tired of livin' and feared of dyin' "; I just go rolling along.

My son Nixon runs the business now. And I wish him luck with it.

# CHAPTER SEVEN

## THE STAGE, THE GARDEN,
## AND THE MOVIES

In the 1930s, after sixteen years in the investment business, I really became a rolling stone. Traditionally, rolling stones gather no moss but, according to some people, they usually acquire a lot of polish. By some unwise trick of fate, my own experience seems to have confuted both of these statements. At one time or another in my life I have gathered quite a lot of moss but, rolling along as I have, I have not accumulated much polish.

I began to grow tired of finance, but the more tired of it I grew, the more enthusiastic I became about the entertainment business, down whose aisles I had occasionally strolled in my youth. Some wag once said that during the twenties I had often undertaken uptown ventures only to lose the profits that I had made downtown. But in the thirties things were different. I had to go uptown to balance the losses that I was taking downtown. Thus it was not surprising, in view of my keen interest in the theatre, and after some years of association with Katharine Cornell and her director-husband, Guthrie McClintic, that I welcomed the opportunity suggested by my old friend Conger Goodyear, a sybarite businessman, founder of the Museum of Modern Art and of the American National Theatre and Academy, that we form a company to finance the plays that Miss Cornell and her husband hoped to produce.

The result was the Cornell and McClintic Productions Company, familiarly known as C. and M.C. Its original capital was about $25,000, and its first production was *The Barretts of Wimpole Street*, which opened in 1930 at the old Empire at 39th Street and Broadway. *The Barretts* ran for several years and, what with motion-picture rights, revivals, and stock receipts, made close to a million dollars. Its distinguished company included Brian Aherne, Margalo Gillmore, Brenda Forbes, and that lovable canine actor, Flush. He was a magnificent actor and thoroughly a show-off; who survived many revivals and lived to a ripe old age, finally going into a decline at Kit Cornell's country place at Sneeden's Landing.

Gorged with the success of *The Barretts of Wimpole Street*, C. and M.C. Productions went on to lease the old Belasco theatre on 44th Street, where the ghost of its founder looked on us with critical eyes. Goodyear and I had offices on the second floor, at the top of a steep flight of stairs. They were so long and steep that many actors had accused Belasco of designing them so that the poor players in quest of work would be exhausted by the time they reached the executive offices and would agree to accept any salary Belasco offered. Goodyear and Griffi.. ..re as useful to the company as a mosquito to a bald head, but we had a lot of fun nevertheless. From the profits, Miss Cornell established the Katharine Cornell Foundation, which for twenty years has come to the aid of many struggling artists and theatrical organizations, and I think that Goodyear and I are still directors both of the Company and the Foundation, which holds regular meetings about every ten years.

It was probably because of my experience in show business that sometime in April 1934, Floyd Odlum, head of the Atlas Corporation, called me up and asked if I knew anything about Madison Square Garden. I told him that I had occasionally been there for prize fights and so on, but I added that I knew nothing whatever about it from a business angle. He told me

that the controlling stock of the Garden, owned by the estate
of Dick Hoyt, its former chairman, was about to come on the
market, and that John Hammond, who once managed the New
York Rangers, had come to him with a proposition to buy the
Garden. The plan was that we should buy the stock and that
Hammond should operate the place.

I told Odlum to send me the figures, and promised him that
I would study them and give him a ring. The next morning I
called him and said, "I've spent some time on these figures, and
it looks to me like quite a deal." I added, "I don't think that
we can make any money out of it, but I think we'll have a lot
of fun. Let's go." This was the most accurate business prognostication I ever made. We closed the deal, went gardening
on Eighth Avenue, had a lot of fun, and never made much
money.

Madison Square Garden has had a fantastic history. It began, of course, in Madison Square itself, where it was not only
a sports center but also the scene of many sensational political
conventions, including the famous Al Smith-McAdoo dead-
lock in 1924, as well as of various non-political shootings, including the murder of Stanford White by Harry Thaw.

When the Garden moved to Eighth Avenue between 49th
and 50th streets, with its highly publicized "Club of 200 Mil-
lionaires," it flourished under the management of Tex Rickard.
When Tex died, a man named Bill Cary ran it for a while, and
when we bought it, General John Reed Kilpatrick was its
president.

We were not long in running into internal trouble, for no
sooner had I settled down there than William Greve, an old
friend of mine, called on me to say that he and his fellow
directors, particularly Walter Chrysler and Bernard Gimbel,
were determined to retain Kilpatrick as president because of
their personal loyalty to him. They greatly resented Hammond's entry into the situation, and they also resented our
purchase of the Hoyt stock without their having had an op-

portunity to buy it. Greve told me that they all proposed to resign from the board. I did not want them to leave and told them so, and the upshot was that they agreed to remain for six months, at the end of which they would permit me to make the final decision as to whether Hammond or Kilpatrick was the proper man to head the Garden. If my decision was for Hammond, they would loyally stay along with it.

It did not take me, nor did it take many others of the new board members, very long to realize that Kilpatrick was for many reasons the proper man. A violent stockholders' fight followed. Hammond was backed by many wealthy friends, including James Norris of Chicago, and those of us who turned to Kilpatrick's side were driven to purchase thousands of shares of stock at extremely high prices in order to hold control. We began a bitter stockholders' meeting on September 24, 1935. It was probably one of the longest stockholders' meetings in history. It lasted four days, each well into the night, but when the smoke cleared away we were in control and Hammond was out of the picture. At the end of this lengthy meeting on the floor of the Garden, I walked over to Jim Norris and asked him to let bygones be bygones and to join us on the Garden board. A handshake sealed the bargain, and Jim Norris, together with his son and his associate Arthur Wirtz, now holds the chief controlling interest of the Garden.

It was at this time that I received an insight into the loyalty of Walter Chrysler, the great automobile manufacturer, who was my friend for many years and who every Tuesday afternoon came to my apartment in the Carlton House in New York to attend a meeting of the Garden executive committee. We had all been pretty much depressed by the prospects of the approaching stockholders' meeting, and I was sitting alone in my apartment the night before the last day on which we could buy Madison Square Garden stock and thus augment our voting power. The telephone rang and I answered it. My only word was "Hello." The voice at the other end of the wire

said, "Stan, this is Walter, I have to leave for Detroit at midnight tonight. I have told my secretary to send you over in
the morning a check for $100,000. Use it any way you like,
don't let those ———s beat us."

This was the essence of Walter Chrysler. I used the money
to buy the stock, and I loved this man until the day he died.
When I became chairman of Paramount Pictures, I tried very
hard to persuade him to come on the Paramount board, for he
was as great a showman as he was a manufacturer. But he declined. I believe that he went on but one important board besides that of his beloved Chrysler Corporation, and that was
the board of the New York Central. The story goes that at
the first meeting of the Central directors he told the management graybeards that the only improvement that had been
made in American railroad operations in the past twenty years
was the slot in the mens' room for used safety-razor blades.

I became chairman of the Garden after Hammond was
ousted, and I remained in that post for about thirteen years,
until I went to Poland in 1947 and turned the responsibility
over to Bernard Gimbel, who was far more fitted than I to
assume it.

With Tex Rickard's death, the genius of creating boxing
profits vanished. But we tried very hard to carry on the tradition under Jimmy Johnson, our boxing promoter. The Garden
had always been known as "The Temple of Swat" and we
were determined to maintain its reputation. We were constantly harassed, however, by the independent operations and
superior abilities of Mike Jacobs, a uniquely successful promoter, for while the Garden had always controlled the heavy-
weight championship, Mike had signed a contract with Joe
Louis, a rising young Negro known as the "Brown Bomber."
Mike, who was one of the most picturesque figures in the business—clicking his Sears-Roebuck teeth at his listeners—wanted
in. Since we were not doing well in boxing, Gimbel, Kilpatrick, and I proceeded on the principle that when a man is

smarter than you, you had better take him on as a partner. So Mike moved in as promotion manager for boxing in the Garden, yielding his post only a few years ago, when he was laid low by a stroke.

The very mechanical operations of the Garden are as fascinating as its weird contracts with boxers, skaters, hockey players, circus operators, basketball teams, cowboys and cowgirls. It operates about three hundred nights a year, and when one realizes that a hockey game ends at eleven o'clock at night and leaves a thick layer of painted ice on the Garden floor (under which run miles of ammonia-filled pipe to freeze the ice), that a battalion of ice plows and workmen must start cleaning out the arena and prepare the setup for a basketball game the next night, all in a period of about eighteen hours; that later a great political mass meeting must give way in a few hours to the entrance of Ringling Brothers-Barnum and Bailey Combined Circus, with three inches of tanbark; that horse shows, ice shows and rodeos come in rapid succession, we can understand something of the physical problems which we face in the operation.

But even these chores are nothing compared with the Garden's endless public relations problems. During the thirties we rented the Garden to many organizations, among them various Communist groups of one persuasion or another. But we seemed always to deal with the same man, who was apparently the general manager of all Communistic public activity in New York. This situation troubled the directors, and at various times we sent emissaries not only to the President, but to J. Edgar Hoover of the FBI, asking whether or not we should allow the meetings to continue. Everyone agreed that we should, especially in view of the fact that the meetings gave the FBI an opportunity to spot the leading Communists. To-day, of course, this problem has solved itself. It would be impossible, even if we permitted it, to find any Communists who would attend such meetings.

A far graver crisis arose when we rented the Garden to a gathering of the Bund in New York. It was led by men in full black-shirt and Nazi regalia and had all the atmosphere of a meeting in Munich. *"Heil, heil,"* rang continuously through the Garden during the evening. It was a peculiarly obnoxious spectacle. I shall never forget my correspondence with Edna Ferber on the matter. She wrote:

*February 25, 1939*

*Dear Stan,*

You're probably in Florida or anywhere that's not New York in February—which is true of those lucky ones of us who can possibly get away at this time of year.

I'm hoping, nevertheless, that this will somehow reach you.

You are, I know, a director and large stockholder in Madison Square Garden. I, as an American, a Jew, and a civilized human being, object with every fibre of decency and justice in me to your having consented to allow Madison Square Garden to be used for the Nazi meeting of last Monday—or for any Nazi meeting. It may be that you agree with their aims and beliefs. I think—I hope—I know you too well to believe that. You may say that the renting of the Garden is outside your jurisdiction. I don't believe that, either.

I know you are a rich man. It can't be that money would be a consideration in permitting these apes to present in Madison Square Garden the ghastly exhibition of this past week.

I have known you for years, I have liked and respected you. But this I must say to you, and you must believe that I mean it:

If ever again Madison Square Garden is rented for the purpose of a Nazi meeting I shall spend my days and my nights talking and writing to every New York Jew who can possibly be reached by my words and my typewriter, asking that they boycott Madison Square Garden. I have attended hockey games, fights, athletic exhibitions—all sorts of occasions—at the Garden. I know what proportion of your audience is made up

79

of Jews. I won't rest until every one of them has pledged himself to stay away from the Garden.

If this is construed by you as a threat, you're right. It is one. I'm sorry that my feeling of shock, indignation and outraged decency makes it necessary for me to write you in this way.

*Sincerely,*

EDNA FERBER

**MADISON SQUARE GARDEN CORPORATION**
49TH & 50TH STREETS—EIGHTH AVENUE, NEW YORK

*February 28, 1939*

*Miss Edna Ferber*
*The Arizona Biltmore*
*Phoenix, Arizona*

*My dear Edna:*

Although I resent from the bottom of my heart the things that you have written me, and the general tone of your letter, my affection for you of many years standing tells me that perhaps, in an hour of excitement and emotional pressure, you have said things that you would perhaps not have said to an old friend, had you known anything of the circumstances surrounding what he might have done.

First of all, let me say that I have no intention whatever of taking shelter behind any statement that the running of Madison Square Garden is outside of what you speak of as my "jurisdiction." I am fully responsible for anything that is done in, or in connection with the Garden; responsible not only to my stockholders, but responsible to my sense of the relationship which exists between a corporation of this kind and the general public, and to my own beliefs and my own sense of decency—specifically, I take full responsibility for permitting the so-called "Bund" meeting to be held in the Garden.

In order that you may understand the background for this decision, let me tell you that for years the Garden has stood fast to the principle of free speech in America, and the right of any political organization, race, creed, or sect, to hire its facilities so long as it was willing to keep the peace and maintain order. In this, we have always believed that we were following a basic American principle, one of the principles the change from which has resulted in the conditions which exist in Germany today. We have believed that this freedom was what America meant, and so we have rented the Garden to Socialists, Communists, Republicans, Democrats, Jews and Gentiles alike—and we shall continue so to do.

As a matter of historical interest, the lease of the Garden to the "Bund" was made many months ago, with no feeling on our part that the general public would be particularly interested in the meeting. When it became evident that there was going to exist a widespread interest in the gathering and possible disorders of a sort, our first thought at the Garden was to consult with those of our directors who are Jews, among others Mr. Sidney Weinberg and Mr. Bernard Gimbel. These men were firm in their belief that we should proceed with the meeting, that the Democratic processes be permitted to work in an orderly way.

We went further than this. We consulted men like Mayor La Guardia, Morris Ernst, and various Jewish organizations including the American Jewish Committee, which wrote us in accordance with the letter, a copy of which I am enclosing. Not one of our Jewish friends with whom we discussed this matter, but felt that the meeting should proceed.

No one in their senses who knows me, could possibly believe that I have anything but abhorrence for the aims and beliefs of Naziism; but by the same token, dear Edna, I trust that no one who knows me well, and who would have any desire to regard me as fit for the category of their friendship, could feel that I could be either frightened or intimidated by the threats which you frankly state you are making. This, I think, hurt me as much as your feeling that I would evade responsibility, or that for a rental fee I would betray the countless friendships I have with those, who like you are proud of the fact that they are Jewish, "both on their mother's and father's side."

With this quotation suddenly coming in my mind, I am reminded that through the many meetings which were held in my apartment in regard to this meeting in the Garden, you yourself indirectly contributed to some of the discussions in regard to it; for I was reading your latest, and I think most distinguished book* at the time, and made reference to it frequently in these discussions.

Since this famous meeting, I have read many columns of editorial comments and publicity regarding it. I am convinced that more harm was done to the Nazi cause in America by this meeting, than has been done by any agency or group of agencies during the entire Hitler regime. From this you may derive some comfort.

Well, there it all is, and perhaps you don't agree with me in any or all of it. I gather from the violence of your letter that you won't, but I will still trail along with Voltaire and I shall still try to look any man in the face with the quotation which I am probably butchering that, "I disapprove from my heart what you say, but I will defend to the death your right to say it."

Yours for better days on earth,

*Sincerely*,

STANTON GRIFFIS

MZAB14 40 NL 4 EXTRA=BM PHOENIX ARIZ MAR 2 VIA ZG
NEWYORK NY
STANTON GRIFFIS
BOCARATON CLUB
YOU ARE RIGHT STAN AND I WAS WRONG IT WAS AS YOU SAY AN EMOTIONAL NOT A MENTAL REACTION CAUSED BY THE SICKEN-ING EFFECT ONE GOT ON READING THE REPORTS OF THE MEETING AT THIS DISTANCE=EDNA

*A Peculiar Treasure*, Doubleday & Co., 1939.

*Arizona Biltmore, Phoenix*
*March 5, 1939*

That makes it Fifteen All, dear Stan.

But look: If I were you, and owned as much of M.S.G. as you do I'd want to make some public expression of the way I felt about renting my property to Nazis and Communists and other Democracy destroyers. I'd take the money that was my share of those particular rentals, and, by God, I'd use it to buy space in the public prints to state that I believe in allowing the same democratic rights to my enemies and the enemies of the government that are due my friends and fellow-believers. But that in mind and heart and spirit I am unalterably opposed to their policies and beliefs.

*Yours,*

EDNA

I'm leaving here and coming back to New York. Too impatient to look at flowers and boids and mountains and old golf-playing stuffed shirts.

Though our great American novelist finally admitted that I was right and she was wrong, I believe now, as I look back over the years, that she was right and we were wrong. All of us I think at that time underestimated the rattlesnake aspect of the power that was rising in Germany; as we did indeed, the power that was rising in Moscow.

The Garden lives and goes on. It is known throughout the world wherever sports are known, and will, I think, continue so to be. We are charged with every sin in the calendar, from scandal to monopoly; but it is operated as cleanly as any institution that I know. To some extent we are changing from a palace of sports exhibition to a television laboratory; for in recent years our income from television and radio has steadily increased, while our net at the box office has steadily decreased. The directors are still undecided as to whether or not sporting events in New York City should be televised in New York

City, and true box-office judgment is yet to come. But I believe they will find a solution when and if the motion-picture theatres perfect large screen television, and if a device is perfected whereby a person can see a sporting event right in his own home simply by dropping a coin in a slot. Television will become more and more a friend of the Garden, and the Garden will be a friend of television.

In 1935, as I gradually transferred my chief allegiance from sports to motion pictures, I was rudely disillusioned. Anyone who seriously enters the motion-picture industry with visions of continually hobnobbing with beautiful, honey-haired nymphs reclining on moon-bathed tropical shores, as Bing Crosby croons and Bob Hope tells jokes, is in for a cruel disappointment. The motion-picture business is one of the toughest, most competitive of all industries. While a few of its members get the fabulous salaries that have made the land of the mile-high malted as famous as it is, the run-of-the-mill people are paid on much the same scale as that of any other great business. It is, of course, an exciting industry and a colorful one. But success in it depends upon hard work. The glamour is only skin-deep.

Paramount Pictures, the giant of the motion-picture industry, conceived by Adolph Zukor and developed during the twenties by a series of wild speculations, bowed to its excesses at the turn of the decade, and it was just emerging from a long and expensive receivership when I became a director in 1935, again through the suggestion of Floyd Odlum, and with the friendly assistance of Percy H. Johnston, president of the Chemical Bank. Its creditors had bequeathed it a diamond-studded board of directors, made up mostly of railroad presidents, bank presidents and similar tycoons selected, so it seemed, for their complete ignorance of the motion-picture industry. Once more the shades of doom enveloped the enterprise and it seemed about ready to go back into receivership. It was a tragic situation, but it presented certain enticing problems to a business physician, and before long I found myself chairman of Paramount's executive committee, spending days and nights in the Paramount offices; much to the disgust of my partners downtown.

Paramount at that time owned, controlled, or leased in the United States and Canada nearly two thousand theatres; more than the number held by all of its major competitor companies combined. It had another far-flung chain of houses in England, France, and Belgium, and its distributing organization extended into practically every country in the civilized world. At the studio in Hollywood, through a succession of managements and mismanagements, the company had burdened itself with fabulous contracts, such as the series with Mae West and Marlene Dietrich, who received about $250,000 per picture. It was a great sprawling business, a Gulliver rapidly being made captive by its self-created Lilliputians.

But while the parent company had its problems, its Chicago and Middle West theatre subsidiary, Balaban and Katz, managed to escape receivership through the expert management of Barney Balaban and his brother John. Thus we turned to Barney in our extremity and asked him to become president. At a historic and embittered stockholders' meeting held on June 20, 1936, the board was completely reorganized. Balaban was elected president, and Zukor became chairman of the board, while I remained and remain to this day, although nominally now, the chairman of the executive committee. But Balaban's election did not end the strife that continued among the stockholders. During our developing years for example almost all of Paramount's stockholders' meetings were stormy, for the motion-picture business is peculiarly subject to the criticisms of small stockholders. At the second meeting after the company's reorganization, the management found an unknown champion in a visiting stockholder who announced himself as the holder of ten shares of Paramount stock and who paid a high tribute to Balaban and to me. He was an old, al-

most unknown actor, but he told the assembled stockholders of
his appearance with Florence Reed in *The Shanghai Gesture*,
and gave them an imitation of a Chinese merchant telephon-
ing a house of ill repute in Shanghai to make an engagement
with his favorite Chinese doll. He then sang songs of his own
composition, and under cover of the laughter engendered by
his appearance we were able to adjourn the meeting without
further criticisms from the stockholders. I was so delighted by
his performance that for years I sent him an annual pass to the
Paramount Theatres. One year I had no letter of thanks, and
shortly thereafter I read of the death of this old actor, Conrad
Cantzen, who by living in subways and cheap rooming houses
and sometimes sleeping covered by newspapers in parks had,
through careful investment, amassed a fortune of close to
$250,000. He left it with the Guaranty Trust Company as
trustee, "to buy shoes for needy actors," since he believed that
actors tramping from manager to manager wore out their shoes
and could obtain positions only if their shoes were in good
shape.

The meeting at which Cantzen had performed was the turning point in the history of a great company. I lived and worked
for almost seven years in an office adjoining that of Barney
Balaban in the Paramount Building in New York, and com-
muted almost monthly to Hollywood. I can say without hesitation that never in my long business and government career
have I met a man with such knowledge and capacity for work
as Barney had, or with higher principles of conduct, both
public and private. My years of association with him were
happy and fruitful. This son of an east-side Chicago immigrant
taught me much.

Our first move was a fast trip to the studio, where we
studied contracts, budgets, inventories, casting, and studio
operations of all sorts. Barney had an intimate knowledge of
the operations both of theatres and production, and I was well
grounded in finance. Paramount securities were selling at re-

ceivership prices, and the corporation was in a good position to buy itself back cheaply. Harvey Gibson, president of the Manufacturers Trust Company, had joined our board during the reorganization, and as soon as Barney and I had assured ourselves that the situation could be worked out, we phoned Harvey in New York to ask him for a credit of $1,000,000 to be used in purchasing our own securities at the great discounts which then prevailed. Our telephone conversation lasted less than five minutes. Without figures and without details, he said, "If you and Barney feel that it's good, I will let you have a million dollars, and I hope that you will come back to me for a great deal more." We did, again and again. Profits began to come in and public confidence was re-established, and for a while we made a great deal more for the company out of the business of purchasing our own securities at bargain prices than we made by operating our theatres and studio.

Before Balaban entered the situation, the directors had become a bit jittery and decided to obtain an unbiased report on the whole Paramount operation. They selected Joseph P. Kennedy for the job, who, after a long study, delivered us a voluminous and bitterly pessimistic report. Five years later *Time* magazine recalled the Kennedy report under the headline, "Paramount is Paramount Again." The article said:

Paramount Pictures, declared Joseph Patrick Kennedy, "is a chain of incompetent, unbusinesslike and wasteful practices," for which another receivership seemed inevitable. That was five years ago. Last week Paramount stockholders got their quarter report; profits were $3,710,000.00, highest since 1930, and almost double the $1,726,000.00 cleared a year ago. More significant, this net was twice that of arch rival Loew's, Inc. After ten years of tussling Paramount was again the biggest money maker in show business. When Joe Kennedy wrote his epitaph of Paramount, many a Wall Streeter figured he was dead right. Paramount had just stumbled out of bankruptcy without appearing to shed any of the overgrown ineptitude that had put it there.

This week Paramount stockholders were the happiest of a happy lot. Moreover, the very brick and mortar that swamped Paramount in 1933, is now its most profitable possession.

It was shortly before this time that the press picked up a statement of mine that the profits from the popcorn and candy business in the theatres were more than sufficient to pay all our interest charges.

Upon the completion of the Gibson loan and some other banking arrangements, I took a hurried trip to England, where the Paramount investment was in the millions. The British management had gone from bad to worse, and I was the first senior officer of Paramount to visit England in several years. I stopped first in Paris for a short visit and telegraphed the British manager that I would be in his office on Monday morning. He replied that he lived in the country and seldom got to London before Tuesday morning. He said that he would be able to see me on Tuesday or Wednesday, but preferably not Thursday as he usually returned to the country on that day. He was soon among the missing in the Paramount organization.

One of the first chores that I inherited at Paramount sprang from suits for malfeasance that the receivers had been ordered by the court to bring against the directors who held office during the twenties. The suits contained charges of various kinds, ranging from lack of plain business acumen to general mismanagement as well as to the issuance of common stock to be sold to the respective directors or to their firms at prices under the market. The various suits were for approximately eighteen million dollars, and the pile of testimony that I was required to study nightly piled almost four feet high in my Carlton House apartment.

There was some merit in the suits but not much, and I was determined not to permit the unfortunate past financial history of Paramount to be dragged through the courts just when we were trying to rebuild—and rebuild soundly—its financial structure. I felt that the amount of time and money that we would waste in pursuing these suits would provide only a Roman holiday for the lawyers, and I made every effort to settle the whole thing out of court. In this I had the friendly co-operation of John Schiff, who had just become a senior partner in Kuhn, Loeb and Company. He and I went over the voluminous figures, and to end a very unpleasant episode we agreed on a settlement, which we finally sent to the court. It was accepted and a useless and unhappy chapter in Paramount's history came to an end.

Meanwhile I found that our English theatres were, to paraphrase an old movie joke, so heavily mortgaged that they looked like covered wagons. The interest rates were running as high as 9 per cent, but the British bankers by that time knew full well that with the rising tide of Paramount credit we could borrow enough money in the United States at around 3 per cent to repay these loans. So they agreed to lower their rates accordingly, and eventually the earnings of the British theatres themselves paid off the notes.

As it went in England, so it did in the United States. Under the Balaban management, we started with such a burden of debt and issues of preferred stock that the entire load ahead of the common shares amounted close to $125,000,000. But with improved studio production and theatre management, and careful financing through the years, aided of course by ever increasing earnings, Paramount Pictures found itself in the forties with no debt, no preferred stock, a thoroughly comfortable net quick-asset position, and even with its common stock issue greatly diminished by purchase in the open market. Many small fortunes were made by those men and institutions who believed in Paramount during the years of its transition. We had really tried to make it what is known as an investment stock, and even with the threatening advent of country-wide television in the late forties, we were not too greatly shaken.

As long ago as 1938 we had begun to prepare for television. It was a small threat at the time, but we were taking no chances with the new toy. The image was wavering and uncertain, the screens usually about four inches square, and transmission frequently failed for no apparent reason. Coaxial cable development was just starting. However, we refused to underestimate the genius of American engineers, and we knew that sooner or later this newfangled invention was bound to be perfected. We had no choice but to consider it seriously.

With Paul Raibourn, Paramount's technical and statistical expert, I journeyed to England again to study television developments there, which proved to be about as embryonic as those in the United States. Besides such great organizations as Radio Corporation of America and General Electric, only a few struggling companies were attempting to enter the field in the United States. The business was in itself a vicious circle. The consumer refused to purchase any of the few sets that were on the market until he could get good programs. Advertisers, who had fostered the astounding development of radio, refused to spend money to create commercial performances until enough sets had been sold to justify their expense.

Paramount had once before lost a great opportunity in the field of electronics. Before the receivership it had been the owner of a 50 per cent interest in the Columbia Broadcasting System, but unfortunately it was driven by financial pressure to sell its interest long before Columbia became a factor in the battle for television supremacy.

In studying the limited field for television investment in the United States, Balaban, Raibourn, and I found that there seemed to be only one company, Farnsworth, which was developing, and in which we could acquire an interest and thus purchase the ability to receive news of developments as the business expanded. However, we felt that the owners of Farnsworth had a far too exalted opinion of the company's value. We offered them several millions, but they said no. We could not agree on terms and perhaps the history of the Farnsworth company, which soon fell on hard times, proves that this was our lucky day.

At about this time we heard that a downtown broker had worked out a deal to distribute 100,000 shares of the common stock of the Allen B. Du Mont Laboratories, which seemed to be making real progress in electronics. The stated selling price was one dollar per share, but even at that price few people bought the stock. However, we decided to see Mr. Du Mont and his financial representatives, and this time our plunge was not in quite such deep water. The elements of the story are simple. Paramount purchased 52,000 shares of Du Mont common stock, agreed to lend certain additional funds, and was at last on the borders of the television industry. It serves no useful purpose to detail the various underwritings and financial developments of Du Mont during the intervening years, except to say that Paramount still owns approximately 30 per cent of Du Mont, for which it paid little or nothing, and which today is selling for more than $10,000,000. Thus today we have a very large foot in the industry's somewhat larger door.

The entertainment and financial world today is agog with groping and uncertainty as to the ultimate effect of television upon the motion-picture industry. My crystal ball still shines dimly on this question, but I do not think that my beliefs seriously differ from those I expressed fourteen years ago, when in February 1939 I spoke before the National Board of Review of Motion Pictures at the Hotel Pennsylvania and said, "Television is not the enemy but the friend of motion pictures, and will be the source of great profits to the industry. . . . While the future of the new art is still obscure it is bound to be closely correlated with the motion-picture industry, with the probability that each art and each business will complement the other. For the exhibitor we see the televising of great sports and other current events as an important adjunct to newsreel programs. Some day we will use transmission of the world panorama of news for projection directly on our great screens, but I feel that this is a long way off. If we look back, you will agree, I think, that the development of radio has complemented and gone hand in hand with the development of the motion pictures without any great damage to either, and perhaps profit to both. The desire of every man to see pictures of joy and sorrow and happiness and suffering not alone but in the company of his fellow man will prevail and continue. Television will act only as every other development that increases public interest in entertainment and amusement, that is, to aid the greatest entertainment business of all, motion pictures. Although I cannot yet pick up any television broadcasts from future days, and your guess is as good as mine, from the point of view of the film industry, we at Paramount believe that the development of television will bring into being in the studios important new departments, both for the adaptation of old films to television programs, but as well, the manufacture of new specialty films of entirely different nature for the television programs. Our laboratories are already working along these lines, for it is our belief that for the next few years a tremendous percentage of all televised programs will be from films and not from direct photography."

All this I believe today, and in recent testimony before the Federal Communications Commission in Washington, in reference to the continuance of Paramount's interest in the development of television, I stated that there will develop a very happy, successful, and lasting marriage between television and motion pictures, to which each will give much and from which each will gain much.

Paramount's interest in television has been progressive. During the war, following the development of a Balaban and Katz transmitter in Chicago, our partners there developed at their own expense a tremendous school for army students of electronics, and furnished hundreds of electronic engineers as officers in the signal corps. In California a Paramount subsidiary has erected a great transmission station on one of the near-by high mountains of Southern California, and in New York the Du Mont transmission station has become more and more important in the networks of the United States. Paramount and television are bound to go hand in hand.

In 1950 Paramount underwent another crisis when the government ordered it to relinquish its theatre holdings. During the long anti-trust suit that followed we were accused of nearly every conceivable crime; of the violation of laws, when no laws existed, of discrimination against small operators, and of all sorts of other malpractice. I have no intention of going into the long and tortuous history of this case, in which all sorts of charlatans gleefully assisted their government. It is enough to say that Paramount was the first great motion-picture company to bow to the government's wishes, formally separating its production, television, and Canadian operations from its American theatre enterprises.

Accordingly, a separate corporation known as United Paramount Theatres was created under the leadership of Paramount's former vice-president in charge of theatre operation, Mr. Leonard Goldenson, who is presently aiming for a union with the American Broadcasting Company in order to combine its radio and television facilities with his theatre enterprises. I personally believe that Paramount Pictures is no better off, nor any worse off, than it was before the government suit, nor indeed are the various exhibitors who accused us of nefarious crimes. The success of both still depends on management and timing.

The history of Paramount, as of all great companies, is the history of its officers and its loyal employees. I have a deep affection for Paramount, and I have tried to write this brief sketch of my service with it in words of loving kindness. I have spoken previously of Adolph Zukor, the sage of the entire industry, of Barney Balaban, of Paul Raibourn, and of

93

Leonard Goldenson, but there are myriad others who should be mentioned, such as Russell Holman of Paramount's story department, and certainly I cannot forget Austin Keough, Paramount's own Blackstone. A brilliant lawyer, he has guided the company for many years through the mazes of government suits, monopolistic charges, civil suits, and strike suits, which unfortunately have a way of cropping up in this strange industry. Always harassed and overworked, he has never lost his perspective, and I have come to the conclusion through the years that he likes his job.

One of my favorite Paramount suits is the one that arose while we were making a jungle picture. The film starred Dorothy Lamour, and as I watched the shooting in Palm Springs Canyon I noticed another star, an enormous ape, who, when settled on his haunches, was only about three feet tall. The extra girls for the picture, posing as beautiful denizens of the South Sea jungles, were arrayed in thin, diaphanous sarongs and had been warned to keep away from the gentleman ape, who usually showed great charm but occasionally indicated interests of an unusual nature. Nevertheless, one of the girls insisted on petting the friendly animal, and as she turned away, the wind lifted her costume and exposed a particularly luscious portion of her anatomy at about eye level to the ape. Apparently thinking that luncheon time was near, he casually leaned over and took a large bite out of her posterior. Despite our warnings we were sued for a substantial amount, and we had to settle the case for $50,000, presumably on the basis of $100,000 for her two derrière protuberances, of which only one had been bitten.

Great stars and small stars, directors and writers, and technicians of every sort come and go, but they all contribute something to the business. Cecil B. De Mille, whose lifework is to produce "the greatest show on earth," seems to sum them all up. The *B* in his name should stand for Barnum.

There are many arts, and there are many of us who are

The author hard at work—on his boat in Miami Bay

The editor in chief (left) with the business manager of the Cornell *Daily Sun*

The editor in chief and the business manager, Jansen Noyes, still in business forty years later

artists without an art, and so, perhaps in introvert self-defense, I have sometimes tried to create the illusion that one of the greatest artists is the man who is able to become what I call an organizer of art. Out in the studio, and functioning as its head, is one of the greatest of these, the Paramount vice-president in charge of production, Mr. Y. Frank Freeman. Constantly driven and tormented by the problems and eccentricities of his actors, writers, producers, costumers, make-up men, and agents, and by the innumerable unions that infest the business, he has remained placid and unruffled through the years. An incorrigible pessimist, who always manages to make a profit, he is a true southern gentleman, and I know that he will permit me to end this chapter with a brief story of his gentle bride, telling it as he probably tells it, with considerable exaggeration.

Amid all the tumult and shouting which arose in connection with David Selznick's production of *Gone with the Wind*, there developed country-wide discussion as to whether the dialogue of this Civil War picture should be in the good, rich dialect of the Old South or whether it should reach the public in Vivien Leigh's precise British accent. Frank Freeman's wife, Margaret, whose own linguistic expression flows direct from the Suwannee River, was a militant advocate of the theory that the opus should be produced in southern dialect, but she did not know Mr. Selznick. However, when Frank, in a moment of indiscretion, told her that Selznick was occupying a drawing room in the next car on The Chief en route to New York, Margaret decided to approach him on the subject. She spent almost two hours with him, expounding her views on the historic necessity of using southern speech in *Gone with the Wind*, and returned to her own drawing room convinced that she had won her point. A short time later Frank Freeman met Selznick in the observation car, and Selznick observed, "Frank, your wife is certainly very charming. She spent almost two hours with me this afternoon, and I enjoyed meeting her. But I still don't know what she had in mind."

"Why not?" Freeman asked.

Selznick answered, "I couldn't understand a damn word she said."

## CHAPTER EIGHT

## EARLY WAR DAYS AND
## BALL BEARINGS IN SWEDEN

The Polo Grounds in New York has a normal seating capacity of about 55,000 people, but for the football game that took place on the afternoon of December 7, 1941, 88,001 men, women, and children seemed to have crowded in, and of this great throng, 88,000 were authors, each of whom has since written about hearing the Pearl Harbor announcement over the loud-speaker. I was not a writer then. But all these stories read substantially as follows so I shall simply give a composite of them as my own:

The bitter cold wind which swept across the Polo Grounds in New York on the afternoon of December 7, 1941, made it impossible to enjoy the game. I was vaguely disturbed by the great number of radio announcements which had been calling high brass and other officials to the telephone so I left between the halves and started downtown, when all of a sudden I heard on the radio in my car that the Japanese had bombed Hawaii. The war which we had hoped to escape was upon us.

In late 1939, along with thousands of other American tourists, I had been caught in Europe, sunning myself in Monte Carlo when the German army marched into Poland. I reached Paris the day that England and France declared war on the Nazis, and joined the crowds around the booking offices of the steamship lines. I made little progress until suddenly I recognized an old Ithaca friend, "Dusty" Bolam, a booking clerk for the United States Lines, who took me back into his office and arranged for my passage aboard the nightmarishly over-crowded *George Washington*. My accommodations proved to be a cot in the emptied swimming pool, but through more nefarious bargaining I managed to hire the lofty cabin of a Scotch engineer on the ship. Where he slept during the voyage I shall never know, but I am convinced that his mother was a jackknife for his berth was certainly not over five feet long.

With the war intensifying and the United States in a frenzy of preparation to defend itself in both the Atlantic and Pacific, the year 1942 was very exciting. The need for continual financing of Paramount was about over, and on the evening of January 29, 1941, we burned the long-term mortgage on Madison Square Garden. The burning itself took place in the Stanley Cup, the emblem of ice hockey supremacy in the United States.

I had rented the weird apartment of Katharine Brush, the novelist, on East 57th Street. This little gray home had a living room so large that at Miss Brush's housewarming someone had remarked, "What, no Cadillacs?" One social writer had gilded the lily by saying that the apartment "is a breath-taking ultra modern duplex, gold elephants walk across a vast black mirror, couches are islands in the sea of carpeting, the bar is a separate circular room, upholstered in green leather." Fortunately I no longer live there, and I hope that whoever has it now has changed the Joseph Urban decorations to authentic Hammacher, Schlemmer.

From this apartment my son, a member of Squadron A of New York, went off to war. I wondered how I could best contribute, little thinking what a number of far-flung chores I would have before the atom bomb fell on Hiroshima and we entered upon a so-called peace.

Opportunity was not long in coming. Clarence Dillon had been asked by his former partner Jim Forrestal, then Under-

Secretary of the Navy, to take over the task of rebuilding the funds of the Navy Relief Society. This ancient institution, devoted to the aid of navy personnel and their families in time of need, had accumulated over many years a capital of a few hundred thousand dollars, and Dillon was certainly the man to reactivate it. He asked me to take over the job of organizing sports and theatre benefit activities, and what he called "special events," throughout the country. The nation was eager to help, and had we been allowed to run our course we could certainly have raised many more million dollars than we did. The New York organization was located in the Heckscher Building at 57th Street and Fifth Avenue. It grew like a weed. I asked Paramount for a leave of absence and achieved the doubtful honor, as stated in one of the trade publications, of being "the only Wall Street banker who ever got on a major motion picture company payroll, and withdrew —voluntarily."

The Special Events Committee of the Navy Relief Society was something of a Who's Who in sports and entertainment. It included Bennett Cerf, the publisher, Edna Chase of *Vogue*, Bill Corum, the sports writer, Katharine Cornell, as well as John Golden, and Lee Shubert. There was Bernie Gimbel for merchandising, and George Hamid for circuses and carnivals. Sonja Henie, Ted Husing, Ned Irish, Mike Jacobs, and Bobbie Jones took care of sports. Brenda Frazier represented the debutantes, and Gerald Livingston the dog shows. There was another circus magnate, John Ringling North, and in addition, Alice Marble, Grantland Rice, Dan Topping, and Gene Tunney. Nick Schenck of Loew's and all the heads of both major and minor companies represented the motion-picture industry. Each in his own way helped us raise the money we needed.

Finally we had the outstanding services of Louis Marx, master manufacturer of novelties of every kind and possessing a highly agile and sparking mind. The children in half the

American embassies of the world share his beneficent gifts at each Christmas season. He designed the famous glass bank, an inexpensive glass box about four inches square, which, when filled with pennies, nickels, and dimes, held from twenty to thirty dollars. Louis and some of our other associates succeeded in distributing more than fifty thousand of these glass banks in Western Union offices, in chain stores throughout the country, in bars, and in restaurants, and, in fact, wherever there was a space next to a cash register and a possible contributor. The plan was that as soon as the banks were filled the local proprietor would mail them to the Navy Relief headquarters, where we would break them open and collect their contents. The plan was terrific, and we could have raised more than five million with it before it stalled, but the whole idea of the glass poor-box begging money for the Navy in all sorts of chain stores, not to mention dives of every description, was too much for the old sea dogs who were upholding the traditions of John Paul Jones and Stephen Decatur. They ordered us to discontinue the devices, but many thousand dollars had poured in through their silent aid.

Hollywood, eager as always to help, organized the Hollywood Victory Caravan, which hastily put together a show headed by Kenneth Thomson, Charlie Feldman, and Mark Sandrich, with Bob Hope, Jack Benny, and other stars. They toured fourteen cities and grossed more than $800,000. The theatre owners permitted us, along with the Army Relief, to run a week-long collection in the motion-picture theatres, which resulted in a gross of around $2,200,000 to be divided equally between the two services. We staged a great baseball game between the professional players in the services and a team of league stars, and each major baseball club and many of the minors donated us the full proceeds of one of their games.

Katharine Cornell and Basil Rathbone, with their usual generosity, contributed a run of George Bernard Shaw's *Candida*, which played to standing room only. We tried hard to persuade Mr. Shaw to donate his royalties, but he told us that he was paying $55,000 to the United Treasury that year and could not afford any more gestures. However, under the charming pressure of Miss Cornell, Mr. Shaw did relent, and though he still refused to contribute any more money to the government, he donated his royalties for the run to Miss Cornell, who in turn turned them over to the Navy Relief Society.

The Navy Relief Society drive established its own peculiar record. It was, I believe, the only charitable drive that was ever discontinued because it was bringing in too much money, but the powers in Washington felt that we were going too fast, accumulating attention and publicity at the expense of the various other charitable drives that were necessary at that time. I have no idea what our final contribution was. It was many millions. But, in any event, we were told to cease and desist. And we did, but it had all been a tremendous lot of fun.

There followed a brief period of fallow weeks during which all hands were engaged in the usual wartime bond drives. The motion-picture industry used my apartment for a fabulous breakfast, at which the industry promised to purchase fifty-five million dollars' worth of bonds. Charles Laughton recited Lincoln's Gettysburg Address and Grace Moore, my old tarpon-fishing companion, sang "The Star-Spangled Banner." One of my better-looking waiters offered to buy a hundred-dollar bond, whereupon one of the starlets present kissed him in an ecstasy of patriotism seven times. Miss Moore remarked that it was very fortunate for morals that he did not buy a ten-thousand-dollar bond.

Meanwhile Colonel, now General, "Wild Bill" Donovan was busy in Washington forming the Office of Strategic Services. He was convinced that the nation should create and maintain a comprehensive secret intelligence organization with men trained for special and highly hazardous enterprises behind enemy lines. His operation grew and flourished under the friendship of President Roosevelt, but, unfortunately, it never received the wholehearted support of the armed forces, or of the State Department. It was always regarded as a wheel outside rather than within another wheel. But despite its nicknames and its reputation of being a cloak-and-dagger outfit, it achieved good results in many countries and became, I believe, the seed from which our present Central Intelligence Agency has grown. Paramount Pictures, although inoperative in many countries throughout the world, held great quantities of foreign funds, and since the OSS found it hard to acquire such funds we agreed that Paramount should put its foreign holdings at the disposal of the Office of Strategic Services to use as it desired. To carry out this plan I became a member of Donovan's organization and took my first trans-Atlantic flight to England during September 1942.

Bill Donovan was an easy boss, and I was put pretty much on my own resources to do my own job and make my own decisions. In England the OSS was headed by David Bruce, later to become our ambassador to France, but I made my headquarters largely at the Paramount office while awaiting transportation to Sweden, which I had decided was to be my first stop before I went south to Spain and Portugal.

In working with the British Ministry of Information to learn about the various countries which I was to visit, I became friendly with the Right Honorable Brendan Bracken, its head, and I received much useful counsel from Lord Beaverbrook, whom I had met some years earlier. It was "the Beaver" who suddenly surprised me one night at a large dinner attended by a number of British Government officials by asking, "Who is Ilka Chase, and what is her great interest in you?" He turned to his butler and asked him to bring in a copy of Ilka's book *Past Imperfect*, which had just been published, and soon proceeded to read some passages regarding our friendship.

Ilka, indeed, had always been my good friend. She was married on my boat in Long Island Sound, and has, I think, probably given me more gratuitous publicity in her books and on her radio shows than I have received from any of my business or diplomatic adventures. General Marshall once told me an amusing story that occurred when an intimation of my possible appointment as ambassador to England had come from the White House. Marshall, to the surprise of absolutely no one, had never heard of me and asked one of his staff to prepare a dossier on me that evening. It so happened, however, that that night, following his habit of reading himself to sleep, he picked up *Past Imperfect* and obtained a far more complete, if somewhat more Technicolored, story than he got the next morning. I did not get the job—but I always regard Ilka Chase as my best, and in fact my only, press agent.

A few days after the Beaverbrook dinner I learned that my passage to Stockholm finally had been arranged. The RAF flew me to the gloomy, granite city of Aberdeen, where I waited for a plane to fly me across the North Sea. German forces, of course, held all of Norway and the only transportation to Sweden was by an occasional flight of Liberators, piloted by young Norwegians who had escaped Norway to England or had been brought back from Sweden, and who made the hazardous trip whenever the nights were dark and starless. Their returning cargoes were usually other Norwegian pilots who had filtered into Sweden, and frequently they carried shipments of ball bearings that were greatly needed by the British factories. After a series of disappointing delays I finally learned that it would be impossible to fly from the field near Aberdeen, and I was to proceed to the town of St. Andrews to await further news. I did not wait long.

At the damp, blacked-out Station Hotel, I was picked up at midnight by some Norwegians who spoke no English whatever, but who smiled grimly as they drove me to the blacked-out field and loaded me, complete with parachute, Mae West, and all of the other impedimenta of flying, into a dark plane.

The night was black and our plane was sealed so that no ray of light could give away our presence to the enemy.

The Liberator flight in those days from the Scottish coast to the Swedish capital took anywhere from five to seven hours, depending on wind conditions and the evasive actions of the plane. I recall that we made the trip in about six hours, and morning breaking over the clean and beautiful city of Stockholm was a happy sight. A large part of Sweden's traditionally neutral population was pro-German because of geographical and family ties, and it was necessary for me to hide my identity under what intelligence circles call "cover." I represented myself to the curious newspapermen as not only a representative of Paramount Pictures on my usual world rounds, but an emissary of Madison Square Garden trying to persuade the great Swedish runner, Gunder Hägg, to come to New York and race in the Garden. In the meantime, Reed Kilpatrick, president of the Garden, was co-operating with me by sending Hägg wires of urgent invitation. Because of this, Swedish newspapers published ostensibly amusing interviews and cartoons—showing me dressed as Uncle Sam, waving great sheafs of bills under the noses of the country's athletes, and later plodding down the long railroad line from the north country where Hägg lived, looking discouraged and carrying a butterfly net marked "for Hägg."

In the meantime, however, I was busy working with the local OSS organization, the British Intelligence, and the American Embassy, collecting information regarding Sweden's armed forces, its attitude toward Germany and the allies, its relations with Finland and, above all, with Russia. I was especially curious to know about the shipments of Swedish iron ore, ball bearings, and steel to Germany. It did not take me many weeks to learn that Sweden was pouring vast quantities of its industrial output directly into Germany, to be aimed eventually at the United States and its allies. I sent an exhaustive and probably somewhat violent report to Donovan, which not only guided the OSS and the Office of Economic Warfare but resulted in my return to Sweden many months later in an effort to end the ball-bearings shipments.

From Stockholm I arranged to leave for Finland, the next stop on my tour for the OSS, where I hoped to use Paramount funds for arranging an intelligence network that would relay information from the Russian-German lines back to Allied headquarters. England was at that time at war with Finland though the United States was not, and it was necessary for me to remove my English visa from my passport in order to make the trip. The Finnish ambassador to Sweden, however, was very kind and allowed me to go to Helsinki, although with grave warnings for my safety and strong arguments against my attempting the visit, for Finland was at that time fully occupied by the German forces. I, of course, did not speak Finnish and my only contact in the country was my small, inactive Paramount organization. At the risk of his life, Carl York, our Stockholm manager, decided that if I were to make the journey he should come too, and off we flew in a morning plane.

We stayed at the Kämp Hotel in Helsinki, whose only other occupants were German officers who scowled as I walked through the hotel. My room was ransacked daily but I had no papers whatever and the Germans found nothing. Even today, almost ten years later, it is impossible for me to tell the whole story of my work in Finland, for the men whose subterranean employment I arranged are still there, and Russia is very close. But we did establish a system for a continuous flow of extremely useful intelligence information to Washington.

London had been blacked-out but not bombed during my brief visit there, and it was in Helsinki that I experienced my first air raid. While the Finns always liked to say that one was far safer where he was being aimed at by a Russian bomber pilot than anywhere else, it was not strictly so, and throughout Finland it had become a national law that when plane warning signals were given every citizen must seek the bomb shelters. Trolley cars were left standing wherever they happened to be. Taxis, private cars, and even horse-drawn vehicles were left unattended. When I first heard the bomb alarm I looked around for shelter, but stood outside as I was determined to see the flight of bombing planes and their results. Three times a large and dexterous Finnish policeman pushed me back into the shelter, and three times I escaped into other streets, until I had seen the horrendous effect of great bombs.

My work finished in Scandinavia, I flew back to Stockholm and returned to England in a British air force plane. It was Christmas time and the New Year. I spent as happy a holiday in Claridge's as was possible in beleaguered England, and prepared for my next jaunts to Portugal and Spain.

The flight to Lisbon in the spring of 1943, just after the Allies had invaded North Africa, was uneventful, and in Portugal I found little to do, although Lisbon was supposed to be the center of both Allied and Axis political information. The headwaiter at the Hotel Aviz was supposed to be in the pay of ten governments. Allied and Axis planes arrived and departed from the same airfield and apparently had a mutual "hands off" agreement in their operations. I cultivated the friendship of Bert Fish of Florida, the American minister to Portugal, who was apparently much more interested in the success or failure of his homeland orange crop than he was in Portuguese politics. Although I had planned to produce a newsreel about Dr. Salazar, the long-time dictator of Portugal, and help cement his relations with the Allies, he was inaccessible; and in any case Portugal, Britain's historic ally, was already pretty much on our side. My only diplomatic triumph consisted in taking away a few thousand yen from some chattering Japanese diplomats playing *chemin de fer* at the beautiful casino at Escorial. It was not enough, however, to keep me in luxury at the Aviz, and I left for Madrid, flying over its famed bull ring and registering at the Ritz, with no thought whatever that eight years later I should return there as United States ambassador.

The Franco government, with its hatred for Russia and its post Civil War semi-allegiance to Germany and Italy, was under strong Axis influence. The government-controlled Spanish press was completely pro-Axis, and Allied victories did not feature in the news though the Axis successes were reported in large print. Americans were about as popular in Madrid as skunks at a picnic, and along with the British they were tolerated only because they were providing Spain a quota of petroleum and gasoline, of which the country was in desperate need. Most of the cars around the Ritz burned blocks of charred wood for fuel and had to be restoked every morning and after each fifty miles.

With the beginning of the Civil War in 1935, Paramount had closed up shop, leaving only an accountant and one or two clerks, and a bank balance of a few hundred pesetas. But upon my arrival in 1943, I learned not only that we had paid the expenses of the tiny organization but that our bank balances were close to twenty million pesetas. The reason was elementally simple. The departing management had left a number of old films in storage, and the accountant had merely rented them over and over again to theatres throughout Spain. Pesetas were unexportable at any price, and I was able to live in great luxury during my stay in Madrid.

The United States was represented at that time by Ambassador Carlton Hayes, a well-known historian and a Columbia professor. He was called to the ambassadorship by President Roosevelt not only because of his knowledge and ability as a historian but because he was a Catholic. He was thoroughly courteous and correct with me, although like most ambassadors and ministers during the war, he was not particularly pleased by the appearance of a representative of the Office of Strategic Services. Franco, whom he saw infrequently, was stubbornly holding to his neutrality, despite the German and Italian influences, and I was determined to cultivate him by obtaining a series of news shots and speeches, which I greatly hoped would flatter him and bring him closer to the Allied cause. Then, as now, he lived at El Pardo, a few miles outside of Madrid, and seldom came to his capital. However, I had my photographers ready and talked at length with Ambassador Hayes about my plans. He seemed sympathetic, but whether through blocks in the Embassy or the foreign office or possibly in Franco's personal household at El Pardo, the plan fell through, and I never met the dictator. I returned to Lisbon more determined than ever to get a picture from Salazar.

This time I avoided diplomatic channels and went to a Portuguese banker who knew Salazar well and said that he would arrange an interview for me. He told me that he would call me within the next few days at my hotel, and the very next evening I received a message from him to come at 11:30 that night to a certain bar in the center of Lisbon. I went there with my interpreter and met the banker, who escorted me to the sidewalk where a large limousine was waiting. My new friend told me that he would not accompany me, but that I had an appointment at midnight with Salazar. As I drove out to the surburbs in the dead of night I wondered whether I was going on what the American gangsters speak of as a "ride." But the plot rang true, and from the court of a large house, where numerous guards appeared from nowhere, I was escorted up the steep entrance stairs and ushered into a room completely bare of pictures or decoration except for some red plush chairs and couches and gilt mirrors. Within two or three minutes Dr. Salazar appeared and we sat down. I began by talking about America's great interest in Portugal and its ruler and went on to my plan for making a picture; to which Dr. Salazar, a tall, scholarly, almost gaunt man, seemed to agree. The dictator showed me many other signs of friendship, and the next day sent his secretary to my hotel to guide me through the historic sights of Lisbon.

In the morning I realized that I would unquestionably be in bad repute with Minister Fish, who had, I believe, seen Salazar only once during his tour of duty in Portugal, if I did not immediately tell him the story of my visit. I telephoned the Embassy and told Mr. Fish that by a fortunate circumstance I had met Dr. Salazar and talked with him on the evening before. Fish said, "You have really talked to Salazar?" I told him that I had not only seen him but talked with him at his house for a long time. "My God," said Fish, "are you at the Aviz? I will be right down, I want to hear everything he said." So it may be seen that sometimes an enterprising motion-picture man can accomplish almost as much as an American ambassador, but my accomplishments turned out to be less than I had expected, for Salazar, despite his assurances, never did let me make the movie.

My survey of the countries on the periphery of warring Europe was drawing to an end.

I returned to London and was in the midst of arranging passage home when a late afternoon telephone call came for me from the American Army headquarters. A plane loaded with entertainers making up one of the USO camp-show contingents had crashed in the river Tagus off Lisbon, and the Army asked if I would immediately go to Lisbon to look after the survivors of the tragedy. The voice on the telephone told me that I was to proceed at once to Bristol, where I would be met by an emissary and given my instructions. Almost within the hour I was en route for Bristol; in the station darkness a courier accosted me and took me to a hotel, telling me that a car would call for me in the morning and that I would be flown directly to Lisbon. Somehow the plan miscarried; it was not until the next evening that an ancient British Catalina picked me up at a near-by coast town and flew me to Foynes in Ireland, and from there to Lisbon. I was the only passenger, sandwiched in with supplies of various sorts, including great masses of printed British propaganda. We arrived at Lisbon at four o'clock in the morning, and by daylight I was on my way to the dreary Portuguese hospital to see the few surviving victims of the crash.

I cannot remember all of them, but there stands out in my memory the white and almost unearthly beauty of Jane Froman, lying in her hospital bed, her face untouched but her body unbelievably torn and twisted and broken. In the next room lay the pitifully wounded and bruised figure of the night-club accordionist Gypsy Markoff, who made a faster recovery than Jane, and whose only commission to me was to obtain some new eyebrows from a certain store in New York, as hers had been lost in the icy waters of the Tagus. Some of the survivors went on as good troupers to England, but some, such as Tamara, who first sang "Smoke Gets in Your Eyes," were lost at sea. The officials of the American Embassy and the Portuguese doctors and nurses had done everything within their power for these unhappy people. There was little I could do except call on them and bring them flowers and food for a few days until friends or relatives arrived.

The years 1943 and 1944 marked the dying days of the old clipper planes, and from Lisbon I embarked in one of these lumbering giants with almost sixty other passengers on my longest plane flight, about five days and nights with stopovers, en route to New York. The sea path was along the coast of French West Africa to Liberia; then came a hop across to Natal on the point of Brazil, and thence to Belém, Trinidad, Puerto Rico, and New York. Unfortunately, German agents had destroyed a great tank of gasoline from which the plane had hoped to refuel in Brazil, and since I was traveling incognito as an OSS agent I was off-loaded, with two Portuguese diplomats and some other unfortunates. I was desperate but there was an American army field near by, and with some forced conversation regarding the need of new motion pictures at the field, I learned that a plane was about to leave for Belém; together with my diplomatic friends, I talked my way aboard.

It was a "bucket-seat job" which should have been in the Smithsonian Institution. The Portuguese and I were lying on the floor of the plane as a tropic storm broke and we creaked and crackled and rolled low over the pathless stretch of Amazonian jungles. A man in uniform, walking to the back of the plane, gazed sympathetically at the regurgitating Portuguese but seemed particularly interested in me. As he walked back he asked, "Aren't you Mr. Griffis?" I said, "Yes, I am." He replied, "You fired me ten years ago from Hemphill, Noyes and Company, and I've never forgotten you." The thunder seemed louder and the jungles nearer as with trembling voice I inquired, "Well, er, what are you doing now?" He said, "I am the captain of this plane, thanks, pardon me I have to take over." I welcomed the landing in Belém even in its equatorial heat and with the field inches under water, but I did catch up with and again board the mighty clipper.

Back in Washington, Bill Donovan suggested some new chores, one in Ceylon and one in Argentina, but this time I was drafted for service, not under the Selective Service Act but by the motion-picture industry. Congress, the Office of War Information, and the White House were squabbling about OWI's tremendous expenditures for motion-picture war propaganda, as well as for its general relationship with the industry. Lowell Mellett, one of the personal assistants to President Roosevelt, had retired as chief of the OWI's motion-picture bureau and returned to the White House secretariat. The whole relationship between government and the industry was at loose ends and adrift. When Nick Schenck, the president of Loew's, asked me to come to his office, I found assembled there all the heads of the industry. I knew that I was a marked man. Far better motion-picture operators

III

than I ever was or will be had refused to take over Mellett's job. But I had no reason for declining, and on September 26, 1943, Palmer Hoyt, then of the Portland *Oregonian*, and the director of domestic operations for OWI, announced that I would henceforth "supervise the relationships between the government and the film industry; handle all requests for motion-picture co-operation, war drives and government information programs, and at the same time co-ordinate the film producing activities of other war agencies." Palmer Hoyt was a good boss, as indeed was George Healy of New Orleans, who later succeeded him; and I was given the best type of co-operation by Elmer Davis, that is, I was left strictly alone.

Instead of spending millions of the public's money for the production of government-made films, the motion-picture industry as usual did the work for free. Writers, directors, actors, stages, all sorts of aid, was given us by the industry, which pitched in to produce two one-reel propaganda films a month, to be shown—also at no charge—by the sixteen thousand motion-picture theatres in the United States. They were of every type: some propagandized enlistment in the WAVES, the WAC, or the Marines; others presented stories like that of the preparation of blood plasma; and there were films showing what our soldiers were actually doing overseas, as well as those like *Save Waste Paper* showing what the rest of us should be doing back home.

I have no idea how much time, service, money, and exhibition the motion-picture industry contributed to this work, but it was certainly worth many, many millions. I was a dollar-a-year man, as I always have been, but I cannot remember receiving the dollar.

This was in 1944, and in the spring of that year I left the films again and embarked on what was to be the most exciting adventure of my life, the ball-bearings mission to Sweden.

Almost from the beginning of the war the missions on

economic warfare in the British War Office, and in the Pentagon, had decided that their primary target was to prevent the German war machine from manufacturing or importing ball bearings, for without ball bearings its planes would be earthbound, its gun carriages immobilized, its trucks, cars, and all other instruments of war useless. For this reason the Allies directed their great bombing raids against the German ball-bearings factories both in the heart of the Rhineland and in the French occupied territory. But the Germans knew about the Allied objective, and in one great night raid over Schweinfurt, the home of the greatest German ball-bearings factories, nearly seventy planes were lost. Certainly we did great harm to the plants, but it became apparent as the war progressed that as fast as we destroyed or disabled the German factories, Sweden, which Hitler had kept alive simply for the sake of its steel products, would make up the deficiency, so that the manufacture of armaments in Germany remained practically unimpeded. In vain had the Allied economic warfare groups attempted to stop the Swedish shipments through the purchase of the output of the great Swedish monopoly Svenska Kullagerfabriken, better known as S.K.F. But the company had apparently used its new money and new profits for the construction of larger plants.

The reports that I had made on this unfortunate situation during my first trip to Sweden in 1942 had been brought to Roosevelt's attention by Harry Hopkins, whereupon Lowell Mellett and Lauchlin Currie, two of the presidential assistants, conceived the idea that I should return to Sweden and see what I could do. They asked me if I would attempt it, and I said yes. They asked when I could leave, and I said within twenty-four hours. They asked if I thought that I could do a better job in this situation than the State Department had done, and I said, "I don't know that I can do a better job, but I am sure I couldn't do a worse."

So we made our plans almost within the hour. I was ostensibly to represent the Foreign Economic Administration, with the authority to negotiate contracts for as much as thirty million dollars on behalf of its subsidiary, the United States Commercial Company. I obtained leave from the OWI and once again flew the Atlantic.

In London I was joined by a young lawyer, Douglas Poteat, who was to be my co-negotiator and advisor in Stockholm. I very much resented the inclusion of Poteat in the mission, for I had understood that I was to be permitted to work in the way that I had always liked best, as a lone wolf. However, I was never more wrong, for not only was Poteat a charming traveling companion, but he contributed greatly to the ensuing negotiations and was indeed my strong right arm. I later stole Poteat from the Economic Warfare Commission in London to become one of my commissioners in the operation of the American Red Cross in the Pacific, and he was in turn stolen from me to become operating head of the Red Cross in Washington. Later he joined me as executive vice-president of Memorial Center for Cancer and Allied Diseases, only to die from the scourge from which he was trying to save mankind.

We left London for Scotland within twenty-four hours, and there we awaited transportation to Sweden in a couple of four-hundred-miles-an-hour Mosquito bombers that the British were using on the Stockholm run and that were far faster than the Liberators I had taken on my last trip. But while the Mosquito was faster than the Liberator it was much less comfortable; there was space forward for only the pilot and the radio operator, while I had to climb in through the bomb bay and sit on a small shelf about two feet across, pulling my knees up against my chest while the bomb-bay doors ground shut, separating me from the outside world and all mankind apparently for good. Mosquitoes were not designed for men of my size and I had all I could do to reach around and manipulate the oxygen mask and the intercom-telephone apparatus. The only light came dimly from a tiny bulb over my head.

The RAF had sent two of these tiny planes to transport Poteat and me, and duly loaded down with parachute, Mae West, and flares in case we fell into the North Sea, we took off with a terrific roar. In a few minutes my pilot instructed me to turn my oxygen up first to the ten and later to the twenty-five thousand foot level. I had with me a novel and a bottle of scotch. I consumed both, but I had no memories of either when the pilot told me that we had passed the Norwegian-Swedish border and would soon be in the Stockholm airport.

We opened negotiations with S.K.F. the next day in the Wallenberg Bank, represented by Mark Wallenberg himself and S.K.F.'s managing director, Harald Hamberg. Poteat and I were joined by William Waring of the British Embassy, a young Britisher with a vast knowledge of the intricacies of ball-bearings manufacture, and with a supply of intestinal fortitude the like of which I have never seen since, just plain, stark courage.

The great board room of the Enskilda Bank was a gloomy cavern paneled in dark oak that grew gloomier as the days wore on, and the severe long-bearded bank presidents of forgotten days looked down on us from the walls with disapproval. It was a strange group of men who sat around the great table: Wallenberg, the bank director, once a famous Davis Cup tennis player for Sweden, and my associate Poteat, an equally well-known football player at Duke University, were both well over six feet and retained their athletic appearances. Hamberg, rotund and blond, contrasted with Waring, the wiry under-sized Englishman. Another man who occasionally sat in was an S.K.F. lawyer, whose name I cannot recall and whose knowledge of international law was such that Poteat was always able to catch him in legal errors and misstatements. Strong sunlight occasionally drifted in through the great windows from the Swedish springtime, and we always maneuvered to obtain the seats that put our backs to the light so we could have whatever advantage lay in this strategy. But always hovering over us were Hitler, and Per Albin Hannson, the Prime Minister of Sweden.

Our position was somewhat stronger than that of the Nazis or at least it became so during the negotiations, for while the Swedes had a natural fear of Hitler, they respected our armies, too, and they knew that the invasion was not far distant. But most of Sweden's men in the street still believed that the Germans would ultimately conquer, and for this reason our bargaining position was not always as strong as we liked. The most we could do was to try to convince the Swedes to risk their future on the chances of an Allied victory. But with the Germans still as strong as they were in the spring of 1944 this was not an easy job.

We were determined not to use any of our credit or, at least, as little of it as possible, so we began by stipulating that all ball-bearings shipments should stop until the negotiations were finally completed or abandoned. At first S.K.F. demurred but finally it accepted this pledge and fulfilled it scrupulously. This in itself was very encouraging, for even though our negotiations might eventually fail, we would at least have deprived the Nazis of ball bearings for several critical weeks while the talks lasted.

On the second morning of my stay at the Grand Hotel, a tall gaunt waiter who brought my breakfast announced in a guttural Balkan voice, "I am an American, I will be working for you and will keep you informed. In room 208 are the listening devices to record your conferences for the Germans; in room 302 is Mr. Hamberg of S.K.F., and in room 410 is Dr. Schnurre, the representative of the Wilhelmstrasse for ball-bearings negotiations here. I will keep you informed." I thought, of course, that this was a plant, thanked him courteously, and made no comment. However, I was wrong, for until the day I left this waiter told me of every movement made by either the head of S.K.F. or the German emissary. I first began to trust him when one morning he said, "Mr. Hamberg will break his appointment with you this morning as he has been called to the German Embassy." The appointment was broken ten minutes later. I have never seen or heard from this man again, but I hope that he managed to get to the United States, the land of his American mother.

The tempo of the negotiations rose and fell, punctuated by the constant intervention of the Swedish Government, which, of course, had an intense interest in the whole proceeding because of its touchy relationship with Germany. At one point I said to Hamberg, "You can hold out as long as you like on this matter, but the United States is definitely and finally not going to continue to stand idly by while you make the machines which are used in killing American boys." Hamberg grunted, "How do you know that any of our ball bearings have ever helped to kill an American boy?" Poteat was ready for him. He took from his pocket a handful of ball bearings and laid them on the table in front of the managing director. "Where were these made?" he asked. Hamberg walked to the window in the fading Swedish twilight. He studied Poteat's exhibits one by one and finally said, "Yes, they were all made in our factories, where did you get them?" Poteat said, "Every one of these was taken from a German airplane shot down over London."

I was fortunate indeed that on this mission I was not under the control of the State Department. I could negotiate in my own way. I could use threats of force, yet the Swedes could not know whether these threats were official or unauthorized. I was trying to save American lives in any way I could and I did not hesitate to use methods that no diplomat could have used. Yet often I feared that the Swedish Government would protest officially to Washington and request my withdrawal, though I was fairly sure that no matter what I had said Bob Patterson and Jim Forrestal would have backed me up.

One of the most effective suggestions that I made to the Swedes occurred at a time when Dr. Schnurre seemed to be making more progress than Poteat and I liked. "You know, gentlemen," I told them, "you have a lot of fog on your coast and you know that our bombers sometimes get lost even going to Germany. It would be a very sad thing if a thousand of our great bombers should lose their way along your coast and mistake Göteborg for Hamburg. It would be a very sad thing to wake up some morning and find your factories missing. We would be very sorry to have this happen, and of course we would apologize, and I am sure that many years from now when the war is over and the reparations commissions complete their testimony we would pay for the damage, but those things take time."

In any event the negotiations came to a close during the second week in June. We purchased less than six million dollars' worth of ball bearings of a type particularly needed by Germany at that time, and which the Swedes had already manufactured. S.K.F. agreed, on an approved schedule of sizes, to ship less than 10 per cent of its former quotas to Germany and to send only types that our experts knew were of little value to the Nazi war machine. Poteat and I, in a rain of threatening and anonymous Nazi letters, prepared to leave Stockholm and leave fast, having arranged with others to carry out the checks on whether or not the contracts were observed. The Mosquitoes were sent back for us, and about one o'clock one dark night we started our journeys back toward Scotland. Poteat got through without trouble and was in London the next day. But through some mischance my plane, which was iced from tip to tip, barely escaped a forced landing in Norway, and I found myself back in Stockholm within the hour, again a tenant of the Grand Hotel. However, I made it the next night, at six caught the morning train for London, and at seven that night I was in Claridge's. Completely worn out, I ordered some toast and a bowl of soup and climbed into bed at about nine. But just as I was drifting off, every gun in London opened fire, and the noise continued for a long time. I assumed that the Germans had started their great air raids again, but in the morning we knew that the V-1 bomb had arrived; it was to be with us in Britain for many days and nights to come.

Glad to escape from Sweden and just as glad to no longer face the daily hazard of the bombs, I celebrated the Fourth of July by flying from Prestwick to La Guardia Field and home again.

Because I am frankly proud of them there are two quotations which I should like to include here, although I resent the denial of my glamour in one of them. They have to do with the Swedish mission. One is an editorial from the Washington *Star* of December 16, 1944:

### ADVENTURE OF MR. GRIFFIS

Not many Americans have ever heard of Stanton Griffis. Fifty-seven years old, bespectacled and rather bald, he is not what one would call the glamorous celebrity type. He has led a quiet life for the most part, making considerable but relatively unpublicized success of himself as an investment banker and as an executive in several corporations. Yet Paramount Pictures—one of the companies whose business he has guided—could probably make a highly suspenseful movie out of a mission he undertook last spring as agent extraordinary for our Foreign Economic Administration.

As revealed for the first time by the New York Herald Tribune, the adventures of Mr. Griffis (and the movie might well go by that title, with somebody like Humphrey Bogart or Walter Pidgeon in the leading role) began with the failure of diplomatic negotiations to effect a reduction in the shipment of vital ball bearings from Sweden to the Nazis. The FEA thereupon asked Mr. Griffis to see what he could do through direct contact with Swedish steel manufacturers, and although the assignment was a hazardous one, he did not hesitate to accept it. Secrecy was imperative, and the mode of transportation had to be very special, and so a British Mosquito bomber was called to do the trick.

But since a Mosquito is roomy enough for only two seats—for the pilot and copilot—Mr. Griffis had to stretch out horizontally in the bomb bay, and in that position, strapped down, with his head facing the tail of the ship, he was transported to Stockholm over some of the most dangerous of enemy areas at a speed of more than 300 miles an hour. There, after arriving numb and half frozen, he was active in his task for about a month, during which time—as in a cloak-and-dagger melodrama—a mysterious figure kept constantly on his trail while anonymous notes repeatedly threatened him with death. But he persisted, and last June—on the 13th—he returned to England, strapped again in the bomb bay and altogether successful in his mission. The Herald Tribune account declares that the Nazis would have sacrificed several squadrons of planes to have foiled him, and we can readily believe in that, for what he did constituted one of the great economic coups of the war, depriving Germany of at least 51 per cent of highgrade Swedish bearings—an indispensable, supercritical item in any military machine.

Thus, in effect, this quiet and unspectacular man did a job whose damage to Hitler's war-making capacity may be likened to the work of thousands of allied planes hammering away at Nazi industry in a prolonged offensive. There probably are other Mr. Griffises, all relatively obscure figures, rendering much the same kind of confidential service in behalf of our country, but it is enough to know about this particular one—a gentleman who is certainly something of a hero—to make us proud to be Americans.

Another from a London paper, whose date line I have lost, but which is headed "Stockholm—Friday," reads as follows:

A footnote to the recent ball bearing controversy appears in today's Stockholm Tidningen, which reports that the German diplomat representative who arrived in Sweden recently to counter-negotiate the ball bearings agreement, is now in Shalgren Hospital Gothenburg, suffering from the effect of poison.

The newspaper presumes that he is afraid to return to Germany, and attempted to commit suicide because of the failure of his mission.

It was the good Doktor Schnurre from room 410 of the Grand Hotel.

## CHAPTER NINE

# THE RED CROSS IN THE PACIFIC

I had hardly returned to my home in New Canaan for a rest after the Swedish adventure when a group of well-meaning political friends in Western Connecticut advanced the startling idea that I should oppose Brien McMahon for the nomination for United States Senator in the forthcoming autumn elections. The prospects of defeating McMahon for the nomination were pretty dim, but the remote possibility of being elected to the Senate was alluring, and the McMahon opposition seemed to have no other candidate. Thus I was inveigled into traveling to the Democratic National Convention at Chicago to be looked over, just like a prospective bride visiting her loved-one's home, and to meet the various Connecticut delegates. I listened to the long series of nominating and seconding speeches for Franklin D. Roosevelt, and heard the disturbing chant from the balconies—"We want Wallace." The vice-presidency was, of course, a big issue in the 1944 election and I spent long, hot hours in smoke, discussing the problem with the delegates. Wallace had formidable support, but his views on so many subjects were so farfetched that it would have been no less than tragic had he been chosen to run with Roosevelt. Fortunately, however, Wallace was defeated, and I recall very vividly how I cheered in the humid hall when Harry S. Truman was nominated.

Though none of us knew at the time how important this choice was eventually to be, we were all grateful for it.

Meanwhile, I still had to decide about my own candidacy for the senatorial nomination. I came, I saw, and I ran away. I had a congenital distaste for running for public office and furthermore, though I had been a Connecticut resident for many years—twenty to be exact—I was nevertheless a commuter to New York and a thorough-going Wall Streeter at heart. There remained, of course, the little item of beating McMahon. And my final decision was simple: all this was not for me. I had frightened Brien a little but I think not much, and as the Convention closed I assured him of my decision and of my support, thanked all hands, and departed for Hollywood to resume my propaganda pictures, and the OWI job.

Back in my old stamping ground with an office at the Paramount Studio, I lived on the bounty of my old friend Joan Fontaine, who was in Mexico and lent me her lovely house. I plunged again into my job as a sort of national screen barker. I deftly side-stepped Leo Crowley's flattering offer to take over the job of foreign surplus disposal, for I certainly did not wish to assume any government responsibilities that would last beyond the duration. I regretfully declined again when Ed Pauley flew out from Washington, bearing Mr. Roosevelt's request that I become chairman of the National Democratic Finance Committee. Perhaps one of the reasons why I passed up these jobs was that I had a premonition that a great and thoroughly non-political adventure was about to beckon, and indeed it was, as I resumed my transcontinental commuting and returned to my chores in Washington and New York.

Shortly after the first world war I had joined my Washington civilian chief, Thomas W. Streeter, scholar, lawyer, book collector, and industrial aladdin, to adventure financially in the Venezuelan oil fields. Streeter had selected as our counsel

a rising young lawyer from Dartmouth and Boston, Basil
O'Connor, who during the middle twenties was to form a
partnership with Franklin Roosevelt, a young lawyer then out
of a job, and later was to go on to become one of the great
philanthropists of his time, heading the National Foundation
for Infantile Paralysis and serving as president of the American Red Cross. O'Connor and I had remained friends ever
since the Venezuelan deals.

As I was working in my New York office early in September 1944 he called me on the phone and said, "I want you to
do a job for me, now don't say no before I tell you what it is."
I said, "I won't do it. What is it?" And he replied, "I want
you to take the job of running the Red Cross in the Pacific
Ocean Areas. How about it?" I agreed to think about it over
the week end, but my mind was instantly made up, and I
knew that here was a really great adventure of the war. Harvey D. Gibson, whom I admired greatly, had for some years
been operating the American Red Cross in Europe and I
had had many talks with him about its work in London. I
was flattered beyond belief that I should be selected to take
over the Pacific counterpart of his job. Elmer Davis and
George Healy released me from my OWI commitments, and
I struck out westward, just as I was about to receive a degree
from Union, the college of my ancestors. The degree came
in absentia. My title was Commissioner of the American
National Red Cross to the Pacific Ocean Areas, and my jurisdiction included a vast stretch of sea and islands extending
in a vague triangle from San Francisco to New Zealand,
north to the border islands of Japan, and then back past
Guam, Saipan, and Tinian to the Hawaiian Islands. There
was a separate Red Cross organization in Australia that worked
with MacArthur's armies and eventually entered Japan. But
our work was mostly with the naval and marine forces
under Admiral Nimitz and the marine commanders. One of
our biggest problems from the very beginning was the Navy's

traditional aversion to women on its ships and installations. It was a long time before we overcame this block but eventually we did, though the Red Cross owes most of its success in the Pacific to General Robert C. Richardson of the Army, whose co-operation enabled us to work very effectively with the men in our area.

Because the Red Cross knew that I was completely unfamiliar with its procedures, it appointed Bowen McCoy as my chief deputy, who for many years had run the Red Cross chapter in Los Angeles. I myself appointed Douglas Poteat, who had done such a good job in Sweden, General Conger Goodyear, one of the heads of the New York National Guard, Arthur Meyer, the co-ordinator of the War Activities Committee of the motion-picture industry, and Mrs. Margaret Emerson, whose two sons Alfred and George Vanderbilt were already in navy service in the Pacific, and who had a host of friends in Honolulu, our first headquarters. It was October before we settled down in the crowded Red Cross offices in the Davies Building in Honolulu and began the tortuous job of forging an organization to distribute services and supplies throughout the area. I had flown to Honolulu, again on one of the ancient clippers, with Mrs. Thomas W. Streeter, who had been appointed by President Roosevelt to head the Marine women, as an unexpected traveling companion. I was very much flattered to find in the posting of the berth assignments for the flight that I was given first choice, only to be humiliated when I found that this privilege was granted for age and not for genius.

Almost as soon as we arrived in Honolulu, McCoy, my deputy, took over Red Cross personnel organization; Poteat tackled the job of the storage and handling of supplies; General Goodyear left for Guam and Saipan to accompany Arthur Sulzberger, a director of the Red Cross, on a tour of Pacific inspection; and Arthur Meyer tackled the broad job of public relations and information. Margaret Emerson, always a master of hospitality, joined me in garnering good will for the Red Cross through entertainments, and I still remember our first *luau*, that marvelous feast of Hawaiian roast pig and sea monsters, at which we entertained General Richardson, Admiral Jack Towers, General Harmon, Admiral "Bull" Halsey, who had flown in that night from his great naval triumphs, and some visiting tourists, Commander Gene Tunney of the Marines and John P. Marquand, the novelist.

At the time of our arrival the American National Red Cross, with agencies in England, on the Continent, and in North Africa, had all it could do to organize its services in the Pacific. We struggled desperately against time to provide the necessary transportation, supplies, and personnel to cover the vast Pacific area allotted to us. But naturally the priorities went to the European and North African theatres, and our job was to catch up as well as we could. I quote with sad memories some of my anguished appeals to National Headquarters in Washington:

We are painfully chaotic and disorganized in three major situations. (1) The whole relationship between the Red Cross and the top men of the armed forces in this area is disjointed and undefined; we are at present little beggar boys holding a tin cup to the military for help with supplies of every sort and transportation priorities, complicated by a fantastic overcrowding in this community. (2) Our supply situation has all of the pattern and organization of a good saloon free-for-all brawl. We have been pushed from pillar to post for storage space and there is nothing yet defined as to how or where we can develop a central storage with some order. As I wrote you, our supplies are scattered the length and breadth of the Pacific. We have no inventory control whatever, or in fact, little actual knowledge of what we have or where we have it. Shipments destined for a certain location are apt to be diverted to other locations and never heard from again. Nevertheless some order can and will be brought out of this shamble. (3) We are painfully weak in our club and

*Above*—The president of Brentano's Bookstores, Inc., Nixon Griffis, and his father in the store. *Below*—Miss Katharine Cornell and Raymond Massey presenting a check, representing the profits of their performances of *Candida,* to Clarence Dillon, chairman of the Navy Relief Committee as Mr. Dillon's coworker looks on

The author on location at Palm Springs with Miss Dorothy Lamour and Adolph Zukor, making one of the Paramount series of jungle pictures

*Below*—The Little Flower was always helpful in bond and relief drives. From left to right: The author, Harry Brandt, Nicholas Schenck of Loew, and His Honor

recreation organization, plans and personnel. I understand fully
the desire of most Red Cross recruits to travel the other way—
Eastward, but there is a war out here and it is quite a war, and
the boy coming out of combat in equatorial jungles against
fanatical Japanese, rates almost as good treatment as the boys in
England and France.

I have told you of, or you are familiar with most of our
troubles, but there is plenty of good. In general, this organization
is sound, hard-working, ambitious and has lots of guts; conditions
under which most of these girls and boys are living make their
spirit all the more miraculous; we can't be perfectionists on this
job, but the job can be licked.

Here, then, were our problems in a nutshell. We faced the
endless Pacific with its far-flung islands. We faced a terrific
increase in army, navy, and air force power; we were short
of men, women, and transportation, as well as supplies and
housing. We faced the crying need for more clubs, more
hospital service, more field directors to arrange liaison between the troops and their family problems at home, as well
as to care for their ever-increasing need of comfort supplies.
We battled with National Headquarters for all of these
things. We battled with the Air Force for priorities to fly
nurses and service girls out to the islands, with the Navy for
transportation, and with the Army for storage space. We
built an office building in Honolulu in six weeks, and moved
from the crowded quarters of the Davies Building. By the
middle of December some order seemed to be coming out
of the chaos, and I flew with Poteat, Meyer, and Goodyear
to New Caledonia, stopping for an hour or so at the tiny
island of Canton, and visiting in turn Espiritu Santo, the
Russell Islands, and Guadalcanal. It was on Christmas Day
on this trip that for the first, and I guess the last time in my
life I enjoyed one Christmas dinner on Guadalcanal and another in Honolulu some thousands of miles eastward, as I
flew back over the international date line.

Meanwhile the armed forces were moving rapidly north-west toward Japan. We had already taken Guam, Saipan, and Tinian, and my report to headquarters observed:

It is the irony of Red Cross in an area such as the one which we operate, that as soon as we hit the zenith of service we are apt to have to prepare to fold up and disintegrate. The program in the South Pacific will decline rapidly from this point on, and as you are familiar, we do not expect to requisition any further supplies for South Pacific, nor do we expect to send any further personnel.

General Goodyear had flown on to New Zealand to close up our stations there. The strike for Iwo Jima was imminent and we were busy equipping for it. During January we had been making great plans for a forward headquarters in Guam, with branches in Saipan and Tinian. Through the visit of Secretary Forrestal to the islands the Navy miraculously became much more co-operative, and in Guam and the adjoining islands we were building Red Cross dormitories for men and women, office buildings, service clubs for army, navy and air forces, recreation centers, along with the always welcome clubmobiles that served coffee and doughnuts. The Secretary also lent us a navy public relations man to supplement the already magnificent work of Lieutenant Colonel Ted Deglin, my old associate at Madison Square Garden who had served me well in the Navy Relief, whom Secretary Patterson had sent out to help me in the Pacific.

Late in February I had the thrill of broadcasting from Honolulu to a gathering of twenty thousand workers of the motion-picture industry scattered in eight great studio stages in Hollywood, and the excitement of a tie-up with Harvey Gibson in London, who spoke of the Red Cross work in Europe as the Allied armies closed in on the Rhine. From the Pacific we told of the developments there and pledged to carry on Harvey's great work as Germany collapsed and the whole attention of the American armed forces turned to Japan's defeat. In March I flew westward for an inspection of Advanced Headquarters, visiting Johnson, Kwajalein, Guam, Tinian, and Saipan. From the air-control tower at Saipan I watched the hundreds of B-29's taking off for night raids over Japan, each warming up at the start of the runway after a thirty-second interval and roaring down toward the sea to join still other bombers rising across the blue waters at Tinian. Yet it was a bitter thing each following morning to jeep back to the field for the straggling return and to talk to the weary pilots as they were given hot coffee, dough-nuts, and sandwiches by our Red Cross girls. The fact that every day some of the planes would not return made us realize the horrible necessity of the sacrifices we had made at Iwo to provide a halfway jump for these mighty bombing missions.

Later on I flew to Iwo Jima with Under-Secretary of War Howard C. Peterson, and in my report I wrote:

I flew accompanied by a group of fighter planes, and witnessed one of the most concentrated pictures of horror and desolation which can possibly be imagined. No words of mine can pay sufficient tribute to the fifteen Red Cross men who went in there and stuck it through with the Marines, and to the men who have now come in with the army and garrison forces. Not a tree, not a wooden shack and a green thing exists on the island, which remains a scene of complete human agony, where men must live in a constant cloud of dust and biting volcanic ash that sweep the little dot on the Pacific. The night before our arrival on the island was marked by an attack by more than two hundred fanatical Japanese of the great number which still remained in the caves and crevices, and there is an augment to the general gaiety by the fact that sulphur fumes creep up through the earth throughout a large part of the terrain, and wells bring in a water supply of saline solution at a hundred and forty degrees temperature.

Turning to shipment problems, I wrote:

In this Iwo operation as I have written you, approximately
one third of our supplies were lost through reasons on which I
have frequently written you, i.e., the marking of Red Cross
packing cases with red crosses and the use of packing material too
light to stand the strain of a landing operation. May I again call
your attention to the fact that a red cross on a packing case in a
transport or landing craft is an engraved invitation to hungry
or playful troops to break open the boxes and help themselves.
The general result of the strikes throughout the Pacific Ocean
areas on account of the terrific unexpected casualties was a general cleaning out of all forms of comfort supplies, teaching us
here and I hope at National the absolute necessity of over-
estimating rather than underestimating supply need.

Since the very week of my arrival in the Pacific, the previous October, we had planned for many months with great
care, and with the complete co-operation of the armed forces,
an operation which we called in our budget and requisitions
Zone X. This, of course, turned out to be the last great strike
of the war—against Okinawa. Approximately sixty Red Cross
men went along with the expedition and landed, along with
the marines, on the enemy-held beaches. Clubs and hospital
services followed shortly behind the strike. Although General Goodyear watched the Okinawa operation as an observer
with the 27th Division, I did not get to the island as the
personnel, transportation, and supply situation throughout
the Pacific Ocean area was again becoming desperate, and I
was devoting all my energies to it.

Thoroughly discouraged, nervous, and tired from flying
the islands, and with a growing antagonism toward National
Headquarters, which we constantly charged with favoring
the European theatre and leaving us as the forgotten men, I
decided to resign in protest, and on April 6 I sent the following telegram to O'Connor. He refers to it always as the "Chi-

nese garbage woman telegram." I fully expected that it would
be my swan song in the Red Cross. It read as follows:

*Basil O'Connor, Chairman, American National Red Cross, Washington*

Six weeks ago I sent Douglas Poteat to Washington with
requisitions to explain serious urgency of supply situation here
and shortly thereafter cabled additional requisitions totaling in
dollar volume, two million. I have repeatedly urged expedition of
shipments. Following telephone call upon my return from forward
areas I have this morning received a cable from Washington
HF1054 that with the exception of a few doughnut machine parts
no shipments have been made and I am advised "highly improb-
able remaining items can be shipped in immediate future." We
have been without arrivals of personnel in this area for almost two
months. Upon your instructions we have made strong representa-
tions to the army and navy as to our ability to serve armed forces
which commitments we are now unable to fulfill. The circumstances indicate complete breakdown and lack of support by
National Headquarters if after six weeks of pleading we are told
that not even a tooth brush can be shipped out here in the immediate future. Under circumstances I feel that you should immediately accept my resignation as commissioner which should
serve to voice the protests which would arise from the entire
nation of contributors if they were able to appreciate apparent
abandonment of this tragic war area by the American Red Cross.
Resignation should take effect not later than your arrival here
April 20 or have aged Chinese garbage woman here who could
take over immediately and operate as efficiently as we can without
supplies and personnel. She might possibly be used to better advantage to operate entire American Red Cross.

STANTON GRIFFIS, American Red Cross

O'Connor's reaction was far different from what I had
expected, but it was a joy. It went something like this: "Great,
great—send me more telegrams like that. They are just what
I need to buck up this organization and if you keep sending
them I will get your personnel and your supplies. O'Connor."

He did not mention resignation, and McCoy, who had felt that my telegram would outrage the Red Cross ancients, unpacked his bags. A few days later, cheered but not satisfied, I flew to Washington myself to storm through National Headquarters, and later through its offices in Chicago and San Francisco, fighting for personnel and shipments. In San Francisco I had the co-operation of Charlie Blyth, head of the San Francisco chapter, and General Kells, commissioner of the Port of San Francisco, through whom we received an enormous grant of warehouse space with the necessary GI labor services. We were beginning to roll again, and I returned to the Pacific, although O'Connor, who was to have accompanied me, was delayed on account of the sudden death of his old law partner, President Franklin Roosevelt.

Probably I have spoken overmuch of the long hours, the bitternesses, and the disappointments of the job in the Pacific, with its exhausting flights over thousands of miles of open water, but it was not without its lighter moments. There were always tennis games with my neighbor Major "Duke" Johnson, who named his baby after me, and with his beautiful wife, Cecile, who sometimes cooked our dinner, and with Alfred Vanderbilt. And, of course, there were always the problems that arose from marooning twenty girls with several thousand hungry and healthy men on a lonely island. Frequently it was necessary to keep our nurses and club girls in stockades, and not for their protection against the natives. There were probably a great many emotional tragedies of which I did not hear, but considering all aspects of the situation there were remarkably few biologic tragedies and apparently some biologic contentment.

Fairly early during my tour of duty in Honolulu, my advisor in charge of the Women's Welfare Staff came into my office, obviously perturbed. I was probably pretty gruff as I asked, "What's the trouble this morning?" She said, "I am sorry to have to tell you that Miss X is pregnant. The father is a colonel and unfortunately married." "All right," I said, "ship her back home and call it a day." The woman advisor looked unhappy. "I am sorry to tell you, sir, that she won't go back. She says she is willing to resign but she will not return to the States. She says it is her baby and it is none of our damn business." "All right," I said wearily, "bring her in here, and I'll send her back."

I was shortly confronted by a very determined young lady, who told me in words of one syllable what she had told the woman's director, in effect, that she was about to have a baby, she was very glad of it, she would be happy to resign, but she would see us all in hell before she would go back and tell her family. I said, "I suppose you know I could send for a couple of marines and put you on board a transport, young lady." Weakening a bit she said, "Yes, I know, but you won't do anything like that, please let me resign and have it my own way." I thought, well I guess it's just one of those things, if you want to do that, go ahead and good luck to you.

I had forgotten the incident entirely when about six months later I received a wire from one of the outlying islands. It read as follows: "Stanton Griffis, Commissioner, American National Red Cross Headquarters, Honolulu, Hawaii. Baby arrived yesterday, mother's features father's fixtures. Thanks. Best regards." It was signed by Miss X. What has happened to her since, I do not know.

There were other aspects of Red Cross life in the Pacific that occasionally gave us a laugh. The regulations provided that so far as costume was concerned American Red Cross nurses and club girls were to be governed by the regulations prepared for the government nurses and members of the WAC and WAVES. This meant, unfortunately, that in the hot and humid islands the Red Cross girls were supposed to wear stockings. They did not want to wear stockings, and they said so in no uncertain words. I stuck to my guns and ordered that the regulations be obeyed, and to a very small extent they were, although the girls went to every conceivable subterfuge to escape the rule. They entered the offices surreptitiously and when the commissioner entered they were usually found sitting as yogis so that he could in no way judge the results of his rules. The battle was a long and bitter one, and resulted in a good deal of disciplinary action, but just before I left the Pacific, when the real heat of the summer was approaching, I posted the following notice on the bulletin board, admitting defeat.

Date: July 12, 1944
Subject: Stocking rule
To: All Female personnel ARC—POA
From: Stanton Griffis, Commissioner
   The Commissioner is licked.
   What chance has one man against two thousand women?
   As practically my last official act (and in order to get out of town with my life and health intact) I herewith announce that the stocking rule is waived until further notice.
                              STANTON GRIFFIS, *Commissioner*

Strange odds and ends of jobs came our way and were duly performed. The commanding general of Guam suddenly requisitioned twenty thousand small American flags for the local population to use on Memorial Day. Through the always dynamic energy of Charlie Blyth, in San Francisco, we finally discovered the flags and shipped them within twenty-four hours. An urgent call from Commanding General Jarman in Saipan told us that the hiding Japanese on the island had stolen and eaten every existing chicken and he wanted a new breed to repopulate. A thousand baby Rhode Island Reds went forward by plane the next day. I trust that their progeny now crow and lay long and lustily on this far island. A sudden request for thousands of face masks for the marines at Iwo Jima, who were fighting through clouds of sulphur and volcanic ash, brought all hands in Honolulu to work. As the Honolulu *Advertiser* tells it, "Request for the masks was received by the

volunteer Red Cross Commissioner for the Pacific Ocean area
from the navy at 10:30 A.M. on March 5th, and less than twelve
hours later they were on their way by plane to Iwo Jima, taken
from the reserve surgical supplies of the Hawaiian Red Cross.
The masks were designed for surgical use of doctors and nurses
and made of eight thicknesses of fine mesh gauze kept in place
by tapes at the back of the head."

Germany surrendered and the war turned ever westward.
With Okinawa captured, the plans for the great strike on the
Japanese coast were progressing. My report to National Head-
quarters at the beginning of July 1945, reads:

The month of June, 1945, marked by all odds the high water
mark of Red Cross operations in the Pacific Ocean Area. During
this month almost three hundred new and returning personnel
reached us. Now we have no area excess of personnel, but a
definite local excess due to the conditions in the forward area, and
the constant delays in obtaining transportation from Honolulu
forward. A report of the staff welfare department will give you
an idea of the crisis in our housing conditions, but we have been
able to meet it, not entirely with comfort for many of the girls
but at least they have a roof and three meals a day and are learning much in their training courses while they wait impatiently to
go forward. Together with this tremendous influx of personnel
has come a great wave of much needed supplies to warehouses
both here and in the Marianas which are filling up rapidly.
Okinawa is still a great problem but we are servicing it as much
and as fast as possible. For the first time since the organization of
the present commission, this area is substantially up to tables of
organization in approximately two hundred and fifty Red Cross
installations. Its supplies with the exception of Okinawa are on
the ground in ample amount or en route, morale is reasonably high
and its growth of about two hundred and fifty per cent in nine
months is impressive.

There is nothing more boring than statistics, but at least we
had reached a personnel strength of between two and three
thousand workers scattered over the far Pacific and, as the re-

port states, in about two hundred and fifty Red Cross installations. A recommendation at about this time to National Headquarters reads:

A nine months' study of the situation here convinces me that the tour of duty for both men and women in this area should be reduced from two years to eighteen months. It would be easy to write a long brief on this subject, but sufficient it is to say that my best judgment is that the interests of the Red Cross would best be served if workers were permitted to look forward to a return to the States after eighteen months of the almost intolerable conditions of the tropics and semi-tropics under which they must work here; particularly as to women, only those with the toughest fibre can even last out the eighteen months if they are spent in the forward area.

It is a little gruesome to write in this connection of the poisonous waters of some of the Pacific islands, from which many Red Cross girls contracted a fungus growth that began to spring from their bodies like Spanish moss from southern trees. Nothing could be more frightening to an attractive American girl. Although I would send them back again and again to their doctors in the areas, a girl affected with this strange affliction was not much to be blamed for constantly attempting to stowaway on army planes or navy transports in order to flee the Pacific.

But the war was passing us by toward the MacArthur area, which now included Okinawa. Our job in the Pacific Ocean areas was rapidly coming to an end, and neither O'Connor nor I believed that I should attempt, as we had previously planned, to supplant the magnificent work of the career commissioner who had worked with the MacArthur forces for so many months. After a good deal of argument with my boss, I decided finally to resign and return to the States, but only after having arranged for the appointment of Vice-Admiral Adolphus Andrews, who was then living in Honolulu, to take over the job, for since it had become more and more a naval area, I knew that he could obtain far more co-operation for the Red Cross as a retired admiral than I could as a civilian.

Margaret Emerson, my faithful hostess who had done so much for the morale of our girls, and I gave a great *luau* in honor of Admiral Andrews and his wife on the evening of July 14, 1945. It lasted until 4:00 A.M., and the flaming torches that had been set up on the lawn were unextinguishable. I could not sleep as I left for Hickam Field in the early morning to fly to San Francisco. The flight was delayed but when it started it was a joy to sleep as the great C-54 winged eastward. It was four o'clock on the following morning when I reached the San Francisco airport, kneeled to kiss American soil, and went to the Mark Hopkins.

When I awoke in the morning I found a telegram from an old theatrical friend in New York who wanted me to help angel her forthcoming play. My delight in returning to the States had so unnerved me that, weakening the resolutions of many years, I sent a wire taking a $5,000 piece. P.S. The show never reached New York.

I wrote National Headquarters the following farewell:

The word "aloha" in the Hawaiian language is a word that means good luck, goodbye, thanks for the ᵣᵣ____ity to be here, God bless and speed you. The Commissioner says "Aloha" to all his faithful friends and associates at National Headquarters, knowing that he is leaving the work in able hands which, on account of their long and brilliant experience with the armed forces, will make this area a far higher credit to the Red Cross in the future.

I was indeed pleased by the citation that General Richardson had given me in Honolulu, and even more pleased by the citation that President Truman presented to me through Chairman O'Connor, to accompany the Medal for Merit, one of America's most highly prized civilian decorations.

It was followed very shortly by Secretary of the Navy Jim Forrestal's award of the Medal of Freedom with the usual pleasant citation.

I tarried for a while on the Pacific Coast, visiting old friends and relatives before I journeyed to New York, where, one night when I was dining in the Colony with a very beautiful lady, we heard the news of the Japanese capitulation. We joined the throngs dancing in the street. The great World War II was over.

Seven years later my thoughts on the work of the Red Cross in the Pacific—in addition to the conclusions that I reached at that time and still retain—may be heresy in the Great Marble Palace in Washington where the American National Red Cross holds its councils. They will probably not be shared by "Doc" O'Connor, but I must say that without the most complete and co-operative understanding between the armed forces and the Red Cross, I seriously doubt the wisdom of sending thousands of young women into areas like the Pacific during wartime, and I rather doubt if it should ever be attempted in a navy and marine landing war such as the Pacific operation. Indeed I would go much farther than this, and question the wisdom of ever having civil commissioners in charge of battle areas. Leaders and organizers, of course, there must be; and the people of the United States should not be denied the privilege of giving their contributions, their hopes, and their aid through civilians who will form a liaison between the men in the field and their families at home, who will comfort and cheer the wounded, and the young men going into battle. But I am convinced that the entire working operation of the Red Cross plan should come under the direct command and be integrated completely with the plan of action of the joint chiefs of staff and the leaders of the armed forces. As Patrick Henry, who might have been Commissioner of the American National Red Cross, said, "If this be treason make the most of it."

## CHAPTER TEN

# A TOUCH OF POLITICS AND
# THE STATE DEPARTMENT

The scrapbooks that my secretary kept so carefully for me during 1946 reflect a time of peace and quiet far removed from wars and adventure. They contain only an occasional report of the operations of Madison Square Garden, and a good deal of hullabaloo about Paramount's completion of a third of a century of operation, although I did not actively rejoin the motion-picture industry except to keep my directorship and remain as chairman of the executive committee. There are the usual clippings from the columnists, who insisted then, as they do now, in marrying me off every week or so to some charming lady whom I hardly know. I would lead a gay and festive life, indeed, if I could marry all the lovely ladies with whom the columnists have led me to the altar. But most of the ladies in question are as surprised as I am when these reports appear, and when my friends send me their usual notes referring to "my new-found happiness," I often have not read the reports and am completely in the dark as to where and with whom this happiness is going to lie.

I made a few new forays into the theatre with a fine group known as Theatre Incorporated, which went the way of most small theatre groups. There was a day of considerable excitement when three of my partners and I sent our sons into the old firm of Hemphill, Noyes and Company. It appeared that the birth of the firm itself had directly coincided with the biologically active years of most of its partners, and young Noyeses, young Hemphills, young Strongs, and a young Griffis were ready to carry on the old traditions. I could not wish any of them any happier fate than association, with or without their fathers, in the business of investment banking, which for me is, and will always remain, the happiest of all businesses and certainly the father of them all.

Like so many other warriors and near warriors, I had returned to New York to find myself without a roof tree except in New Canaan. It was the day of the great apartment shortage, with literally thousands of people looking for a place to live. Fussy old bachelor that I was, I had very fixed ideas of where and how I wanted to live, and it was only after a long search that I found the apartment I wanted; a vacant maisonette duplex at 25 Sutton Place, close to the river. Alas, I could not rent it, for a great insurance company that had foreclosed on the apartment house some years back, and had been operating it at great loss ever since, held the apartment as bait. Whoever rented it would have to buy the building. I walked into the trap—with my eyes wide open—and became the owner of a magnificent piece of real estate, a perfect apartment, and a rent roll that was a far figure from the costs of operating the building, paying the taxes, and meeting the interest on the mortgage.

However, I was very happy with my new adventure, even though the months I spent redesigning and air-conditioning the apartment were punctuated by an occasional cry of horror as I read the rent returns and the cost figures from my agents. My list of tenants looked like a concentration of the New York Social Register. I should have taken great pride in contributing to the support of such poverty-stricken individuals as Mrs. Otto Kahn, who occupied the three top floors, and I should have had no regret at contributing to the welfare of

Bob Sherwood, who was busily writing *Roosevelt and Hopkins*, and whom I called my favorite tenant, although he insisted upon calling me his favorite landlord because of the subsidy that I was advancing for his rent.

It was a little later that *Time* magazine sent one of its precocious boy-girl writing teams to interview me. The lady, whose name escapes me, claimed to be interested only in my political philosophies, and we talked about these for an hour or so. When the article appeared, it said: "Resembling an over-sized foxy grandpa, Griffis lives in an over-sized fourteen room apartment on Manhattan's elegant Sutton Place. Five bathrooms are done in various pastels, one in baby blue, décor runs to silver zigzag-patterned wallpaper, thick cream rugs; the bric-a-brac is Brobdingnagian. Twice married, twice divorced, Griffis keeps his current philosophy stitched on a sampler hanging on a wall of his pine-paneled library. 'High hopes faint on a warm hearthstone, he travels the fastest who travels alone.'" No doubt, a lady reporter from *House and Garden* or *Architectural Forum* could write a really good political story.

In any event, this forced adventure into New York real estate had a happy ending. Some years later a more adventurous real estate operator than I purchased the building from me and gave me a lease on my much maligned apartment. Yet I cannot refrain from a friendly tip to all hands who would buy an apartment house just for the sake of living in it. Don't do it; your tenant on the fifth floor is apt to call up in the middle of the night and tell you that the plumbing is out of order. I can sleep better as a mere tenant.

I went for a happy tarpon-fishing expedition in the Panuco River at Tampico, with my pygmy friends, Reed Kilpatrick, and Bernard, that genial patriarch of all the Gimbels, and to visit a very successful investment made in La Consolidata steel corporation with Paul Shields. From there I went over to Palm Beach and dallied among the sybarites visiting Mary and Bill

Greve, and playing many afternoons of "towie"—a version of three-handed bridge—with its inventor, "Rep," the beloved Leonard Replogle.

I returned to New York and spent months negotiating with practically every important publisher in the United States, hoping to purchase an interest in a great publishing house that I could combine with my bookselling business. However, these literary men, content with their own profits, looked down their noses at the thought of being in trade, especially since it concerned their own product. Only Harold Guinzburg of Viking was intrigued, though not to the extent of making a deal; and Nelson Doubleday said at the end: "I would go along with you except that I am absolutely certain that you would not stay put, and would probably run away to Portuguese East Africa or way stations within six months." I fear that there was more than a *soupçon* of truth in his pronouncement, for some months later I sold an issue of preferred stock to aid in the expansion of Brentano's Bookstores and it came back to plague me. The salesman in an excess of enthusiasm had represented to the purchasers that I had committed myself to spend the rest of my days on the floor of the main store, describing the virtues of best sellers to the customers. Nelson Doubleday would have known better.

In late 1946 the Democrats of Connecticut were hard put to find a candidate for United States Senator to oppose the popular Republican Governor Baldwin. I received a series of calls late one night and some more in the morning to come at once to Hartford, where the Democratic State Convention was assembled, and accept the nomination. But my inhibitions against running for public office, which had determined my decision in 1944, were unchanged. I was still a commuter and still of Wall Street and I regretfully declined the opportunity to run against Baldwin, who duly defeated the Democratic candidate and served brilliantly in the Senate. This was in the days before Governor Chester Bowles had engineered the brilliant political

deal that took Baldwin out of the Senate to a state judgeship
and permitted the appointment of his former partner Bill
Benton, thus perpetuating the advertising firm of Benton and
Bowles, though in a different setting, in the Senate. It would
have made me very happy to have represented the great State
of Connecticut in the Senate, and I have had three extremely
vague possibilities of so doing, once in '44 with a Chinaman's
chance of defeating Brien McMahon for the nomination, once
in '46, as I have just written, and once during my term as ambassador to Argentina, when Chet Bowles told me that if Bill
Benton's business commitments would not permit his accept-
ance of Chet's very proper nomination of his former partner
for Senator, he would probably give me the appointment.
Now, however, I will probably never have the pleasure of being sued by Senator McCarthy.

Bill Benton, meeting me one day later in an anteroom off the
Secretary of State's office, introduced me to a friend as the
only rich Democrat, a strange tribute since Bill himself is the
owner of the Encyclopedia Britannica and Muzak, and certainly far richer than I. In any event the reputation that this
sort of introduction had given me was making it unceasingly
apparent that some form of political life was closing in on me.
One afternoon late in 1946 two stalwarts of the Democratic
Party called on me in my apartment and suggested that I
should take more interest in party affairs; they ended with the
stark question, "What would you like to have?"

I told them that there wasn't anything in the world that I
wanted except prosperous obscurity, but after a moment's
thought, added, "Of course, I would like to be ambassador to
England."

That chance remark started a train of events which later led
me to four diplomatic posts, though never to England. While
I had all sorts of assurances from Bob Hannegan, then chairman of the Democratic National Committee, and Postmaster
General, that I would be sent to London, the appointment

finally went to Max Gardner, who died tragically on the morning that he was to have sailed for his post.

Jim Forrestal and again Hannegan assured me that my wishes were now "in the bag," but the resignation of Jimmy Byrnes and the appointment of General Marshall, who knew nothing about me and who was guided largely by the recommendations of Dean Acheson, led to the brilliant appointment of Lew Douglas. Nevertheless, the virus of ambassadorial appointment was in my blood, and as a result I was finally sent to Poland.

Many ambassadors who have received so-called political appointments, as opposed to career appointments, have been accused of buying their ambassadorships through contributions to the party in power. Some of these charges may have been true. I do not know. From the press, one may believe whom he will. The Bridgeport *Herald* at the time of the Polish appointment said, "Democratic bosses are boiling over the Griffis appointment, party leaders claim there is no record of a contribution from him to the Democratic Campaign Fund." This is completely true. Or one may believe the statements of the Alsops in the New York *Herald Tribune*, directed at the time largely against Ambassador James Bruce, but which stated among other things, "In the same way other large contributors, Griffis, Laurence Steinhardt, et al., will ultimately receive as their reward posts in the gift of the American people."

The fact is, however, that not until long after my appointment as ambassador to Poland did I contribute one nickel to any political party, nor since that time have I made any contributions which by any stretch of the imagination could be called large. Nor have I by any subterfuge or loans or contributions through members of my family given any substantial funds to the Democratic Party. Yet I certainly was and am happy to have been a political appointee to the various ambassadorships in which I served.

So, early in 1947, President Truman called me from Palm

Beach to Washington and, a little apologetic about the promised English appointment, asked me to go to Poland. While I
find that according to the newspaper comments on my appointment I attempted to give the impression of being dragged
off in the service of my country on a great popular draft, the
truth is that I was delighted by the whole idea, and overjoyed
to encounter that behemoth of mismanagement and conflicting
ideas, that natural target for all statesmen of the opposition,
the State Department of the United States of America.

One's attitude toward the State Department frequently depends on the angle from which he views it—whether he is a
Democrat or a Republican, a career officer or a political appointee, within the Department or outside it, and whether he
has a big job or a small one. The State Department is enor-
mously complicated, a fantastic network of men, women, and
typewriters, who report to Washington from all parts of the
world on the political, economic, labor, and agricultural conditions of the countries in which they serve. The filing cases in
Washington are voracious eaters and are fed daily from the
great pouches that come in by air from the various embassies;
in the meantime the home team, having properly disposed of
the information from the field, proceeds to write its own endless reports to go forward to the same ultimate fate in the
embassies throughout the world. Hardly anyone, much less an
ambassador busy with constant conferences, the ordinary
housekeeping of his embassy, and the care and feeding of visiting Americans, can read, let alone understand, the flow of
departmental contributions that comes across his desk. Of the
tons of reports on every subject that are rushed with great
haste and at great cost by airplane, I doubt if fifty per cent
serves any useful purpose or contributes anything to the Department's knowledge.

In other words, I believe that the operating cost of the
State Department could be reduced by at least forty per cent,
with a loss of less than five per cent in efficiency, if the job

could be undertaken without fear by someone with full authority who did not have to be concerned for his job or the distinguished politicians in the House and the Senate. Such a man would need unqualified authority and no such authority has been given in our time, and it probably will never be. Senator Vandenberg, who, when the Republicans controlled Congress, was chairman of the Senate Committee on Foreign Relations and who had a vast knowledge of the State Department, pointed up these ideas in his recently published papers when he referred to the brief administration of Stettinius as Secretary of State. Vandenberg said that Stettinius was not really Secretary of State at all, but he was in effect general manager, and it was probably with this idea of efficiency engineering that he was put into office to breach the gap between Hull and Byrnes.

We have had many distinguished Secretaries of State in our time, and a number of fine Under-Secretaries, but we have never had a man who combined ability with the authority to enter the State Department, in whatever capacity, and clean out its Augean stables of bureau piled on bureau and committee piled on committee. In view of the tremendous growth of bureaucracy in Washington, a development of this sort is understandable. But if the State Department is ever to regain its former efficiency, it should be placed in the charge of not one but two men. The first, a secretary in charge of major policy decisions; the other, what Senator Vandenberg described as a "general manager," one who would really be a general manager and see to it that the Department did not bog down under its own dead weight. Perhaps Carl Humelsine, the Department's top organizer, can accomplish this job. When Secretary Marshall appointed him, the State Department felt that the five-star general was trying to establish a sort of general staff with military methods and objectives. But Humelsine is only human. While he has done a tremendous job, he still remains saddled not only with departmental housekeeping but with the preparation of the budget of the Department for submission to the watchdog committees of the Congress; and it is a strange but inexorable fact of the calendar that no sooner does one budget become approved for a fiscal year than another year and another budget start. Neither Humelsine nor anyone else has the time, or indeed the power, to do the clean-up job in the Department that everyone knows should be done. The jobs of both the Secretary and the Under-Secretary are man-killers, and no one man should be expected to play every instrument in the band.

For the defense, Eddie Miller, my most beloved boss in the State Department, takes the position that—while all this over-staffing and over-reporting may exist—the answer lies in the exorbitant demands made upon State by the departments of Commerce, Labor, and Agriculture, whose representatives clutter the United States embassies throughout the world. However, this is only partially true. I have never served in any of these government departments, but I have had ample opportunity to watch their work in the different embassies which I have operated, and perhaps under the circumstances I can properly apply the same general criticism of overstaffing, over-reporting, and over-expenses to nearly all of the departments of our government. I am sure that the average taxpayer will agree with me. Certainly a great part of the reports sent in through the State Department by the various representatives of other branches of the government are a waste of time and effort.

Every ambassador must know of many cases where a thorough incompetent is sent from post to post rather than removed from the service not only for his own good but for the good of the Department. Such men are known as "poor old Joe," and in those strange documents known as rating sheets, which annually carry a great output of fiction from the field to the Department, they are carefully protected lest the man who is writing the rating may some day find himself in a similar situation. Ratings from the Department and the field ultimately reach a promotion board, and determine the future of career officers. They are wonderful things to behold. There is no middle ground allowed in the answers to the voluminous questions they ask. Answer yes or no to each of the following question: "Does he wear a red necktie with a diamond-studded horseshoe pin with his morning coat?" or "Does he wear absolutely correct Brooks Brothers suits?" How do you answer? There is no exact repetition of the ancient query "Has he stopped beating his wife?" but there is the most careful inquisition into the habits, clothing, entertainmentship, general health, and fertility of the man's wife, whose social ability is considered highly important by the Department.

Many of these questions are, of course, taken lightly, but ratings are the bane of every Department officer. The system is not perfect, in fact it is not even good, but for some strange reason it sometimes happens that the better men gradually work up through the field. Yet sad indeed is the case of the hard-working, able career officer who somewhere along the line has picked up an adverse criticism on his record or incurred the displeasure of a sour and ancient ambassador. Sometimes all the perfumes of Araby cannot deodorize an unhappy paragraph, and the State Department is no exception to the rule that every business is crowded at the top.

But with the fabulous growth of bureaucracy in Washington there is little, if any, incentive for a high officer of State or any other department to save a few million dollars by cutting down the number of his employees. The drive in every government department is for larger and more expensive endeavors throughout the world, and it has become a cliché to comment on the fact that a business corporation operated in the way that great government departments in Washington are run would go broke within six months.

Even Forrestal, trained all his life in business and in the

economy of business, finally admitted that he was a bureaucrat where any question of economy was concerned. During the war every branch of the service had its own public relations unit that photographed everything in sight at a tremendous cost to the taxpayers. While I was in charge of the motion-picture end of the Office of War Information during the latter years of the war, and came constantly in contact with these duplicated operations, I told Forrestal one day that if he would let me try to coordinate the various photographic services of the different branches of defense I could save the defense budget more than fifty million dollars a year, and probably close to a hundred million dollars a year. His answer was very direct: "What is a hundred million dollars in war?" Obviously the job did not seem worth the effort. As good a man as he was, he could not quite face the pains of unification; indeed no man has yet appeared who is willing to accept the responsibilities and punishment of businesslike integration of the Department of State.

Strangely, however, the State Department more than all others manages to maintain a mysterious glamour about all of its works. To the young student of history or politics or to the career girl from Keokuk or Albuquerque it brings dreams of soft, far-off beaches in the shadow of waving palms, the mysterious bazaars of the Near East, the spicy smells of the Orient, the boulevards of Paris, or the mysterious Balkans and the charms of working for young and intriguing diplomats. The aroma remains until the realization comes that adventure usually means heat, fleas, bad living quarters and food, bottles of sulfasuxidine for "gippy tummy," and the declining excitement of Latin or Oriental male interest in the American State Department girl. But who am I to deglamorize the far-flung embassies and ministries and consulates of the State Department. Fortunately, I shall fail in any event, but even for an ambassador there comes the realization that through the ages diplomats remain much the same and it is probably true that taxidermists gaze upon most of them with a certain professional envy. It is sadly true that the glittering, romantic diplomatic corps throughout the world have a certain dull sameness. The ambassador from Shangri-la stationed in Warsaw is likely to look and talk exactly like his cousin, the ambassador from Shangri-la stationed in Guatemala or in Singapore. The sturdy representatives of His Majesty's Foreign Office in Whitehall are astonishingly similar the world around, as are the smiling Italian linguists with their never failing magnificent cuisine of spaghetti variations.

Every ambassadorship carries with it the responsibility of a great celebration on each ambassador's national holiday, and since there are ordinarily about fifty ambassadorships or ministries in each great capital, it is easy to see that at least one such observance a week is sandwiched in with the innumerable cocktail parties, small lunches, and large dinners. An ambassador has but one liver to give for his country. Nothing is so completely terrifying to an American plenipotentiary as the thought of his great Fourth of July party, to which he must invite all local Americans, who develop a mighty thirst over the weeks in preparation for the event. My Fourth of July party in Madrid, to which I invited all the local Americans, was particularly successful. It produced about thirty Americans of the Mayflower variety, and exactly eight hundred and forty-nine delegates from Puerto Rico.

Probably the most amusing picture of the State Department at work is the comparison of its operations with the love life of elephants, a bon mot which is attributed to Bob Lovett. The analogy is simple, but astonishingly true. It falls into three phases of comparisons; the first, that all important business is done at a very high level; secondly, that any developments are accompanied by tremendous trumpeting; and thirdly, that if any results are accomplished, the period required is from eighteen months to two years.

As I waited for the Senate to confirm my appointment, I

studied daily in the Department of State and I gradually ab-
sorbed a good deal of knowledge not only about Poland but
about the Department itself. I learned a great deal because I
looked for things to learn. I did not join an organized class.
Unfortunately, in the Department an ambassador is an ambassador and a junior official is a junior official, and never the
twain shall meet. Nor does there seem to be any machinery
existing for the real indoctrination of new political arrivals,
though there certainly should be. Nor indeed was I ever given
a clear, concise statement of what the policy of the Department was toward any of the countries to which I was appointed; though in nearly every case there was usually an
ancient paper known as a policy statement, or a document
being developed that was supposed to state a policy. Ordinarily
the plan seemed to be to pick it up in bits and pieces as I could.

As I browsed around the Department there was one man in
the division of Eastern European Affairs who, I think, was so
terrified at the thought of my going into one of the countries
for which he was responsible that he really went out of his
way to indoctrinate me. His name was Llewellyn "Tommy"
Thompson, who now serves as ambassador to Hungary. As I
recall it, Tommy's sagest advice to me was never to underestimate my counselors. A counselor, he said, is exactly what
he is called. His job is to counsel the head of the embassy and
to give him every benefit of his experience, his knowledge, and
his logic. It was good advice and in general I have followed it.

I have been extremely fortunate in the list of counselors with
whom I have served. Ned Crocker, bridge player extraordinary and recently ambassador to Iraq, was with me in Poland,
and in Egypt I had the brilliant services of Jefferson Patterson,
now serving as a representative at the United Nations. In
Argentina there was my good and able friend Lester Mallory,
and in Spain John Wesley Jones, one of the best men in the
Department, affectionately known as Johnny. Tommy
Thompson, horrified no doubt by some of my pronounce-

ments as to how I intended to approach the Communistic government of the Poles, quoted at length to me one of Talleyrand's essays of advice to young diplomats, which included the key phrase "And above all, young man, not too much zeal." With these words of counsel, I began to realize that perhaps Thompson and Talleyrand had something after all, and I asked Tommy if he would have this phrase lettered in motto form so I could keep it on my desk in Warsaw. This he did, and it has followed me ever since. It is the best advice I know; not only in diplomacy but everywhere else.

I learned, too, there is today hardly a post in the world where the ambassador cannot lift the telephone and in five or ten minutes be in communication with the committees in Washington that really determine all his major decisions. The limit of his initiative lies in his personal relationship with the foreign minister, the ruler, or the other ministers or plenipotentiaries of his accredited country. As far as the State Department is concerned, he is part of a pattern, but the drawing board, the pencils, the T-square, the compass, and the triangles are in Washington.

The really distressing part of it all, at least to an extremely active and individualistic American businessman who finds himself in the State Department, is the fact that inevitably the diplomat's career progresses toward inaction and long periods of indecisive communing with Washington, while the inefficient system of promotion suggests that if the diplomat does not do anything at all he will never do anything wrong. The constant conferences between State Department employees and ambassadors is always summed up in the word "don't"— never in the word "do"; even an ambassador can't go wrong if he doesn't do anything, and the suggestion of a sharply defined course of action made from the field to the Department always carries a thousand corollary reasons why it should not be done, and very few reasons why it should.

There is nothing in this writing which I have not said to my embassy associates a thousand times. I have called my first secretaries master surgeons, having watched them with clean and unerring knife at least attempt to emasculate completely any direct statement in my cables to the Department on political and most other subjects. My good but terrorized friends in a number of the embassies can tell you of a thousand cutting and curetting operations on my cables, but sometimes to their horror I have really let loose in my comments to Washington and obtained some results.

And even before I went to Poland I learned another grim truth of political life, which upset me nearly as much as my discovery of State Department inefficiency. I was to speak in Hartford one night before an enormous audience of Polish Americans. The evening was devoted to raising funds for Polish relief, and on the platform with me were Chester Bowles, later to become governor, Clare Boothe Luce, and a distinguished Pole from Chicago. The audience was heavy-lidded and dreary. The night was hot. The Pole had announced that he would deliver half of his speech in English and half in Polish, and though many minutes had drifted off into eternity the English part was not yet finished, and there was not a laugh in a carload. I was to be the next speaker, and I whispered to Clare Luce, who was sitting next to me, "This is terrible, I am going to lighten this thing up and give them a laugh here and there." She answered, "Please don't do that. You will be making a terrible mistake. I know these people," she added, "and I know that if there is a lot of humor in your speech they will regard you only as an extremely frivolous ambassador." Then she gave me some advice that Joe Martin, the Representative for Massachusetts, had once given her. Martin, she said, had never seen a politician with a constantly and openly expressed sense of humor survive in public life.

This, of course, is an exaggeration, for some of our great politicians have made their constituents laugh and been elected nevertheless. But I have found that among heavy-minded diplomats and their staffs that Martin's theory is approximately right. But I love to laugh, and I was struck with the truth of one of Elsa Maxwell's comments about me that appeared in her column. "So few ambassadors," she wrote, "have real humor. It seems to be hidden away by most diplomats as unbecoming to their dignity, but humor is like butter on bread, it smooths the paths for politicians; if Griffis can make the Poles laugh he will be a prince of diplomats." I didn't make the Poles laugh, nor in fact, the Egyptians, nor in general the Argentines and the Spanish, but I myself laughed a good deal, and the experience of having done so has certainly added years to my life. If successful politician or diplomat I cannot be without laughter, then I do not want to be a successful politician or diplomat. I guess now I don't want to be one anyway.

Yet there are famous stories of the diplomatic service that are not without humor, and my favorite was told me by August Rust-Oppenheim many years before I had any thought that I might some day be called Your Excellency. It is about the British admiral who anchored his flagship in the bay of Tunis, and received word that the ruler of Tunis was about to come out and make an official call upon him, further that the ruler spoke only French, which was, of course, the official diplomatic language. The British admiral spoke only English and regarded anyone who spoke anything else as a bit immoral. Accordingly, he arranged for one of his junior lieutenants who spoke fluent French to translate during his meeting with the Bey of Tunis. The conversation filled with amenities and innocuous comments dragged on for a long time, and the admiral, bored and sleepy in the afternoon sun, finally said to his translator, with a feeling of complete linguistic safety, "For God's sake tell this nigger to go ashore, I can't stand this any longer." The suave lieutenant translated this remark to the Bey, saying that the admiral again wished to express his pleasure at being in Tunis and having the delight of viewing its beautiful scenery and meeting its distinguished ruler and so on, ad infinitum—punctuated with the renewed English suggestions that the ruler be on his way. Finally the interview was concluded, and the following Saturday night when the admiral was about to return to his ship, after a magnificent garden party given by the Bey, filled with good cheer and the Bey's champagne, he made his adieu, expressing in execrable French his delight at having been present at the party; whereupon the Bey answered in perfect Oxonian English, "My dear admiral, I am delighted that you have enjoyed my party, but I do feel that you have missed your calling. You should have been a diplomat."

Though my five years with the State Department may qualify me to criticize the cumbersome and squeaky mechanism of its management, I do not feel that I have any business to attempt, especially in a book of this character, a critique of the Department's foreign policy. A multitude of half-baked writers, a good many publishers, and certainly every man or woman who runs for public office in the United States— whether for municipal garbage collector or senator—have had much to say about our recent foreign policy. Few of them have the slightest idea of what they are talking about, but the American public is avidly interested in the subject, and they have their reward. The gross sales of my bookstores would drop off considerably if authors were suddenly required to write with verity and knowledge.

So for many reasons, particularly within the confines of a short chapter in a book confined largely to the rambling observations of a rambling businessman and ambassador, I shall abstain from any general comments on foreign policy. Certainly one of the best reasons for my abstinence is the fact that I have never served in what might be called a friendly, or even a normal, post. I have always been a diplomatic trouble shooter, accredited to dictatorships; the Communist police government of Poland, the absolute monarchism of King Farouk, the gradually rising slavery of Juan and Evita Perón, and the absolute dictatorship of Francisco Franco. So I shall leave it to those theoretical writers and speakers who have never seen these lands to criticize the hard-working upper strata of the State Department.

There are three types of this literature that I resent deeply. One is the work of that ever-growing number of writers—growing indeed as the prospective royalties increase—the re-formed Communists who carried a card for a while but who saw the error of their ways, particularly when they finally understood that there were many men in Hollywood and elsewhere who regarded them as vipers in the bosom of the nation. Secondly, I am weary of that great mass of Baker Street irregulars who prowl the halls of the Department of State looking for Communistic employees. Certainly there have been Communists in the State Department at one time or another. There were probably Communists in a great many of the large American corporations and in the grocery stores, and in the barber shops. Perhaps they were even more likely to gravitate toward the State Department because of its intellectual allure, and the fact that Communism was a fetish of many half-baked intellectuals in the thirties. Yet during my entire term in the State Department I never met a Communist so far as I know, nor did I ever have any man or woman in any of my embassies who I believed nurtured Communistic ideas. Perhaps I am just an unobservant old gentleman, but I am bored with the Hisses and nauseated by the Chamberses. A curse on both their houses. I wish that they would quietly crawl back into their respective pumpkins and stay there.

Most of all, I am bored with the five-years-later quarterbacks who criticize the action of the President and of our State Department representatives at Yalta. Certainly we made mistakes at Yalta, mistakes as grave as permitting the Russians to take and hold their section of Berlin and accepting their solemn promises to permit free elections in Poland. But has anyone never made a mistake? We made a far greater mistake during the war when we came to the aid of Russia in such a way that she was able to destroy the German armies. It would have been far better if we had simply enabled the Russians and Germans to exterminate each other. But here again we made the mistake of just being Americans and expressing our naïve belief in all human nature, our belief that Russians are people.

The best answer to Yalta is simply to imagine oneself as a high-ranking officer in the Pacific at the time of the conferences who knew from the studies on the proposed attack on the Japanese mainland that millions of young Americans were bound to die in the assault. Such an officer might have known something about the atomic bomb, but even if he were the highest echelon he could not have been really sure of its power. He knew only that the nation and the world were weary of war, that hundreds of thousands of Americans had already been killed, and that the attack by Russian armies on the Manchurian front was almost certain to end the Pacific horror in short order. At the time, of course, dear old Uncle Joe was our good and trustworthy friend, and thus it is easy to see what prompted the Yalta decision.

There is a deep-rooted tradition in the minds of the American people that only rich men accept an ambassadorship. This theory, I think, is greatly exaggerated. I doubt if the rewards of statecraft are much different from those of most businesses. Even Hollywood and Wall Street, which once constituted an exception to this rule, are getting pretty tough nowadays. An ordinary secretary in the foreign service receives as much as, and usually more than, her counterpart in business, considering her basic salary, her living allowances, and her traveling costs, and the same is generally true for attachés as well as for first, second, and third secretaries. And certainly an ambassador can live comfortably on his salary and allowances in most countries, though if he has a private income there is certainly opportunity enough for him to spend it. Jokingly I have sometimes referred to the opulence of an ambassador's career, stating that he received a salary of twenty-five thousand dollars, spent fifty thousand dollars in living and entertainment, and out of the balance paid his income tax. But this is far from the strict truth. An ambassador usually receives a fair salary; he is given either an existing house that is owned by the government and maintained by an adequate staff of servants, or else he gets an adequate household allowance to rent and carry on his own establishment. The government always pays his transportation to and from posts and arranges to ship his household goods. He also gets an adequate allowance for entertainment and parties. Unfortunately, as every ambassador knows, the entertainment and parties are the real horror of his existence. In order to collect for them, he is supposed to entertain the dignitaries of the country to which he is accredited, although he is allowed a sprinkling of Americans. It should be exactly the other way. He should be allowed his largest allowance for the entertainment of his visiting fellow citizens. Certainly it is no treat for an overworked minister of foreign affairs or for the ambassadors of important countries to have to come to additional dinners and cocktail parties at the American Embassy. I myself have seldom, if ever, seen these celebrations result in any increased good will or accomplishment. But the tradition remains and the entertainment can be made as lavish or as primitive as the ambassador desires. Unfortunately, the whole theory of "we must have a cocktail party" spreads through the corps down to the lowliest secretary, and in the last analysis that is what sometimes makes the diplomatic life expensive. Yet no one who really loves the game of diplomacy, no one who would deeply desire to spend his life with the State Department, should ever refuse it on account of its cost. An outside income will not do him any harm, but he can, in most places, get along without one.

# CHAPTER ELEVEN

## THE IRON CURTAIN AND I DESCEND ON POLAND

Contemplating a peaceful re-entry into government service, I had blithely overlooked the fact that every man who enters public life in the United States immediately assumes the position of the unfortunate gentleman who pokes his head through the hole in the canvas at the county fair, and thus becomes a target for any number of would-be pitchers. The only important differences are that in public life the yokels are replaced by the columnists, and the gentleman who made the mistake of looking through the hole has a better opportunity to dodge than the man in public life.

Some five or six years before the Polish appointment I had been dining quietly in New York with my long-time friend, tennis opponent, and physician, Dr. Foster Kennedy. There were only two others present at the dinner, Mrs. Kennedy and another guest. The conversation turned to politics and became one of those strange arguments that seem always to hover along the edges of violence. In this case the tendencies to violence were augmented by the doctor's large and tasty martinis. The years have dimmed exactly what was said at the dinner, but following a discussion of *Mein Kampf*, I remarked that Hitler had one of the important minds of Europe and was one of the greatest organizers in the world. The statement ended a long-time friendship and I completed my dinner at home.

The story grew and spread, turning from a small cloud on the horizon to a tempest. It grew into charges of pro-Naziism and its corollary, anti-Semitism. One of our more obnoxious columnists, who had had the story for years, unleashed it for the American and Swedish press on the very day on which I started negotiations with the Swedes on the ball-bearings question. However, in 1947, I felt that it had been consigned to limbo, when I was suddenly called by the Foreign Relations Committee for examination in reference to my fitness for the Polish nomination. Both Senator Vandenberg, who was then chairman and Senator Tom Connally, the present chairman, were extremely fair to me before the committee, and I thought that the ghost was properly laid until I began to read in the papers that my former dinner companions had been summoned before the committee. It appeared from the report of that hearing that a gentleman well-known in journalistic circles in New York had telephoned Senator Vandenberg to protest my appointment, leading to a hue and cry that lasted for many weeks.

Meanwhile, a good many columnists jumped into the fray, making it a sort of a New Orleans battle royal over what had been said or what had not been said. In any event, through the gentle intervention of my old friend Clare Luce and a number of others, my nomination was finally confirmed unanimously by the Senate. Into the record were read a series of commendatory letters from Admiral Nimitz, with whom I served in the Pacific, from Bob Patterson, the Secretary of War, who had been deeply interested in my Swedish negotiations, from my old friend Jim Forrestal, then Secretary of the Navy, and from "Doc" O'Connor, President of the Red Cross, who observed that the gentleman who had made the original charges against me greatly needed the services of a good neuropathist. Not to be forgotten, too, was the public statement of one member of the Foreign Relations Committee that "he was inclined to agree that Hitler showed organizing ability."

All of this *opéra bouffe* transpired five years ago, but to this day, several times a year, the story rears its head in columns or in columnists' broadcasts, particularly kept alive by the columnist who originally sponsored it. I think it would have been better perhaps if I had robbed a bank or committed a quiet murder, if the Shakespearean theory is correct that "the evil that men do lives after them, the good is often interred with their bones." If stigma I must have, I would like at least to have some honest charge of misdeed attached to my public life.

On the day that I presented my credentials to President Beirut of Poland, the Kremlin called a play and gave orders to its satellites that have changed the whole course of history. In the month before my arrival in Warsaw the first stirrings of the Marshall Plan began, and every country in Europe was invited to attend a parley in Paris to discuss ways and means of putting it into successful operation. Poland was the first European country in the Russian zone that expressed readiness to co-operate in the Marshall Plan for European recovery, and it had formally announced its intentions of sending a delegation to the meeting. Foreign Minister Zygmunt Modzelewski had confirmed this intent to me on the evening before my presentation to Beirut.

The cavalcade of a few bedraggled cars drove me and my staff up to the Presidential Palace in a pouring rain. The two or three hundred feet of courtyard which separated the palace entrance from the street was lined with Polish troops, all vigorously presenting arms as the rain dripped from their uniforms and guns. I had been instructed by the Minister of Protocol to walk halfway to the entrance, stop in the center of the line of troops, raise my silk hat, and shout *chowem yownieze*, which in Polish means "Hail to the troops," and which I had vigorously practiced shouting for the past twenty-four hours. I had not been told, however, that the whole soldiery were to shout back to me in Polish "Hail to the ambassador," which so unnerved me that only a miracle saved my silk hat from falling into the street in my embarrassment.

Poland was the only country in which I served where the old custom of the ambassador's reading a speech to the head of the state, and in return listening to a speech from the dignitary to whom he was accredited, prevailed. Everything went off very pleasantly. I read my speech in English, of which President Beirut understood not a word, and he responded with what was no doubt a magnificent speech in Polish, of which I could understand nothing. I was then escorted in to a small antechamber where we were supposed to have a private conversation, and where I immediately burst into my appreciation of the Poles' attitude in sending a delegation to Paris. President Beirut seemed to freeze a little, and said that it was not yet decided whether they should go or not but that he would advise me during the evening. The blow fell when I was called to the Foreign Office at nine that night from a dinner which I was giving for Eric Johnston of the Motion Picture Association. When I got there I was told that the Poles for no apparent reason had changed their minds and would not appear in Paris. When we received news the next day that the Czechs, and in fact all of the Russian satellite countries, had sent exactly the same message at exactly the same time, we realized that Russia had laid down its dictum, given orders to its slaves, and determined that since East is East and West is West, never the twain shall meet.

It was a bitter blow, but it had personal compensations for me, for the first cable I sent to the State Department that night, and which apparently went directly to Secretary Marshall, led to the beginning of the Secretary's kindly interest in the new ambassador. He has chuckled over it and reminded me of it many times since. It ran something like this: "Secretary of

State, Washington [as all incoming State Department cables are addressed], my first day of diplomatic effort has resulted in a perfect score—one hundred per cent failure."

Shortly after this episode I was to meet most of the Polish ministers, including Prime Minister Cyrankiewicz, whose head resembled a billiard ball with eyes. Cyrankiewicz, a dyed-in-the-wool Communist masquerading as a Socialist, played the role of the trained steer that leads its constituents up the runway of the stockyard, only to move on for additional duty as the ax falls on the head of his followers. It was not many months later that he showed his true colors, developing a merger of the Socialist party with the Communist party. The Socialists were no more. But at the time he was, in public, a Socialist, and as one Socialist to another Bevin called on him on his way to England from the ill-fated Moscow conference. Cyrankiewicz, so the story goes, protested to Bevin against the British Government's policy of giving asylum to renegade Polish politicians in England, and it was then that Bevin, assuming his most comfortable position, the larger part of his anatomy on the seat of the chair and his knee on the floor, clapped Cyrankiewicz on the back and said to him, "You are a young man, Mr. Cyrankiewicz, some day you may need asylum." Unfortunately, this has apparently not yet happened.

Except for Modzelewski and Cyrankiewicz, I had little or no personal contacts with government ministers except for Hilary Minc, the Minister of Commerce. Only once during my stay in Poland was I invited to enter any Polish home, either governmental or private, except for Chopin concerts at the Palace. Government officials living in small threadbare apartments claimed that they had no place to entertain, and non-political Poles in private life were too frightened of their government to think of inviting the American ambassador to visit them. Meanwhile, whenever I invited a Polish minister or officer to my house, he would invariably hesitate before accepting and say that he did not have his appointment book handy, but that he would call me shortly. Invariably, he would call back and say he would be very happy to accept but he would like the honor of bringing with him his good friend, General ——— (a general obviously appointed by the government officials to spy on my guests, who would spend the evening observing everything that went on).

As the Iron Curtain descended and the rising tide of anti-Americanism rose, my diplomatic chores became less and less, and I turned to the happier job of Embassy housekeeping and reorganization in an effort to make my long-suffering staff as comfortable as they could possibly be in the horror of Warsaw's rubble. Some of these efforts have been humorously described by Jack Iams in an article published in the New York *Herald Tribune's This Week* magazine, on December 5, 1948. It described the ambassador and was called "Whirlwind in Warsaw." I never had the pleasure of meeting Mr. Iams, and since he wrote his piece after I had left Warsaw, I assume that his information came from Embassy officers. It gave me many a laugh and I quote part of it as follows.

At the intersection of Marshal Stalin Avenue and Pius XI Street, two items brighten the jagged desolation of Poland's capital city. One is a battery of American flags, the other a honey-blonde lady cop who directs traffic with provocative twirls of a short skirt. Undeniably, a certain cheerful showmanship has cropped up behind this segment of the Iron Curtain, most of it traceable to recently departed Ambassador Stanton Griffis. Griffis never failed to tip his hat to the blonde cop, and she never failed to salute his limousine.

The new chancellery is surrounded by an attractive garden, full of lilacs and syringa, with gravel walks under the chestnut trees, but it is the basement which offers the main attraction—the commissary. It's a fabulous bazaar, offering drinkables from American canned beer to vintage French champagnes, cigarettes of all major, and some minor, brands, Havana cigars, canned goods of every variety even to rattlesnake meat, and such dainties as pâté de foie gras from Strasbourg, with truffles.

Prices are extremely reasonable, and the facilities are made available to almost any American who pauses to pay his respects and isn't suspected of selling blueprints to the Russians.

Adjoining the commissary is a milk bar, serviced by the embassy's own pasteurization plant. The milk bar, temperance groups will be pleased to know, does as thriving business as the liquor counter.

Most of the embassy staff lunches in a pleasant mess hall set up in the partially restored former chancellery. Next to it is a comfortable recreation room which, three evenings a week, is transformed into a movie theater with seats for 100, including leather chairs for the upper echelons and tolerably new films, flown in from Berlin or Paris. Attendance is large and faithful.

In back of this still charred and bullet-pocked building is a spacious, a grassy compound sprinkled with so-called Swedish huts, well-heeled first cousins of the Quonset variety. The largest collection of huts provides apartments for about 30 girls of the staff, who double up in units of two bedrooms, living room, kitchen and bath, each with its maid-cook. The apartments are cheerfully furnished in a chintzy way, and one even boasts a baby grand piano.

Across the way, on the other side of Pius XI Street, is a row of three more American buildings, containing the U.S. Information Service and the accounting and consular sections. Whitewashed and flag-decked, the buildings present a snowy façade with red, white and blue trimmings, while at one end, the presence of the U.S.I.S. is announced to Stalin Avenue in gigantic letters, both Polish and English. There are those who wince at this touch and wonder if it doesn't smack of an advertisement for Lee Tires, of which Ambassador Griffis is a director.

A few blocks away, on Emilii Plater Street, is the elegant ambassadorial residence, in the drawing room of which Griffis introduced a built-in bar. In various other parts of the city, the embassy has bought or leased, through war-surplus negotiations which, in some mysterious way, didn't seem to have cost anybody anything, some half-dozen two-family houses or small apartment buildings which accommodate most of the remaining personnel.

The Polish Government has been surprisingly co-operative in

seeing the Americans well-ensconced, especially when you consider that Poles are living two and three to a room. One cynical embassy official claims this to be a subtle and insidious policy designed to portray Americans as parasitical voluptuaries.

The physical advantages which the embassy enjoys are almost entirely, though sometimes grudgingly, credited to Griffis and his high-pressure businessman's methods which, though he departed last July, still hover legendarily about the place. His whirlwind arrival in July, 1947, brought a change not only in the material setup but also in diplomatic punctilio.

One story about him, vouched for by witnesses, involves the first formal call paid by the Russian ambassador, a stiff and elderly professor. Griffis offered him a cigar, but the Russian said he didn't smoke. Griffis suggested a highball, but it seemed the Russian didn't drink either. Irascibly, Griffis demanded, and the interpreter faithfully interpreted, "What do you do to smell like a man?" The rest of the interview was strained.

(This yarn is slightly on the imaginative side, although I saw much of the Russian ambassador. Because of our diplomatic ranking in Warsaw, we were inevitably seated together at the receptions and cocktail parties given in the corps and at Polish celebrations, where the Poles sit at small tables lined with bottles of vodka and the thimblelike glasses for its consumption. The ritual between the Russian and American ambassadors was always the same. He would fill two glasses of vodka, raise one, and toast me in whatever jumble of Russian sounds means "good health." I would shortly return the compliment in English. Because neither of us understood the other, making conversation impossible, the frequency of toasts increased as the level of the vodka bottles decreased. It grew into a scintillating game before we both, but not together, glowingly wandered out into the night. I never did get up enough courage to joke with him over the fact that to my certain knowledge all of the telephone wires from my house and from the chancellery were monitored through the Russian Embassy in Warsaw.)

But if Griffis was considered unorthodox as a diplomat, as a businessman he was viewed, at least by the career officers on his staff, as all too typical. Everything had to be done in a tremendous hurry—"Keep pushin' 'em" was one of his favorite phrases.

Among the things he wanted, and wanted right away, was the movie theater, the lack of which is said to have struck him as inexplicable. The task of remedying the omission as fast as possible fell to the first secretary in charge of U.S.I.S., a placid man named Walter Schwinn who used to write editorials for the Hartford *Courant*. He still shudders as he looks back on the theater assignment. Building materials were scarce, local contractors slow, the projection equipment arrived with vital parts missing, the power system proved to be inadequate, and all the while Griffis stormed and fretted at the delay. "What's that contractor's name, Snail and Company?" he once roared at Schwinn. However, the theater did open on schedule with a gala showing of "Gone With the Wind," which had been flown from London and mislaid for 24 hours in Berlin. The opening was voted a great success by everybody but Schwinn, who had taken to his bed, and Griffis, who had left for consultation in Washington the day before.

Another rapid-fire project, worthy in its way but a cause of untold misery to underlings, was the milk pasteurization plant. The burden of getting the plant set up in the Griffis tempo was borne by the agricultural attaché, a serious student of crops and soil named Edwin Raymond. The job was done, but Raymond like Schwinn, was a nervous wreck at the end of it and was greatly relieved to be transferred to Cairo.

But if Griffis' methods left their scars, they also left a solid monument in the way of comfort, health and general contentment among the staff, an investment that would seem to have paid off in harmony and efficiency. There have been no resignations in over a year, which is probably a record for any American diplomatic establishment.

As Clare Luce had told me, I quickly found that it was unsafe and dangerous to have a sense of humor, especially in Poland. I had formed a sneaking admiration for Foreign Minister Modzelewski's stoutness in sticking to his Communistic principles, however thoroughly I disagreed with them, and I think he had a friendly feeling toward me, because we minced no words and every conference usually involved our walking up and down the room, shaking our fists at each other but ending with a smile. I thought I had reached a point at which I could joke with him when one day he complained about the continually rising expenses of his government. I volunteered that I could save him a very substantial amount if he would let me, and he immediately jumped at the suggestion. I told him what my plan was. I said, "You have exactly seventeen secret police in my embassy, disguised as messengers, chauffeurs and whatnot. Every Friday afternoon they report to their bosses all of the goings on in the Embassy and then I have to make them repeat that all to me the next day so that they know I have them spotted. You are just wasting these salaries, so why don't you come over to the Embassy every Friday afternoon and I'll let you read all my cables to the State Department and their answers. It will save you a lot of time and money." The humorous Mr. Modzelewski saw no jest in this suggestion and angrily contended that he had nothing to do whatever with the famous U.B., the Polish secret police.

It was Modzelewski nevertheless who, while definitely reserving the right of his government to attack every American principle and policy through its press, promised me that so long as I was in Poland I would never be personally attacked, and he kept his word, though once again I learned the danger of laughter behind the Iron Curtain, through an incident that caused the Polish press obliquely to break their agreement by quoting a headline dated in Prague that was unquestionably of Polish origin. I had never seen any of the Nazi prison camps in Poland, and toward the end of my stay I felt that I would like to see at least one, so with my military attaché, Colonel Betts, and the distinguished and much-decorated correspondent of the Associated Press, Larry Allen, we journeyed one day to Lublin and thence to Majdanek, one of the Germans' most vicious and horrible torture houses. We were shown all of the hideous exhibits, including the crematory, the great piles of human ashes, the gold teeth that had been extracted from the dead, the piles of shoes. We were finally escorted to the gas chamber. It was a great, solid, concrete room, with shower nozzles on the ceiling. There were no windows of any nature and only one door, a great mass of concrete swinging on heavy hinges, which could be opened only from the outside. I entered the chamber first, thinking that my associates would follow me, but my jokester friend Allen closed the door on me and remained outside. My terror was understandable, and when a few minutes later he opened the door to let me out, I expressed my relief in nervous laughter. The laughter was a mistake. This was the story that the Poles picked up with the headline "Only the American Ambassador, of the thousands of visitors to Majdanek, thought it was funny." Never laugh behind the Iron Curtain.

It was during my tenancy of the Polish Embassy that I had my only long and losing battle with the State Department on diplomatic theory. Early in 1947, Secretary Byrnes had made his famous speech in Stuttgart, wherein he offered the Russian Government a forty-year defensive and offensive peace pact, which the Russians refused. I had listened to so many diatribes from the Polish Government to the effect that the United States was the warmonger, and Russia the great exponent of peace, that I felt that the Poles might really have come to the point where they believed this foolishness. I conceived the idea of making official representation to the Polish Government whereby they would consent to act as intermediaries between the Kremlin and the State Department to bring about a settlement of the differences between East and West, based on Secretary Byrnes's offer. I thought that the plan offered two possibilities. First, it had a possible chance of success, but at its worst and if it brought no results, I felt there was a possibility that the Poles would finally realize the Kremlin's double-faced policies. I argued with the State Department in every possible way in order to get permission to proceed with this plan, but for good or for bad I was refused. Certainly if there is no decency or honesty whatever in the Kremlin, we will never have more than a nervous peace. But if there is any integrity at all in the whole Russian system, it seems to me that stronger efforts along the lines which I have sketched might have prevented the impasse that we are now in.

I met Stanislaw Mikolajczyk, the leader of the great Peasant Party, only once. At the time of my arrival he was anathema to the Polish Government, the only remnant of opposition to the Communist government. Every Pole knows his story, and most Americans who have any knowledge or contact with the recent history of Poland know of him and of his losing battle for democracy in his country. The story of Mikolajczyk stands out as a light in the Communist darkness.

Following the death of General Sikorski in 1943, Mikolajczyk had become the premier of the Polish Government in exile in London. At the insistence of Winston Churchill and Franklin D. Roosevelt, he returned to Poland in 1945 to become Vice-Premier and Secretary of Agriculture, and again to head the Peasant Party, which probably constituted at least seventy per cent of the Polish electorate. It was on Mikolajczyk and his party that the United States and England depended for the fragile hope of any real democracy in Poland, and for the vaunted "free elections" that would express the honest judgment and vote of the Poles.

The story of shattered dreams, of the falsity of Russian promises, and of Mikolajczyk's failure are all too well known. Mikolajczyk had to flee. The smoothly oiled curtain was descending with a terrible ruthlessness, and I have no doubt whatever that when Mikolajczyk fled from Poland, he was a

marked man. Had he not escaped the country he would not
be alive today. Nikola Petkov, the Bulgarian anti-Communist,
had recently been erased; Jan Masaryk, the great Czech
who was almost an American, was to die a few months later.

I would not tell you the story of his escape if I were not
sure that all of the American actors in this drama had long
since left Poland, and that the Polish Government, through
its arrest of Mikolajczyk's friends, had already obtained the
true story of the historic flight. By this time they are either
actually dead or among the dead who live in Polish prisons.
President Truman himself has seen fit to tell the story in
public, so I suppose that now it is no longer a top secret.

It was on the evening of October 17, 1947, when I was
having a preprandial drink with the beautiful and talented
Polish soprano, Victoria Calma, that there came a loud ringing at the Embassy bell, denoting the arrival of George Andrews, my first secretary, who had been the point of contact
between the Embassy and Mikolajczyk. Andrews was greatly
agitated and told me that just as the Embassy was closing
that afternoon an emissary of Mikolajczyk had arrived asking
him to come at once to Mikolajczyk's apartment. There
"Mik," as he was called, stated that he had received definite
word that with the opening of the Sejm, the Polish Congress,
the following week, criminal charges were to be made against
him, and he was to be liquidated. Mikolajczyk asked for our
advice and help. He was our man, our duty was clear, and
we were not long in aiding him.

All during the next day, Saturday the eighteenth, we discussed the project and how we could best deal with this
extremely ticklish diplomatic situation. Our responsibility to
Mikolajczyk was clear. We had arranged and fostered his
return to Poland, he was the hope of the great democratic
nations, and it seemed to all of us that, diplomatic hanky-
panky notwithstanding, we had to save this man from death.

The first plan was that I should carry Mikolajczyk in the

trunk of my large Chrysler, although Mikolajczyk himself was of considerable size, and deposit him on the Czechoslovakian border. But this plan was abandoned in view of the possibility of the definite involvement of the American ambassador, and a new one developed.

On the morning of the next day, October 19, we had planned a ceremony for American war fliers whose bodies had been found in Poland through the offices of the American Graves Registration Service. A long cavalcade of trucks had come from Berlin. The bodies of the dead were to be loaded therein and a high religious ceremony was to take place with a symbolic casket in the center of the Carmelite Church in Warsaw. I suggested to my military attaché that he ask the commander of the cavalcade to come over to the Embassy, following the ceremonies.

The commander was a young captain not more than twenty-two or twenty-three, and his Americanism and his courage impressed me as nothing impressed me before. He came into my library in the Embassy and I said to him, "We want you to do a very dangerous service. We want to get out of Poland a great patriot and a great democrat whose life is in danger. Would it be possible to put him in an empty casket in one of the trucks, and carry him over the German border to Berlin when your cavalcade leaves at midnight tonight? I want you to understand perfectly that if you are discovered in this operation it may cost you your life, but this is a matter of world importance. Can you work this out for us, realizing that you are in grave danger?"

Never in my life have I been so moved as when this youngster saluted and said, "Yes, sir." We transmitted the news to Mikolajczyk, but he refused to accept the plan, telling us that he felt that his duty was to inform his various associates in the Peasant Party of his plans and give them an opportunity to attempt escape at the same time he made his own break. So we had to hatch an entirely new scheme.

The new plan was somewhat more difficult though less bizarre, but time was passing quickly and Mik's death was almost upon us.

We had learned that a ship was sailing to England from Gdynia, on the north coast of Poland, on Tuesday morning a little after seven. Quickly the naval attaché acquainted the captain of the ship with the arrangements. Mik had until Monday night to advise his colleagues of their peril and of his departure, and at about six-thirty, Monday, as darkness descended on Warsaw, a truck loaded with household goods ostensibly for shipment on the vessel was to be found apparently disabled at a certain corner in Warsaw. The chauffeur, one of our trusted employees, was to be tinkering with the engine, and Mikolajczyk was to walk along the street in disguise and crawl into the truck, surrounding himself with household goods, when the occasion seemed propitious.

Mik agreed to the plan and it worked. As darkness came the truck roared through the night toward the Baltic Sea. I provided the driver with a hundred thousand zlotys in case he had to bribe his way through any of the road blocks. He nearly had to use the money when one of the Polish sentries objected to the sewing machine as a possible implement of war. Mikolajczyk, carrying only a toothbrush and a revolver and wearing a battered old American raincoat and slouch hat that I had sent him, arrived safely at Gdynia, where he was sheltered from 4:00 A.M. to 6:30 at the home of one of my friends. He was entirely without fear, and apparently enjoyed his morning coffee though I suspect my friends did not. We had learned that the Polish guard always stationed around ships in the port of Gdynia was to change at seven in the morning. At a quarter to seven, three men—Mikolajczyk, the chauffeur, and my friend in Gdynia—ascended the gangway to the ship, and had coffee with the captain. The guard changed at seven and, as we had hoped, forgot to advise the new guard of the number who had ascended the gangplank.

A little after seven, two men descended. Mikolajczyk remained in the captain's cabin, and a few moments later the ship heaved anchor and was on its way to England. Some days later a plane from a Berlin airport stopped at the corner of a British field and took aboard Mikolajczyk, who was standing quietly in the shadows, and taxied him up to the arrival office to present him to the newspaper correspondents who were gathered to receive him. The job was done, and at the Embassy we nervously awaited developments.

They were not long in coming, for we had the news of the arrest of three of Mikolajczyk's friends on the Polish border, including a high member of his party and his wife and Mikolajczyk's secretary. It was with some regret that I recalled that Mikolajczyk had begged me to let him take his secretary with him, but I felt that the responsibility to my government extended to him only, and I could not run the risk of permitting a double hazard. But there it was. I knew the Communist methods of obtaining confessions, and I obeyed the summons to the Foreign Office, fully aware that the secretary would already have signed statements involving me.

But I was reasonably sure that the foreign ministry could not have obtained all the facts, and as Modzelewski read me the secretary's sworn confession I showed increasing anger, telling Modzelewski that this charge was the last insult of many heaped upon the American Embassy since my arrival. Nevertheless, he stuck to his guns, and stated that as Bill Blake, our second secretary, had unquestionably been involved in the escape, he was now persona non grata to the Polish Government. In diplomatic goings on, this is a sentence from which there is no appeal, and it becomes incumbent upon the government whose representative is declared non grata to remove the man to another post immediately. I could not shake Modzelewski's decision and returned to the Embassy with a heavy heart.

A night of worry brought me to a course of action that

I put into effect the next day. I asked for another audience with Modzelewski and proposed to him the following plan. I told him that the relations between Poland and the United States were tenuous enough without adding the risk of a final breakdown if he persisted in his course of asking me to remove my second secretary. I suggested that he withdraw his request upon my personal assurance to him that Blake, whose tour of duty was about to end anyway, be transferred with reasonable promptness from Poland to another post, without all of the sensational headlines that would result from his being banished by the edict of the Polish Government. Modzelewski, with his facts obviously incomplete, consented to this, and I was thus enabled to tell the curious newspaper correspondents the next day that I did not hold any request from the Polish Government for the removal of Blake, who later went to Rome for a well-earned promotion. But Mikolajczyk was safe in England. We devoutly hoped that the incident, as far as we were concerned, was closed, though a few days later the Polish Parliament deprived Mikolajczyk of his seat in the House, denounced him as a traitor to the Polish State and declared him banished for life. I am sure that he is happy indeed to remain banished.

Shortly after the Mikolajczyk incident, I flew to London and thereafter to Washington at Secretary Marshall's invitation. While in Washington I successfully evaded the kindly efforts of the President and Averell Harriman to persuade me to become chairman of the Civil Aeronautics Board, which had become vacant through the expiration of James M. Landis's term. I am allergic to airplanes, and I had no desire to be involved in this particularly difficult job. Even the dullness of life in Poland seemed preferable, and I returned to Warsaw after a few weeks.

The best record of my Polish experiences occurs in three long letters that I wrote at various times during my ambassadorship to friends back home. John Reed Kilpatrick suggested that I do this and I am grateful that I took his advice. The first was written in the summer of 1947.

AMERICAN EMBASSY<br>*Warsaw, Poland, August 7, 1947*

*Dear Joe:*

A month ago yesterday I reached Warsaw and here is the story of life in Poland as seen through the eyes of a freshman Ambassador who has literally covered the waterfront—the Polish Government, the Polish cities and towns from the Czech border to the Baltic, the diplomatic corps in Warsaw, and the prevailing political and economic situations.

When the tide of battling Germans, Russians, and Poles swept through Warsaw toward Berlin, two hotels of any quality remained in Warsaw, one, the Bristol, which is being reconstructed but which has not yet reached the stage of heat or hot water, and the other, the Polonia, a third-rate hotel which would be known in an American city as a railroad hotel. Here I am ensconced in two rooms with most of the minor diplomatic corps and an entire floor occupied by members of our Embassy.

For a fussy old man who all his life has made a fetish of a quiet room for sleep, the nights at the Polonia are nights of sheer charm and ecstasy. Stenches of every known kind of Polish garbage waft through my bedroom, which is practically on the street. Large Polish horses dance tangos on the cobblestones every night and motorcycles and trucks get under way about 4:30, followed by a line of rattling Polish carts. Occasionally, during the night the other noises are punctuated with little shootings, mostly from trigger-happy soldiers who are roaming the streets.

From my window and just across the street, the twisted girders and steel work which was once the Warsaw station lie in a pit of rubble and on the skyline are silhouetted a long line of brick shells which were, in happier days, office buildings and apartment houses. Beyond lie the countless blocks which were the ghetto. Now not even the shell of a house remains, only piles and mounds of bricks and mortar under which are supposed to lie the remains of close to 30,000 Jews, entombed in the ruins of their own houses. On hot days the odors are still not those of new-mown hay.

In all of Warsaw I have not seen one house which is not pock-marked by bullets or shrapnel and hardly a house escaped some damage. The local statistics are that the destruction amounted to about 80 per cent. You know, of course, that this destruction came only in a very small degree from the bombing and battles which encompassed Warsaw during the German attack in 1939 and the Russian counter-attack in '44. It came largely from the vicious, vengeful and planned destruction by the Germans in their anger and hatred of the Poles, following the Polish insurrection in late 1944 while the Russian Army stood on the eastern bank of the Vistula and waited and cheered. I came here feeling that my arrival in Warsaw must be a happy surprise because the picture could not fail to be better than the worst which I had anticipated. I was wrong.

With the desire to see something of Central Europe I drove across from Paris: the first day through the bountiful fields and beautiful countryside of a France substantially untouched by this war; then across the German border at Strasbourg through many towns which gave silent but terrible evidence of the efficiency of the Allied Air Forces. From Strasbourg to luncheon in battered Stuttgart and thence by one of the great German autobahns to Munich. Remembering many happy vacations in Bavaria and the unbelievable charm and comfort of the Four Seasons Hotel, it was an hour of sheer horror to find myself in this same hotel battered beyond recognition and only a small part of it remaining amid the horrible destruction of the once beautiful city. Throughout Germany, however, and on the next day's trip to Prague in Czechoslovakia, crops were good, peasants were working industriously, and except in the cities which were scenes of destruction, the only recollection of the war appeared in an occasional rusting and abandoned tank in the fields or solitary crosses topped by a German helmet. From Prague it was a fairly long run to Krakow in southern Poland and the next day to Katowice and Lodz (pronounced Wootz), thence into Warsaw.

My first days in the Polish capital brought me an initiation the like of which I doubt has ever been received by an incoming Ambassador. I was hit squarely in the face by the Poles' refusal to attend the Paris Conference, which came 24 hours after I had been assured by the Government that they would be there. Within a few days thereafter our Government announced that Poland had been stricken from the list of European countries selected for relief and the Polish repercussion was immediate and vigorous. The Air Attaché's plane, which has been for the use of the Ambassador, has been ordered out of the country and as a result of these few incidents my conferences with Government officials have not been all peaches and honey.

The patterns of government here are defined and unmistakable. Most of the high members of the Government are young, almost without exception in the forties. Many of them spent a large part of the war in prison or concentration camps. Their languages are usually Polish and Russian or Polish and German, which they will not use. A mere handful speak some English and some French. While there is much talk of a coalition government of communists and socialists, actually the domination is entirely communistic and the trend, despite constant talk of merger of the two parties, is definitely toward a gradual elimination of the socialist influence. In a nation of 22,000,000 people it is said that probably less than 50,000 are actually communists but with the Russian alliance in the background, with a pitifully small Polish Army far outnumbered by the Russian Army in Poland, the Government has become even more strongly entrenched by the tragic results of American gifts of more than $500,000,000 through UNRRA, which, it must be understood, distributed its largess through the Government. One may easily guess the results in strengthening the power of the few men who controlled the distribution and who now dominate the Government and the country.

There remains also the little matter of countless secret police, of continual political arrests and imprisonments extending even to many priests and Catholic clergy, many of whom are held incommunicado and without trial. Altogether, the atmosphere is surcharged with nervousness and fear, and walking through the streets of Warsaw at night one almost has the feeling that the planes should be overhead any minute now.

Yet some of the Poles accept their control and their troubles with a sense of humor, for the favorite old joke in these parts is that "Poland is the largest country in the world. Its western borders are on the Oder. Its capital is in Moscow, and its population in Siberia."

The Russian trained, indoctrinated and sponsored Polish Communists have not sought to control Poland through a seizure of power in the classic Marxist sense. Rather their approach has been gradualistic; they have sought to insinuate themselves into power, presumably reserving ruthlessness for the *coup de grâce* instead of using it consistently as a political weapon. The choice of this technique has resulted inevitably in a piecemeal approach to their problem, and this in turn has necessitated an intricate scheme of political maneuver aimed at keeping large and diverse elements of the population controlled and quiescent, while selected groups were to be either dominated or liquidated.

No one, least of all I, can predict the future but, in judging it, you must realize that since before the Napoleonic Wars when Poland was divided between three Great Powers, Russia spent a hundred years trying to russify the Poles; Germany spent the same century trying to germanize them; and Austria, in its small way to austrianize its part. All of them failed. Then out of the First World War arose a new Poland. Certainly, from 1926 until the Second World War, Poland never had a free government and now after the Second World War, with the nation reduced from 35,000,000 to about 22,000,000 people, the Polish people are back in the ring fighting as Poles.

As completely clear and defined as the Government and its Russo-Polish ideological pattern is the propaganda served the people unceasingly in the almost entirely controlled Polish press. It plays only a few strings but these are incessant: (1) that the United States, that monster of capitalism where the poor downtrodden workman is striving daily for the growth of Communism, is rapidly approaching a complete financial debacle; (2) that Poland may rest content for its future prosperity and safety under the gentle and all-embracing umbrella of its great and powerful ally, the Soviet Union; (3) and this is an exact quotation from the leading Warsaw newspaper of July 29: "The American policy wishes to have a strong Germany—stronger than all her neighbors.

It wants Germany to become the greatest industrial power of Europe." This latter is, of course, an extremely powerful piece of Goebbelism in reverse, for the Polish hatred of Germany is far more deep-seated than its hatred of Russia, and its fear of German aggression far more intense. In my first press interview I told the Polish reporters that their policy reminded me of a man who approaches an old friend on the street and begs him for help and for loans, punctuating the request by smashing the friend in the nose. In other words, Poland has its left hand extended for help and its right hand is a fist constantly attacking the United States and everything American.

On the other side of the picture in Warsaw and the other cities, and throughout the countryside, is witnessed a modern miracle of reconstruction. The industry of these people is unbelievable and in Warsaw you can literally see the city growing back into a semblance of order day by day. It reminds one of an anthill swept aside with your shoe and which an hour later appears again apparently undamaged and swarming with worker ants. While all land is theoretically owned by the State and can only be leased to occupants for construction for a period of 60 or 90 years, nevertheless, in some strange way some titles are held and the whole question of who owns what is a complete Chinese puzzle. As an example, the four-story house which I was to occupy is now occupied on two floors by part of our Consular Service and the upper two floors by some fifty people who have merely moved in and live there as squatters. The Chancery building which we occupy is reputedly owned by the Bulgarian Government, and the Bulgarian Minister makes life miserable both for the Polish Government and for me and yet we are allowed to stay. It is all very quaint and yet with a will many things can be accomplished with American dispatch. One of our Consular buildings, reputed to be owned by some expatriated Poles in London, has now been assigned to me by the Polish Government as a residence. Within one week's time reconstruction plans were drawn and approved. Within another week bids were received and a contract awarded, and sixteen days after we started to work on the matter, reconstruction was actually started and I am hoping against hope to have a fairly decent place in which to live before the snow flies.

In the present plight of Europe the keys to reconstruction are, of course, coal and grain. With its position of one of the great coal-producing countries of Europe, the economic position and the probable rapid development of Polish economic power cannot be overestimated. It must be realized that Poland will produce this year about as much coal as Germany and about a third as much as Great Britain. To be sure, a large part of this production now goes eastward to Russia but if a great percentage of its future production can, through one means or another, be guided into a general plan for the rehabilitation of all Europe, a very substantial tie between East and West will have been developed.

Zlotys, the Polish currency, constitute a major and daily headache. The official government rate for zlotys is 100 to the dollar. The black-market rate varies according to the political and economic fortunes of the country, from 700 to 1300 to the dollar. The real buying power is probably approximately 600 to 1. Every conceivable kind of exchange rate exists. When we are in the favor of the government, we have ample zlotys at a fair rate and then occasionally, apparently without reason, we are subjected to a period where no American can live on his salary and at the 100 to 1 rate a decent meal costs around $20 a meal. All of this you may rest assured is being cured so far as the Embassy is concerned, or will be cured if my old battling power holds out. On the other hand, with ample zlotys in the pocket the food is probably the best in Europe except for Sweden and the black-market restaurants in Paris, although there is an utter sameness about it, an unending richness and a final revulsion at the wide variety of Polish sauces and garniture in which every dish is wrapped.

For news we are dependent on the daily State Department Radio Bulletin, the London *Times*, which comes anywhere from four to five days late, and the Paris *Herald*, which, on rare occasions, reaches us within ten days. Mail to or from New York or Washington takes from an average of two weeks to an occasional 30 days and Wednesday, when the diplomatic pouch comes in from Berlin carrying the Army Post Office mail, is a day of suppressed excitement and very little work in the Embassy.

For amusement there is always eating, which is quite an important going on in Poland. In the summer there are week ends in the little restored villas in the country, and presently, if I hold out, there will be an Embassy motion picture theatre with new pictures sent down from Stockholm and which Bedell Smith in Moscow has already heard about and is crying for. Then, the great indoor sport is an occasional diplomatic poker game, in which the winner and champion is the Chinese Minister, whom we call "the Chink in the Iron Curtain."

Around the corner from the Chancery is the busiest institution in Poland, the American Embassy Consular Service. From early morning until late at night lines are formed on the sidewalk, consisting of myriad Poles who either claim to be American citizens, who have relatives in the United States, or who (and this class embraces the entire Polish population) desire to immigrate to the United States. The establishment of American citizenship here is a long, devious and paper and red-tape packed journey to final exit permit and visa. The effort to obtain a number in the immigration quota now results after months of investigation in a strong position in the line of immigrants, which will get to the ports, according to my lightning calculation, about five years from Thursday, but hope springs eternal in the hearts of these people despite the complete determination of the Polish Government to keep every Pole within the borders of the country.

Like everything else, the care of orphans and every type of humanitarian work in Poland including private American agencies comes under the control of the Government. During my first week here I offered to finance personally an orphanage for fifty children and pay all the expenses as to food, shelter, education, and medical care so long as I was permitted to screen the children and select only the sons and daughters of the intelligentsia, such as of artists, writers, or others having a background susceptible to development by both physical and hereditary gift. The decision on this, of course, had to be made by the government and despite innumerable talks and conferences, I have yet to receive permission to establish this orphanage. I very much doubt that I will receive permission on account of my desire for a selected group and my unwillingness to accept the run of the mine, which is the essence of Communism.

After almost four weeks in Warsaw, I came this week to the north coast on the Baltic and am writing this from a laughingly-called luxury hotel in Sopot, which lies halfway between the old Polish port of Gdynia and the now Polish port of Gdansk, which was formerly the Free City of Danzig. My hotel lies directly on the ocean and this is really the Southampton or Palm Beach of Poland in its shabby unhappy way. Here are the crossroads between the old East Prussia, Poland and the Polish Corridor. Russia is a stone's throw away. I came ostensibly to attend what was advertised as a great international fair at Gdynia and expected to spend some days studying its exhibits of the life and industry of Poland. Unfortunately, it was a bit over-advertised and in general would compare unfavorably with a fair-sized county fair in upstate New York. Yet here the political and social pattern is the same, except in this resort there seems to be some tendency for the few wealthy Poles and their families to appear in decent clothes without the ubiquitous necessity which apparently exists in every Polish city to answer to the secret police as to why and how one has a new suit of clothes.

Another two or three weeks and I shall start on a tour of the well-known western lands between the old Polish border and the Oder, which, in the minds of all Poles, is the ultimate western boundary of Poland. In this pre-war German territory has been the scene of the greatest mass migration in history, the forced eviction of more than 5,000,000 Germans and the repopulation to date of more than 3,500,000 Poles, mostly from east of the Curzon Lines, and others, from all parts of the world. The question of the western borders, with their rich agricultural lands and with many of the old German coal properties, is the one and only subject on which all Poles are united. It is literally not fanciful to say that the determination to occupy and hold these lands is such that even the pitiful Polish Army might take to the field if the United States, the Great Powers, or any human agency attempted to return them to German control.

And how have you been?

*Sincerely yours,*
STANTON GRIFFIS

183

AMERICAN EMBASSY
*Warsaw, Poland, October 20, 1947*

*Dear Joe:*

More than two months ago on August 7 I wrote the first long
letter on the adventures of a rising young American Ambassador
in Poland and I have had so many friendly responses to it that it
seems possible to believe that you can by this time take the punishment of another philippic on this rose-garden playground behind
the Iron Curtain. I hesitate to attempt this letter, for life here during the months of August and September went on in the classic
pattern of Communist infiltration and there is little or nothing to
add to the description of the patterns of government here which
I have already described. The development has been slow but
inexorable and with little or no deviation from the basic blueprint.

Many years ago I had an uncle who was somewhat on the eccentric side, particularly as to physical culture and the body beautiful.
He was a theologian living alone in one or two rooms, and having
made himself an outstanding expert in the then popular art of
Indian clubs and dumbbells, he still felt the need of additional
exercise so he installed in his bedroom a stationary bicycle. For
two hours a day he pedaled the bicycle with tremendous and exhausting vigor and I may say that the progress which I have made
with the Polish Government has been about the same as the progress which Uncle Horace used to make on his bicycle, the only
essential difference being the number of hours I have pedaled
every day.

I doubt that in the history of diplomacy any Ambassador can
point to a more perfect score with the Government to which he
has been accredited. So far as I can see, the curve of degeneration
in Polish-American relationships has been unbroken since the day
of my arrival until the present date. Beginning, as I pointed out
previously, with the refusal of the Poles to go to Paris and, shortly
following, the refusal of the United States Government to include
Poland in the list of relief countries, there came in late August the
inability of the Poles to obtain grain allocations, and last week
from a meeting of Communists held in Poland came the now
famous announcement of a revival of the Comintern. It will be
interesting perhaps for you to know that while this meeting was

held right under our noses and attended by leading Communists from all over Europe it was kept so secret that, so far as I know, no Embassy here nor, in fact, any member of the Polish or international press knew about the meeting until the announcement was made which, in the words of Mr. Lovett, so violently "maligned the aims of the American and British people in the recent war and carried to new lengths the distortions of United States policy with which the Communist press everywhere has recently been replete."

Some weeks ago before the Minister of Foreign Affairs, Zygmunt Modzelewski, left to attend the meeting of the United Nations in New York, I called on him for the purpose of thoroughly discussing the malignant and completely unnecessary nature of the constant attacks on the United States by the Polish press. At this meeting I was assured that the Minister agreed with me and that these attacks should and would be discontinued or at least tempered. Far from being the case, the rising tempo of vicious attacks on everything American has continued in the Polish press and I would say that at least 50 per cent or more of all editorial or essay comment—which represents the bulk of the Polish newspapers—is devoted to these attacks. Just offhand I will give you a few of the headlines or the sentences which have been served to me by the Polish press with my morning coffee during the past month:

"Spontaneous anti-American demonstrations at the Conference of the World's Federation of Democratic Youth."

"U.S.A. draws Turkey into the fight with Greek nation."

"Conference of 9 Communist and Labor Parties in the defense of independence against American imperialism."

"Under pressure of U.S.A. changes in the Greek Chief Command announce ruthless terror."

"Who is enemy of peace—War fattens American capitalists."

"The specter of Wall Street over the world is the specter of resuscitated imperialistic Germany over Europe."

"Sober opinion of the world press. Paris Conference—a cold shower bath. Marshall's Plan—a smoke curtain."

"The value of gold soaked in blood will be calculated in dollars and will be used to finance American export to Europe. This is good business. It is known that gold does not stink, and to the 60% of gold reserve of the whole world kept in the Knox Fort will be added a modest amount made up by gold coins and bars of gold made of wedding rings, teeth and jewelry of the victims of Majdanek, Oswiecim, Mauthausen (Concentration Camps in Poland and Germany)."

"The gold confiscated from German looters and murderers is stained with the blood of Polish citizens murdered in a bestial manner in Oswiecim and Majdanek. It is an incontestable property of Poland and nobody gave to the American Government authority to dispose of it, and what is more to do 'welfare' at our expense."

"This is called democracy. Americans do not allow a representative of South African Negroes to enter the U.S.A."

"Already the criminals in the General Staffs of England and the United States are active to put up a new plan for a war against the Soviet Union."

"Truman Doctrine is a source of new hope. Strasser wants to resuscitate German Fascism by order of Wall Street."

"We understand that they only long for a war so as to give Poland over, with the assistance of foreign bayonets, as a booty for American cartels."

"One thing we shall never resign—even at the price paid in American dollars—it is the sovereignty of our country."

In addition to this kind of tripe, the daily and weekly tabloids and magazines are filled with cartoons maligning the United States, Uncle Sam, and particularly President Truman. The one I have before me from this morning's tabloid shows President Truman first dressed as Alexander the Great, later as Julius Caesar, Ivan the Terrible, Frederick the Great, Napoleon, and finally as a haberdasher selling neckties on the street for 5 cents each. The cartoon is headed "President Truman's dream and reality."

As I pointed out before, the chief basis of Polish propaganda is the never-ceasing harping, from various angles, on the theory that the United States, contrary to the Potsdam Agreement, is building up Germany at the expense of Poland and that it is all part and parcel of those vicious Wall Streeters who are fomenting another capitalistic war.

For a long time I besieged the State Department to issue a complete statement on the American-German policy for the benefit of the Poles and this was finally done on September 30 in answer to a Polish note of protest regarding this policy. On that night, simultaneously with the release of the note in the United States, I called all the members of the Polish press to the office and gave them a verbatim copy of the State Department pronouncement translated into Polish and challenging one and all to print it verbatim. The newspaper boys stayed for two hours, asking me all sorts of carefully phrased trick questions and today, many days later, appeared the first garbled publications of part of the American note, following the printing of the Polish note in full. It was identical in all newspapers, proving completely that it had taken the Minister of Propaganda exactly ten days to work out his publicity.

From the newspaper clippings which have reached me I gather that the press has had a lot of fun with my battle with the squatters. The story is pretty much factual, for about seven families had moved into various Embassy properties and the Polish Government, despite repeated promises, showed not the slightest willingness to remove them. I started by making each one of them a substantial cash offer to move out into other apartments which we had been able to find for them but the answer in every case was "no dice," and it became a little game as to the amount for which they could hold us up. Accordingly, as the Associated Press man here put it, on the theory that "Music has charms," I started four radios operating in rooms adjoining the squatters and these radios were turned full blast 24 hours a day in six or seven different languages with a few assorted types of music and an occasional shot of static thrown in for good measure. It took more than five weeks of this kind of goings on to bring the squatters to terms and they collapsed about the same time as my own organization in the same building who, one and all, said that they were willing to get out too. Anyway, I only have one left, who is camping in the gatehouse of my new residence and who is demanding a million zlotys to move from a small room and bath. I suspect that he is going to be with me for some time. He likes music.

On the other hand, the question of real estate titles here is entirely a question of "Button, button, who's got the button" and we are squatters ourselves in our Chancery, which the Bulgarian Minister claims that his Government owns. The Bulgarian Minister calls on me weekly trying threats, cajolery, and the rights of small countries. Unfortunately, the Bulgarian Minister speaks only Bulgarian and his secretary only Bulgarian and Polish. The Bulgarian Minister speaks to his secretary in Bulgarian. His secretary translates it to mine in Polish who, in turn, transmits the message to me in English. By the time the answer gets back to the Bulgarian Minister any relationship to the original conversation is purely coincidental. We really have a lot of fun.

Also, we are having our usual jolly little game of Zlotys, which, on account of the fantastic fluctuations in exchange, means that one day we are all very rich and the next day the Embassy staff hasn't got enough to eat. Zlotys, in what is politely called here the outside market—never the black market, were floating along a couple of weeks ago at about 700 to the dollar. Suddenly all the newspapers published a story that the United States Government was about to call in all dollars and issue new ones in exchange only to those who could prove that they legally held the dollars. I feel confident that this was a very bright dream of some young man in the Propaganda Department of the Government and, in any event, the zlotys dropped overnight to 350 to the dollar and dollars were offered cheaply and clandestinely all over Poland. My telephone rang night and day with calls from harassed dollar holders until I finally shut it off. In any event, I denied the story and the zloty is again pursuing its tortuous way up.

In September, General Bedell Smith, American Ambassador to Moscow, wrote me that I should come over and see him and as he described it "meet his constituents." During a lull here, around the first of October, his plane picked me up on the way from Berlin to Moscow and I flew over the endless plain which constitutes eastern Poland and Western Russia, across dreary wastes of the Prypec Marshes into Moscow. It is almost mysterious to fathom how anyone, whether it was Napoleon, the attacking Germans or the advancing Russians, could have transported and fed an army through this terrible wasteland, and if you will study the map, the distance, and the topography between Berlin and Moscow, you cannot but wonder at the magnitude and the unbelievable difficulties of the operation, especially during the almost Arctic winter, which is beginning to set in here now.

I landed at an airport about ten miles from Moscow and drove in to the city with Ambassador Smith, closely followed by a Russian secret service car. After a few moments at the Chancery, Ambassador Smith and I started out for a walk and were immediately joined by three gentry, one of whom walked in front of us, one behind, and one on the other side of the street. These friendly companions stayed with us night and day during my three days there.

No words of mine could describe the incredible poverty, filth and degradation of Moscow and its citizenry. In the very heart of the city people live in indescribable slums; countless families live and cook in deserted churches; mud and puddles fill the streets; and a Communistic Vogue or Harper's Bazaar would delight in the completely nondescript clothing which consists largely of padded sacking, ancient and much-darned skirts and trousers and felt boots or—merely rags. The whole atmosphere to me was one of such horror that even Warsaw seemed like "Home, Sweet Home" to return to and its people, tragic as they are, like the Easter crowd on Fifth Avenue as compared with the denizens of Moscow. On the other hand, when on the second night we went to see "Swan Lake" at the Ballet Theatre, we entered an entirely different world of astounding artistic beauty and performance. The "Borshoi" was crowded to suffocation. The dancers are among the very highest paid of the Russian comrades and the people of Moscow told me that in many cases weeks and months elapse before they are able to obtain ballet seats. The depression of the trip was almost insignificant as compared with the charm of this one evening.

On the last day I called on Mr. Lenin lying deep in his glass tomb opposite the Kremlin. Although a line of Russian comrades extended, two by two, for almost half a mile in order to walk through the tomb, I was permitted blithely to drive up to the head of the line and go immediately into the presence of the great Lenin. The guide told me that he had been embalmed by a brilliant French scientist and, accordingly, his body has remained unchanged since his death 24 years ago. My more cynical friends at the Embassy told me that after the body was taken away from Moscow to a hiding place during the threatened German invasion, it came back for exhibition obviously with a new blush of youthful health and vigor in its healthy cheeks. The whole goings on is extremely bizarre and spooky and it is my personal belief that the body represents a finer piece of waxwork than ever existed in Madame Tussaud's.

The Moscow Embassy staff live under conditions even worse than ours here in Poland. They should receive the grateful thanks of the nation, being as they are subjected to all the rigors of the Russian climate, the continual insults of its Government, and the isolation imposed by the fear of any Russian citizen to have any contact with the American Embassy. Poland and Warsaw are no sweet beds of roses, but, believe me, the plane out of Moscow for home was a little bit of heaven despite the fact that we had a pretty tough flight back. To my great astonishment the Poles had broken out the American flag over the airport on my arrival. Ambassador Smith and his party went on to Berlin.

Back in Warsaw the astonishing rebuilding of the city goes on apace. A great many groups of people give up their Sundays to clear away ruins, bedecked for the day with the flags of their organization or their party. Every day is tag day on the plea that the money goes for the rebuilding of Warsaw, and collections, some voluntary and some a little on the forced side, are taken up all over Poland for the cause. The stores are beginning to show an increasing amount of consumer goods and the whole scene of ant-like activity continues.

Yet, as I have pointed out, the violent outcry of the entire Polish press apes the Russian with a "me too" denunciation of everything American and Capitalistic. Wall Street, which you and I know, has been on the ropes for the last fifteen years would be very honored to realize that it controls all the wealth of the world and both parties in the United States; that it lies awake at night plotting to seize the vast wealth of democratic Poland and Russia as well as the blood-stained gold recovered from the dental fixtures of the former occupants of the concentration camps. There is constant talk of war, the thesis always being that the United States will attack Russia.

Does this all mean that there will be war or that Russia and its satellites want war? I do not think so nor does Ambassador Smith; nor do I believe do any thinking people and particularly those who realize the tragic economic condition of Russia and its satellites. You and I know how the fear and dangers of war unites and co-ordinates a nation, and probably a great deal of this absurd propaganda is for home consumption. The pronouncements of the satellite press are almost verbatim those of the Russian press and perhaps the attitude of the Polish-Russian newspapers and of the Russian spokesman in the United Nations is reminiscent, and this is a quotation, of the advice given by the lawyer to Chichikov in Gogol's "Dead Souls," when the law was about to catch up with him:

"Remain calm, let nothing embarrass you, however bad things may get. Never despair of anything; there is no case that can't be saved . . . if you see that the matter is approaching decision, don't try to justify and defend yourself; no, just mix things up by bringing in new elements. Mix things up, and mix them up again, that's all. Introduce extraneous factors so that others get involved as well as yourself. Believe me, when matters get critical, the first thing to do is to complicate them. Why, you can complicate things, if you want to, so that no one will ever be able to make head or tail out of them. And, after all, you can only catch crayfish in muddy waters."

This letter has been interrupted by the arrival here of a very charming and able gentleman from California, Senator Knowland, who is a member of the Senate Appropriations Committee and who is really doing a job on his own in the study of European conditions. As he wanted to see the so-called "recovered territories" to the West and as it was necessary for me to see them in order to make a report to the Secretary as an eye-view witness, we started off last week to cover the northern half of the ground between Warsaw and the "new" German border. We traveled many hundred miles over incredible roads covering substantially all the Polish cities between Poznan in the center and Szczecin [Stettin], the great port on the north. We reached Szczecin one day about two in the afternoon and after one whiff of the hotel there (the town water supply had broken down and there had been no water for some weeks), we decided to attempt to return to Poznan. Through a fog that was reminiscent of London in the deep winter and with three punctures from the nail-strewn roads, we finally returned to Poznan towards midnight and reached Warsaw yesterday after a really murderous trip. Of the four of us who made the trip only the Senator could "take it." My chauffeur and my Polish secretary are both under the doctor's care and I am dictating this letter from my bed—between coughs.

Cities and countless small villages in the northwest country received a terrible battering in the war and we counted literally hundreds of rusting and abandoned tanks and pieces of artillery. Particularly around Szczecin with its destroyed bridges and ruined villages could be read the story of the final German defense of the homeland against the attacking Russians. Unfortunately I am not able to give you a complete report as to how fully the Poles have carried out their repopulation and cultivation of the country for this section cannot be judged without an equal study of Upper and Lower Silesia, which constitutes the southern half of the so-called "recovered territories" and which must be included in an analysis of the whole picture. A visit to Silesia will be my next Cook's Tour. Sufficient it is to say that there are probably less than 5 per cent of the former German settlers remaining and that the Poles are making valiant efforts to till and people the lands. On every village cottage is painted a letter and a number showing that it has been or will be allocated to a new Polish settler.

In the meantime, during the last few days, the long-suppressed and feared battle between Church and State has broken out in Poland. We had all hoped that there would be some semblance of peace between the Communistic Government and the Catholic Church here, but the Church, realizing all too well the slow infiltration and gradual piecemeal approach methods of the Communistic Government, decided to attack first, and on September 28 there was read in all the pulpits of Poland a "Proclamation of Polish Bishops to the Faithful" signed by Cardinal Hlond, the Primate of Poland. Referring to the gradual undermining of the parochial schools and the religious instruction in other schools, to the continual attempt to indoctrinate communistic principles among the youngsters, particularly the thousands of orphans in state institutions, the desecration of the Sabbath, and the gradual disappearance of civil rights, the Cardinal summed up in stating "There is such a series of these phenomena that one gains the impression that there exists a carefully directed hidden struggle with God and the Church."

So, coming from Moscow, where I saw the great sign which Lenin erected many years ago that "Religion is the opiate of the people," I found that the Catholic Church in Poland had at last decided to strike out in defense of its life against the Lenin doctrine.

Whether you are Catholic, Protestant, Jewish, or of any other faith, you must realize that the great hope for a democratic Poland lies in maintaining the strength and power of the Catholic Church here. The people are historically Catholic to the extent of 85 per cent of the population, and Communism and Catholicism are hereditary and sworn enemies.

Last week we completed another one of our strange repatriation operations, returning between 600 and 700 "American citizens" to the "home country" by steamer from the Baltic ports. This is a to-do which is hard for me to understand, but the benign Government of our nation holds that American citizens in Poland if they can legally obtain passports and exit permits are, if they wish, to be brought back to the nation at the expense of the Government although they are required to give notes for their transportation. Now, most of these "American citizens" are the children of Poles who emigrated some years ago to the United States, where the children were born. Through this geographical accident of birth they became American citizens but later were brought back to Poland by their parents. Few, if any of them, can speak over a half dozen words of English. None of them have any understanding of the nation which gave them birth, but "they come," and the great resources of the world's melting pot which you and I inhabit will no doubt absorb them in its virile bloodstream.

No one realizes better than I that there is not much of the lighter vein in this letter, but while this whole job is discouraging to a degree and sometimes appears utterly hopeless, we live on, perhaps in idle dream that time will heal. After all we have accomplished some few things since the middle of July. We have to a degree kept the peace and so far prevented the possibility of one of those dangerous incidents which sometimes touch off a world powder barrel. We have finally negotiated with the Polish Government the right to keep the Embassy plane in the air for use on trips from Warsaw to other European capitals, and although it must be based in Berlin, we have so far brought it in twice for trips to Prague and Vienna. We have negotiated the first commerce between Poland and Germany through the sale of 50,000 tons of potatoes from the Polish Government to the Military Government of Germany, and are fathering many other deals. We have finally worked out an agreement with the Government whereby we are permitted to visit bona fide American prisoners, who have previously been held in jail incommunicado and without charges. Some have already been released. We have developed a building program for the staff so that now, with the winter setting in, we expect to have all hands housed in at least reasonably comfortable apartments prior to Christmas. The squatters are pretty well cleaned out. The new motion picture theatre for 35mm projection will be ready by December first and will be used as a mess hall and club room for the staff during the day. We are giving four motion picture performances a week of the 16mm films, to which we invite the staff, the journalists, the Polish Government officials and the foreign diplomatic corps. Not much of a record to be sure when the major relationships disintegrate daily but I assume that our only purpose in being here is just to be here and show the people that we are here.

I have no illusions whatever of the dangers and virtual untenability of my position in Warsaw but here we are and perhaps some magic of diplomacy, economic development of the Marshall Plan, some miracle of sanity in the police states, or some act of God will restore a semblance of peace on earth. However, adventure it is and high adventure at that, and as I hope to move into my new house tomorrow, I can at least now be warm and have an opportunity to dream in front of my own fireside of the charming lives which you live in the United States albeit it may be a fool's paradise. It was mighty cheering to read in this morning's *Radio*

*Bulletin* Secretary Marshall's magnificent speech before the CIO and particularly his homely and Lincolnesque conclusion.

"Above all things a regard for the American tradition is required, the typical American readiness to assist those in need of help, to discount vicious propaganda and outrageous criticism, and in the end to seek only to do what is right, so far as we can determine the right."

One thing I wish you would bear in mind, that in this far-off corner of the world letters from home are like manna in the wilderness but letters addressed merely to the American Embassy in Warsaw take from four to five weeks to arrive and are all opened and censored by the Polish Government although stamped that they arrived insufficiently sealed. Mail comes fastest—in ten days to two weeks—in the diplomatic pouch if addressed as follows:

> Stanton Griffis
> USPOLAD OMGUS
> (Embassy, Warsaw, Poland)
> APO 742, c/o Postmaster
> New York City

Groggy but still in the ring,

> *Sincerely yours,*
> STANTON GRIFFIS

AMERICAN EMBASSY
*Warsaw, March 11, 1948*

*Dear Joe:*

This is the third and I devoutly trust the last of a series of pastoral letters dealing with adventures and containing assorted chitchat of an American Ambassador behind the well-known Iron Curtain. The series might well be entitled "Mr. Alice in Blunderland."

On a dull and fog-laden Saturday in the middle of December I was sitting quietly at my home when the Embassy telephoned me a typically verbose telegram from the Secretary of State, which said "Come London soonest. Marshall." In five minutes I was on the telephone, arranging for the plane to be sent in from Berlin but unfortunately I could not leave for forty-eight hours as I had appointments at the Foreign Office Monday morning.

Our arrival at the Templehof Airfield in Berlin that afternoon was an experience never to be forgotten for we had hit a blinding snowstorm and came in by radar. Through a deep milk soup, only a voice on the loud-speaker saying "Turn left. Turn right. Turn up. You are doing fine," a mixture of science and psychology, brought us to an exact target on the runway, which we saw at about 200 feet before we hit it.

In London the next day I found that the Foreign Ministers' Conference had adjourned *sine die* the night before. The Secretary, however, was his usual calm, confident, unruffled self and to my great delight invited me to ride back to Washington with him on the well-known Sacred Cow. Well-berthed in the Cow's interior, we departed on Thursday evening, December 17, together with Ambassador Douglas, Counselor "Chip" Bohlen, and various secretaries, arriving in Washington at 9 o'clock on the minute the next morning. With the knowledge that the Foreign Ministers' Conference had failed, the President with his usual thoughtful human viewpoint met the plane with the entire Cabinet to greet the Secretary at the airport. It was a magnificent demonstration to a great Secretary of State.

You will not be interested in my six weeks in the United States. Coming direct after six months amid the poverty, the bitterness and the depression of Eastern Europe, the Colony Restaurant was almost as great a shock to me as it was after my return from a year in the Pacific war. But that is neither here nor there.

On February 16, following a rough, rolling trip on the Queen Mary, and by air from London, via Paris and Berlin, I flew back into Warsaw to greet one of the astounding anachronisms of the Poles. My crew had not been able to obtain Polish visas, but we were advised by radio that the airport would permit them to land to drop me off on the condition that the plane return immediately to Berlin that night. The airport was lighted up for the first night entrance of any foreign plane since the war and I had a great welcome from the Embassy staff. But there was a slight pay-off. Without any warning whatever, the Polish Government arrested the entire crew, stating that the airport had no authority to permit them to land and that they had violated the sacred laws of Poland. With all the contradictions indicated in the situation, the boys were held incommunicado at the Hotel Bristol, the best hotel in Warsaw, well fed and permitted to return to Berlin the next day. I suspect this kind of thing was the original musical comedy plot, but the overtures of this kind of music are grim and vicious to the American ear.

However, it was pleasant indeed to get back to the comfort of my home in Warsaw. All the servants were lined up in the hallway to greet me Polish style, and they are the same seven servants regarding whom I have taunted many American housewives because for the seven the total monthly payroll is around $65 per month.

In former letters I have written you of the intense Catholicism of these people. In the front of the concierge's house at my Warsaw residence is embedded an almost life-size statue of the Blessed Virgin lighted day and night by an electric bulb. During my absence some of the electrical equipment in the house failed to work on account of damp wires, and the light on the Virgin went out. For a day the street was quiet but the next day there was a tremendous furor and we were called on by a large delegation of the neighbors in protest. This block on the street called Emilii Plater is a sorry one at best, but, except for three out of its four corners, it escaped destruction during the war although every house is pockmarked with shrapnel and bullet marks. Yet the neighbors firmly believe that my special Virgin saved the block during the insurrection and as soon as the light was restored, we were called upon with all manner of offerings of appreciation—fruit, cookies and sweets.

During my absence and since my last letter the Communist juggernaut has rolled on swiftly and efficiently in Poland and adjoining countries. It was on the date of my last letter, October 20, that Mikolajczyk, the great Polish leader, having decided that it was better to be a live politician than a dead statesman, escaped from Poland. The Ambassador and the American Embassy were immediately the storm center of many charges and countercharges regarding the departure of Mikolajczyk and his followers. At the opening of the Polish Parliament the following week,

Mikolajczyk was described as "Poland's best export." Puppet pro-Communist leaders immediately moved in to control his organization, the Peasant Party, and its newspaper, and October 20, 1947, substantially marked the end of legal or organized opposition to this Government in Poland.

It will be remembered that it was Mikolajczyk who apparently in the minds of both the United States and Great Britain was meant to be the catalytic agent between Russia, the Lublin Government and the Polish Exile Government in London. Roosevelt greatly admired him and according to the famous history "Defeat in Victory," written by the former Polish Ambassador to Washington, backed him in every way with help and promises until he felt it necessary to make certain concessions to Stalin at Yalta. Mikolajczyk fought hard for his party and to obtain voting control of the Government, but the famous "free elections" of January 1947 substantially ended any hope of power which the Peasant Party had and Mikolajczyk was relegated to a minor ministry and to finally an obscure but active position in the Parliament. We have no way of being certain that the stage had been set for "rubbing him out," as the New York gangsters say, but popular opinion here is to the effect that he was marked for elimination.

During the last three quarters of 1947 a series of political trials were conducted involving about 100 alleged members of underground secret organizations who had been arrested in 1946 and early in 1947. Charges invariably involved treason, espionage for "foreign powers," and collusion with Mikolajczyk and the Peasant Party. Defendants were uniformly convicted and death sentences were pronounced in a majority of instances. A number of these death sentences were not carried out. Consequently, the condemned as well as several hundred untried conspirators now in prison, serve as hostages for the behavior of their associates who remain at large. The chief result of these trials was to intimidate the remaining conspirators and to make all members of the underground doubly cautious, with the result of slowing up communications and organizational activity.

In the purely theoretical event of the withdrawal for any reason of Soviet support for the existing Polish regime, the internal conspiracies and the numerous Polish anti-government organizations operating in various foreign countries probably have the ability and sufficient organization to overthrow the Government and to form promptly and fairly effectively a representative popular government. In other words, they are prepared to occupy a vacuum but little more. Of course, there still remain in the south of Poland and on the Ukrainian border various small roaming bands who, together or in conjunction, frequently make life miserable for the secret police and the small villages.

On the thirtieth anniversary of the Russian Revolution, Warsaw was ablaze with interwoven Russian and Polish flags. There were tremendous if somewhat synthetic demonstrations, and banners broke out all over Warsaw reading in effect "The future of Poland is safe in the arms of its great ally, the Union of Soviet Socialist Republics."

The next important event on the political calendar was of course the failure of the London Conference, followed by a new wave of attack by the Polish press on everything Anglo-Saxon and highlighted by peculiarly vicious attacks on the French Republic and its government, aimed at splitting off the French from the Western Allies.

Last week came the long expected Communist coup in Prague, following immediately a meeting of the Foreign Ministers of Poland, Czechoslovakia, and Yugoslavia to protest violently against the present meeting of Deputy Ministers in London, the Marshall Plan in particular, and the long alleged violation of the Yalta and Potsdam Agreements. The passing of Czechoslovakia into Communist control has been expected and predicted for almost a year and together with the Russian insistence on a military pact with Finland seems to close the backgammon board with Russian markers from the Baltic to Greece and Turkey. In Asia and to the east and south of the U.S.S.R. lies now the battling Communist-Nationalist armies of China. To the south lies a turbulent India and proceeding westward Iran, Turkey, Greece and Italy. West of the Russian Zone of Germany lies Bizonia or Trizonia, the Low Countries, and France. The vermilion of the map of Eastern Europe—in fact from Vladivostok to Berlin and Helsinki to the Black Sea—shows no open spaces. The next move is in the hands of God, the American Government and the Kremlin.

Last week, simultaneously with the Czech developments, we had another bit of musical comedy in the visit of a great Rumanian Delegation headed by the Prime Minister and by the famous woman Minister of Foreign Affairs, Madam Pauker. Madam Pauker is a little on the Amazonian side, with a terrific mane of iron-gray hair, and one can well imagine the timidity with which the tragic little King Michael faced her when he was invited to abdicate. One of the minor diplomats, no doubt with exaggeration, told me that he had watched her taking her daily exercise throwing pianos across the Vistula. The Swiss told me he had come to the reception to see the two Foreign Ministers dance together as Modzelewski, the brilliant Polish chief, is a little on the small side. In any event, the Poles outdid themselves on hospitality and the Rumanian Minister wound up the goings on by a dinner, at which I roughly guessed the attendance at about 400. We were flooded with caviar, pâté de foie gras, and rare viands, together with buckets of champagne, all of which I roughly estimate cost starving Rumania in one night much more than the entire entertainment allowance of the American State Department to the Warsaw Embassy and all its officers for a full year.

It is reported around the diplomatic corps here that the Rumanians brought all of their food, secret police as waiters, two bullet-proof automobiles, and an entourage of 150 people directly by special train from Bucharest to Warsaw. It was expected and announced in the press that Rumania and Poland would sign two treaties, one of cultural relations and one of mutual defense. The cultural treaty was signed amid great fanfare but in the midst of conferences, the newspapers suddenly stopped discussion of the mutual aid pact and apparently none was signed for reasons unknown to this deponent.

Per contra, the new French Ambassador gave a large reception upon his arrival here to which all of the Polish Government was invited but which was boycotted to a man on account of the fact that this happens to be anti-French month in Poland.

In my former letters I have not, I think, explained the rationing system in Poland. It is entirely different from a rationing system as we know it. There are no black markets here except in currency and anything that is for sale can be bought at a price. But out of about 24 million inhabitants, about 11 million hold "ration cards" which permit them to buy staple goods at Government stores far below the prices which ordinary citizens and the foreign element can purchase. It may be easily visualized how it works in providing faithful allegiance to the Government, and a defense of it can be understood in the following translation from a Warsaw newspaper article:

"The author analyzes the ration system in Poland financed by the state. Although the sum of 90,000,000 zlotys assigned for this purpose in the state budget is a huge expenditure and constitutes 30% of the budget, he considers that it serves a more useful purpose than increased wages: The state is able to buy essential foods either at wholesale prices or at cost prices and distribute them among the working population, while if the above amount were used simply to increase lower wages it is doubtful whether the persons concerned would be in a position to buy such foodstuffs as are indispensable for their health. The author concludes by saying that on the whole the food situation has improved but the living standards are still too low—the average amount of daily calories per head is 1822 but it is expected to increase them to 2101. He believes that the proposed reform of the diet will greatly contribute towards a general improvement, mainly by replacing less nourishing foods imported from foreign countries with more nourishing home foods."

Personally, I do not believe these calorie figures at all. I believe that the Poles in general are the best-fed nation in Europe, both in the cities and on the farms. I personally do not know any Poles who do not seem to have the habit of overeating and my mind throws back to the early days of my stay here when a highly publicized American Commission came to Poland to estimate its food relief needs. There was much criticism by the Polish Government and newspapers when the Commission only stayed four days before returning. I myself was a bit startled and on the last day I asked the Chairman, a celebrated food expert, how he could make his judgment of a nation's food needs in four days. He answered, and I think with great truth—it was very simple. He simply went to four parts of Poland and looked at the "behinds" of the citizenry, male and female. Confidentially, they are uniformly large.

Within the last month, too, the Polish Government has trotted out a rather new plan with which you, bowed down though you may be by taxes, have not yet been honored, that is, a compulsory savings act whereby, in addition to income taxes, all Poles with an annual income of 400,000 zlotys (which is $400 or a thousand dollars, depending on the rate of exchange used), must deposit savings ranging from 1 to 3 per cent of their income in the Government banks. Rates for industry and trade, already heavily income-taxed, range from 4 to 18 per cent per annum. I am not entirely sure that this would not be a good plan in the United States.

At the Embassy during my absence almost all of the temporary building projects were completed and today we have substantially all of the staff who really wish to get away from hotel life housed in small apartments or houses. As apparently is happening all over the world the Embassy birth rate has taken a substantial jump and the stork dashes among us with constant arrivals or impending arrivals. Because last December we were excluded from the only semi-sanitary hospital in Warsaw, we immediately started in to build a small Embassy hospital. It is nearly completed now with a three-bed ward, a two-bed ward and a private room together with X-ray and operating equipment and a great mass of hospital supplies which we were fortunate in obtaining from the Paderewski Fund mobile hospital, which, after many months of inactivity, finally decided to permit the distribution of its equipment throughout the various hospitals in Poland. We are going to be pretty proud of ours and I believe that it will be the best small hospital in Eastern Europe. God knows under the conditions of sanitation, unrefrigerated food and bad water, terrible climate and, in some cases, inadequate housing under which our people live, they are entitled to the best of hospital care. The new young Army doctor is serious and able and the staff seems to have confidence in him.

The Embassy motion picture theatre and mess hall are completed so that all the boys and girls are able to have a good hot luncheon in the middle of the day close by the Embassy and with a recreation hall for games. The 35mm motion picture projectors are operating and we have showings four or five times a week for the staff, for the diplomatic corps, and the Polish Government. In addition to the 16mm films which the Government sends us, my motion picture friends of all the major companies in Paris are sending us weekly good current pictures.

The far-famed Embassy dairy, which really buys its milk in Warsaw but which pasteurizes it in a homemade machine in the Embassy basement, has grown by leaps and bounds and our business is now much in demand with the other Embassies, especially for the officers and attachés with youngsters. However, the Polish press now attacks me as stealing the milk from the mothers and children of Warsaw although, of course, the fact is that we use approximately 150 litres out of approximately 100,000 litres which come into Warsaw daily.

While it has been an open winter, the strong and highly justified gripe of the Embassy is about the mail. As I have previously written, the mail comes in from Berlin once a week by courier plane and that is a day of great excitement but, during the last two months, which have varied from dreary fog to bitter cold, there have frequently been low ceilings at Templehof in Berlin or the field here and the mail has failed to arrive for days at a time. Today marks the 14th day that the plane has failed to arrive from Warsaw and officers and clerks alike are cross; tempers are wearing thin, and the piles of outgoing mail increase. Some happy day there will be a direct train service through the Russian Zone from Paris to Warsaw and this horror will end. In any event, after a winter of alternating moderation and intense snow and cold, an early spring seems to have come to Warsaw. Flower stands are appearing again on the corners even if their stock is only evergreen and pussywillows. Tulips are appearing in the flower store windows, and like the Swedes the Polish people stretch themselves in the sunshine at midday.

My car remains the seventh wonder of Poland. Although it is only a stock Chrysler limousine and I have been here approximately eight months, it is still, so far as I know, the only limousine in Poland and still attracts crowds wherever it is parked. With a small American flag on one side of the fenders and the blue-starred Ambassador's flag on the other, it seemed at the beginning pretty ostentatious, but the Embassy boys persuaded me I should keep the flags and I think that they were right, for everywhere I go the flag is greeted with bright shining smiles, both by men and women, who stop along the street to look at it. Their greeting is welcome compensation for the glares of Government officials as they pass me in their fleet of 500 Chevrolets imported from Denmark. The deep affection for the United States still remains in the people however much the Government may attempt to destroy it. It is partly a reflection of the fact that per unit of population of Poland today, there probably is a higher percentage of Poles and people of Polish descent in the United States than of any other nation.

The black market in zlotys continues its merry whirl. The dollar dropped violently when a bill was introduced in Congress during the winter to call in for exchange all American currency and then climbed again when the bill was not taken seriously. This was met by a series of Government propaganda articles to the effect that a large swarm of Poles had been arrested at the coast ports, bearing thousands of dollars of counterfeit American money. So it goes. The Government is making Herculean attempts to hold the zloty at 400 to the dollar, using every known legal device, but like the franc, water cannot be made to run uphill and it must inevitably find its real level. What seems to me to be an amusing episode occurred when I made a donation to one of the Catholic bishops for his orphans. Asking him whether he would prefer zlotys, dollar currency or dollar check, he responded without a moment's hesitation that he would prefer the currency. Later in talking to one of the American relief officers here who had introduced me to the bishop, I expressed the hope that the good Father could exchange his dollars at a fair rate of exchange. The direct reply—"Don't have any worry about that. He is very astute in these matters, and will hold on for the best market." I trust that the good Father does not go to the hoosegow on my account.

When I went to the airport last Saturday to welcome John

Boettiger, President Roosevelt's son-in-law, who is here on a free-lance newspaper expedition, I suddenly realized that it was the first time that I had had an American visitor of almost any sort since last Autumn when the swarm of locusts representing American Congressional Committees and countless newspapermen descended on us. It is an astonishing commentary on the isolation of the Iron Curtain that this could be the case. To get to Warsaw one has the choice of flying to Berlin and there perchance be marooned for many days before the flight can be resumed to Warsaw, or to fly to Prague for a 20-hour rail trip to Warsaw, or to take the bull by the horns and take the Orient Express from Paris via Prague, a delightful journey of two days and two nights on a cold, dirty and drafty sleeping car—the trip punctuated by hour-long stays and all kinds of interrogation at the borders. The Russian Zone presents a far more formidable barrier to cross-European transportation than does the City of Chicago, as depicted in Bob Young's diatribes to the effect that a "pig can travel from New York to San Francisco by rail without change but you can't."

The Jewish situation in Poland is changing somewhat. I have hitherto referred to the fact that out of 3½ million Jews who were Polish citizens prior to the last war only about 88,000 remain but by some strange process of reasoning the Polish Government has up to this time permitted free access to and exit from Poland to any Jews who desired visas. Now this is changing with the growing determination of the Polish Government that all emigration must be stopped, and the head of the Jewish Relief here told me this morning that he believed within two or three months no emigration, either Jew or Gentile, would be permitted from Poland. At present it takes from six to eight months for a Pole to obtain a passport, if indeed he obtains it, and I am deluged with letters from Senators and Congressmen who cannot understand why I am not able to wave a magic wand as American Ambassador to Poland and restore Maria Jankowski to the waiting arms of her sister, Sophia Nowicki, who has a good job, a good husband, and a home waiting for her in Bridgeport. The Consulate staff answers these letters, running about ten a day, and tries to phrase them as though I had spent my entire working hours for a week looking into this case. They come across my desk always in the late afternoon to be signed personally in an effort to show my great interest in Maria's case.

Anyway, I have accomplished one great result for I have definitely determined the reason why the East and West, or to put it more simply, Russia and its satellites and the United States, fail to get along or understand each other. I feel confident that it is because here in the East of Europe there is so little human happiness or sense of humor. There is no laughter. I earnestly believe that if the Russians and the Slavs could learn to laugh they could more nearly understand us and we might live together in peace and understanding.

It is now almost a year since the Big Boss in Washington asked me to come to Poland, I have said many times that it was like the man having ten children, that I wouldn't have given up the experience for a million dollars but I wouldn't give a nickel to do it again. It is with deep depression that I watch the crevices in the curtain being closed and the general situation going from bad to worse. I pray daily that some miracle may change it but I find myself unconsciously humming the old California song "When the swallows come back to Capistrano, I'll be coming back to you." I don't think it will be long now.

I'll be seeing you.

*Sincerely yours,*
STANTON GRIFFIS

In the late spring of 1948, I had been writing to Bob Lovett, the Under-Secretary of State, that I felt strongly I was wasting the public's money in remaining as ambassador to Poland. Our diplomatic efforts had slowed to a walk, and constant Communist pressure against everything American was rising. The quality of mercy that always falleth from Bob Lovett is not strained, and I was permitted to return to the United States and supposedly to private life. On reporting to Washington I found, however, that Secretary Marshall had recommended to the President my appointment to another spot, warm in every sense of the word, in the shadow of the Pyramids. The great Secretary made me very happy by telling me that I was no longer to regard myself as a political appointee, that I now had the confidence of the State Department and was one of them. In fact, as the President has told me the story a number of times, the Secretary told the Boss that the Department needed the appointment of the man whom they did not want to accept for Poland the previous year. The fire yawned as I jumped from the frying pan.

# CHAPTER TWELVE

## EGYPT, PALESTINE, FAROUK,
## AND THE REFUGEES

Very few envoys in the history of diplomacy have faced a more hostile attitude than the new American ambassador faced as he sailed into the peaceful harbor of Alexandria on August 24, 1948. Egypt was at war with Israel; there was an atmosphere of hatred of all things American, permeating Egypt, its government, and its people. There was little to choose between the bitterness of the Russian government in Poland toward the capitalistic United States, as against the hatred of Egypt toward us because of our Palestine policy. The situation was not aided by the fact that practically all the Americans, who were old hands in the Near East countries, were opposed to our government's policy, and were very free in so expressing themselves to their Egyptian friends and business associates. They were pro-Arab to an extreme, and they felt that the American Government was making one of the great diplomatic mistakes of history in alienating the Arab world in its policy toward Israel.

It was not long before my arrival that an American tourist had been stoned and killed while visiting one of the Arab mosques in the streets of Cairo. Egypt was seizing ships coming through the Suez Canal on the pretext that they contained goods for Israel; and one of my first duties in the Embassy was to delegate guns, tear bombs, and defense positions to every male employee of the Embassy, and to make plans to protect ourselves against a possible attack by the Arab mobs, which were frequently making demonstrations of wild bitterness against all Americans. The age-long Egyptian hatred of the British had been transferred in toto to America, to the United States Government, and its people. The Embassy officers were very doubtful that I would be received at all by King Farouk, and the whole atmosphere was one of terrific nervous tension.

However, His Majesty apparently decided to be correct with the new American ambassador in public, and even to un-leash his great personal charm upon him in private. I was duly received on September second, when I presented my cre-dentials at Abdin Palace in Cairo, and I was accorded a private audience with the King on September eighth through the medium of a letter couched in diplomatic French, reading as follows:

*Office of the Grand Chamberlain, Abdin Palace, September 7, 1948*
Mr. Ambassador, I have the honor to inform Your Excellency that His Majesty the King, my august Master and Sovereign, will receive you with pleasure on Wednesday, September eighth, at four o'clock in the afternoon at the Palace of Koubbeh.
Be assured, Mr. Ambassador of my highest consideration.
GRAND CHAMBERLAIN

One might be interested, in considering this letter with its ancient and feudal verbiage, to ponder the remoteness of the possibility of receiving an appointment letter from Matt Con-nelly, Secretary to Mr. Truman, wherein he would refer to the President as his Sovereign and Master.

I greatly enjoyed my conference with the King. He smoked his *cigarros* and I smoked my pipe as we talked in his small library in the towering palace, and I enjoyed future confer-ences with him although they accomplished little toward solving the all-pervading problem of Palestine. However, I shall write little of him, for his story during the past year has been blazoned to the world and his kingship is over, perhaps forever.

Even in my time, four years ago, stories were current throughout Egypt that steam was continually kept up on the royal yacht in Abukir Bay, that the craft, prepared and manned, was always ready for a quick exit from Egypt of the royal family in case it should become necessary. However, there were a few more signs than usual of the approaching end during the past year as the world watched Farouk's antics at Monte Carlo, his new marriage, and the subsequent production for his people of a son and heir. There were riots and burnings in Cairo. There was the failure of the American and British efforts to arrange a tripartite defense of Egypt following Egypt's new attempt to abrogate the treaty of 1936 with England and drive out the wise and carefully operated military control of the Suez Canal. Rumblings there were, but the opposition to Farouk was not consolidated, and could not be until one strong man of courage emerged from the masses, as he always must. The strong man was, as the world knows, General Mohammed Naguib, and at his very forceful suggestion, backed by a picked group of Egyptian army officers, Farouk stepped aboard the royal yacht *Mahroussa* at precisely six o'clock in the evening, July 26, the time to which he had agreed in his abdication documents. As the *Mahroussa* steamed toward Capri there was a king no more in Egypt, except the infant child to be known as King Fuad II, ruling through the hastily constituted regency of a royal cousin, a jurist, and a representative of General Naguib's junta. No student of the kingdom on the Nile can safely predict its political future, but were I to venture a prediction, it would be that the troubles of Egypt are far from over. Yet one may hope that if the promises of the regency that they will close the gap between rich and poor are realized, and Egypt's new rulers will recognize the kindly and helpful political influence of England and the

United States, there may be better times in the land of the Pharaohs.

In the last analysis, Farouk fell, I believe, not on account of his lack of the qualities of kingship but on account of his lethargy and absolute unwillingness to employ the mental brilliance that he unquestionably has. The world during our generation is beginning to realize that no ruler, whether dictator or otherwise, can long exist unless he has a real social consciousness and a desire to improve the living conditions of the masses of his people. Of this social consciousness Farouk had absolutely none. Despite his squabbles with England and despite the debauchery and corruption which permeated his court, he might have survived had he made the most elemental effort to feed his people, and indeed, look even ever so casually to the welfare of his army, which existed to protect the throne instead of seize it.

During my period in Egypt, Farouk was in the throes of getting a divorce. He spent a small amount of his time in diplomatic and political work, but he was a constant devotee of the Cairo night clubs, almost always accompanied by beautiful women, and sometimes attempting, to the great consternation of American and other diplomats, a *droit du seigneur* attitude. Being a Moslem, he was forbidden by his religious tenets to partake of alcohol, but he was the best customer that the Coca-Cola Company had in Egypt. His capacity for the drink was unlimited.

One of my employees, a youngster who did not realize that where beautiful women are concerned royalty is a one-way street, involved both himself and the Embassy in great difficulty. His sin was in sending a card to one of the girls at the King's table at an outlying night club, asking her if she would ask His Majesty's permission to dance with him, and in the unhappy hours that followed this episode he maintained that the young lady had given him a cordial smile. When the next dance started, the young man moved across the dance floor and started to put his hand on His Majesty's shoulder. So many armed guards jumped out of the palms that it seemed as if the Egyptian Army had begun maneuvers, and the poor youngster was hustled into the night. The next day one of His Majesty's secretaries called on me and maintained that the King had been insulted. Abject apologies written by the unhappy youth served nothing. I was merely told again that the King had been insulted. I understood that the boy was accredited also to Turkey, and since I earnestly desired to avoid a diplomatic incident whereby the boy would be declared persona non grata, I asked him if he was so accredited. He told me that he was, and I asked him when the next plane left for Turkey. He said, "At four o'clock this afternoon. I have been looking it up." He was able to make the plane. The incident was closed.

The gay social life in Cairo went on in the embassies and in the homes of the rich pashas, while hunger and famine and cold stalked the Arab refugees from Palestine to the north. Terrorists and assassins were active both in the Arab nations and Israel. The new Foreign Minister of Egypt, the great Nokrashy Pasha, was assassinated, and on September seventeenth, less than a month after my arrival, we heard the tragic news of the murder of Count Bernadotte in the streets of Jerusalem. Bernadotte, acting as the United Nations conciliator, a neutral angel of mercy covering both Arab and Jewish lands, had received many threats of assassination, but he was a man without fear, a man of great good will, and he did not believe that he should be armed or protected in either Arab or Jewish territory. I have been criticized many times in foreign lands for arming myself and accepting guards when anti-American fanatics were threatening my life. But I believe that I have been right in so doing, and I believe that Bernadotte would be alive today had he permitted any of his convoy to carry arms. As it was, the assassins had to search through three cars until they found the totally unarmed Bernadotte. They pushed a Bren gun through the window of the car and killed him in cold blood.

In my scrapbook reposes a map of Palestine, with proposed borderlines marked in Bernadotte's own writing, outlining the territorial arrangement of his famous plan. But Bernadotte is dead, and the Bernadotte Plan died with him. The Jewish forces, aided by great contributions from the United States, continued their victorious campaign. They spread upon and held the land, far beyond the lines of Bernadotte's map. I remember later sitting in Ben-Gurion's library in Tel Aviv and asking him why the Jews wanted the Negeb, that triangular piece of land stretching below Gaza to the Red Sea. I told him that I had flown over it many times, and that I doubted if a prairie dog could live there. Ben-Gurion with his intense idealism and optimism said to me, "You come back here in ten years; I'll make a date with you ten years from today, and we will go over the Negeb together; it will be a garden, it will be an Eden." I hope he is right, and I am told that some progress is being made there. Certainly something good should come out of the horrors of the Near East in 1948.

Yet the murder of Bernadotte will remain forever a black and disgraceful mark on the early history of Israel. Apparently it seemed wise to the existing government not to attempt to punish the assassins, but I believe, and believe firmly, that their identity was, and remains, well known to the Israeli Government. I was told that on the night of the assassination lights burned late in the Czechoslovakian Embassy in Tel Aviv; and one could find, if it were possible to look in the files of the State Department, a list of almost twenty Palestine terrorists who were given Czechoslovakian passports and flown out of Israel within twenty-four hours after the murder of Bernadotte. But nothing was ever done, though perhaps someday justice will prevail, for Bernadotte died a very great man.

We were all deeply stirred by the events of September and October. So long as the Palestine matter remained unsettled, there was little of a diplomatic nature that the Embassy could do. Our minds turned more and more to the suffering of nearly a million Arab refugees from Palestine who were wandering through the Near East, unfed, unclothed, and unsheltered. And so it came about that my diplomatic activities, in fact, my active ambassadorship in Egypt, lasted for less than three months before I was given leave of absence and began organizing the United Nations Relief for Palestine Refugees, which took all of my waking hours for many months thereafter. Later in this chapter I shall include two letters that I wrote to friends at home, like those written when I was in Poland, which will describe my feelings and viewpoints in Egypt. There are many things in the letters which I perhaps would not say today. My attitudes toward Zionism and the Bernadotte Plan seemed to me right at the time, but I may well have been mistaken. Nevertheless, I am including the letters completely unexpurgated, without a word changed although my views have changed in the meantime.

It was about the middle of November when I was called to Paris and later to Washington to organize the Arab relief activities. The United Nations had voted $32,000,000 for refugee relief, but they had neglected to raise the money. So it became my job not only to organize the relief, but to purchase supplies, and then to hunt the world over for the money necessary to carry on the operation. At last the United States, as usual, voted $16,000,000 of the $32,000,000 necessary. England was extremely generous, as finally was France, and I received many donations either in cash or in foodstuffs or clothing from many other nations throughout the world. But I did not receive one ruble nor one ounce of food from Russia or from any of its satellites, nor did I receive any contribution of substantial amount from south of the Rio Grande. Surprisingly enough, Egypt itself was one of the chief contributors to the United Nations Fund. Not only did it contribute, but it permitted me to buy foodstuffs of all kinds at very fair prices from the government stores. Some other Arab nations which shall be nameless were less charitable, especially since they permitted their merchants to overcharge disgracefully for relief supplies for their own people, although we made every possible effort to buy goods and food at low prices. I shall not dwell on some of their other tactics, such as the disavowal of agreements we made with them, the blocking of passage of food trucks through their territory, and the many other atrocious delays and deceits which slowed our work and increased our burdens.

Israel won the war but found an uneasy peace, a peace that rises and falls like the wind in the desert. Israel won not only because of American dollars but because it is very hard to beat crusaders. It is very hard to beat a nation that has a great principle; it is very hard to beat a country that is smart enough to carry out the policy of divide and conquer—Israel knocked out most of the Arab nations one by one.

The Jews were fighting an Arab world torn by jealousies and hatreds, and the result was for good or for evil; I hope, for good. There is this much to be said on the Arab side: that when the United Nations ordered that no arms be shipped to the embattled Near East, the United States, Great Britain, and the Arab states meticulously obeyed. No arms were shipped from neutral nations to the Arabs. There was a tremendous flow of arms to Israel from Czechoslovakia, not, I think, from Communistic urges, but for profit.

The Arab armies were small and untrained. I asked my senior military attaché to tell me the size and strength of the army of one of the small Arab countries. He may have been a bit cynical, but his answer was, "They have about five thousand men under arms, about half of them are usually absent without leave, and the other half are looking for them. When they find them they change places."

They had no real will to fight. The Arabs were not impelled by the urge to defend this homeland as the Jews were. And so the world witnessed the astonishing situation in which fewer than one million Jews were victorious against a Moslem world of two hundred and eighty millions.

The result is part of the new map of Europe today.

### THE FOREIGN SERVICE
### OF THE
### UNITED STATES OF AMERICA

AMERICAN EMBASSY

*Cairo, Egypt, October 30, 1948*

*Dear Joe:*

Somehow it all seemed very familiar—the sights, the sounds and the smells, the soft delayed muted music, a long line of camels padding by, the countless donkeys and donkey carts and vari-colored costumes of the natives. I suddenly realized that memorials of long-forgotten expositions were flooding back into my memory with the inevitable "Streets of Cairo" on the Midway. I was in Cairo for the first time but I am afraid I remembered Paris in 1900, Buffalo in 1901 with McKinley driving in the day before he was assassinated, and St. Louis in 1904. My God, I am getting old. Perhaps I had better find myself a quiet little pyramid and lie down beside one of the Pharaohs.

I took the easy way to come to Egypt, the luxurious way but not the fast way, for I could have done it in less than 36 hours by air. But I chose comfort as Kravchenko chose freedom, and took the long way round: by the Queen Mary to Cherbourg . . . a pleasant drive across France to the sunshine and smiling waters of Monte Carlo, where I stayed for ten days turning the Casino's unfortunate financial history of 1948 into black ink . . . then to Rapallo and Porto Fino to revive those happy, carefree days when dollars were peanuts and I lived on a boat in the Mediterranean . . . thence to Genoa. Out of Genoa I traveled on a beautiful reconstructed Liberty ship, the pride of the Egyptian Marine, owned by Abboud Pasha, the richest pasha of them all, who had kindly given me his personal cabin and sitting room, a private deck, and an unbelievably charming four-day voyage to Alexandria.

Suddenly, as we dropped anchor in the harbor of Alexandria and the series of port launches came up to the ship's ladder, I realized that I was an American Ambassador in an unfriendly country, a country that considered itself at war with the State of Israel and which had become antagonistic to the United States and all its works, so strongly did the Arab nations blame American political policy for support of Israel. The knowledge was brought home to me by the arrival of ten Egyptian guards, who closed around me and never let me out of their sight, night or day, during the 24 hours I spent in Alexandria.

When I met the American Colony in the garden of the American Consul General, these guards stood quietly in the bushes, and when I swam in the Mediterranean, they stood at the water's edge. At the train the next day they handed me over to a group sent down by the Governor of Cairo to look after me. All this is more than two months ago, and they are still with me, night and day. On the street below my apartment at the Semiramis Hotel they stand with tommy guns. Outside my door one sits through the long hours of the night, and in the morning my most faithful shadow climbs into the car with the chauffeur, and whether I am through work before dinner or at one or two o'clock in the morning, he is still with me until I disappear through the door of my apartment.

Well, I have got used to it now. I still do not know what would happen if someone cried a loud "boo" to one of these gentry, but so far there has been no outward demonstration of animosity anywhere and they are highly useful for my household in running errands, and will not permit me to carry a book or a tennis racquet for more than ten feet. Of course, I have to put them on my personal payroll, for the Egyptian Government only pays them about six Egyptian pounds a month, 18 bucks to you, and with my slight addition they are vastly envied among their fellow cops.

So, two months ago, started my work in Cairo in a beautiful chancery, an excellent staff, hard-working and loyal, and a climate to be envied of the Gods. The summer heat of northern Egypt is certainly no worse than Washington or New York and now in the autumn comes a succession of cloudless days and there is never any doubt as to exactly what the weather will be. I have yet to see a drop of rain and sometimes the sunshine becomes so monotonous that we almost beg for clouds of rain, but my weather bureau friends say that I will only see a few showers during the year, perhaps in January.

The first two weeks—because I had been warned of demonstrations against me in Egypt—I stayed at the Mena House in the shadow of the Great Pyramids, about 20 minutes' drive from Cairo, an ancient hostelry which I think was built by Joseph when his brothers came to see him in Egypt in Old Testament times. It has not changed much since. It is spooky with gloom, out-at-elbows in furniture, and living there is altogether like living in Endor or wherever those witches came from. However, the advantage was the peerless sight of the Great Pyramids in the moonlight, a few hundred feet away, and the Sphinx gazing quietly toward the Nile just beyond. The Sphinx always makes me think of Bill Greve's expression "You never saw a deaf and dumb man in jail." Unfortunately, the Egyptians during the past few years have insisted on excavating the Sphinx to a point that its derrière, and a pretty dull derrière it is at that, has been fully exposed, thus ruining Joe Ripley's favorite story of the love affair between the camel and the Sphinx. Unfortunately, too, when you have seen the Sphinx and the Pyramids, the flat cotton fields of the Nile and the Nile itself, you have seen about all there is to see of great interest in northern Egypt barring the museums, and very few of my visitors here ask for them. Accordingly, what with visiting Congressmen, Generals, Admirals and miscellaneous guests for the past two months, I roughly compute that I have driven around the Sphinx and the Pyramids 314 times and it will be all right with me if I never see them again. In any event, the gruesome atmosphere of Mena House was too much for me, and while the Semiramis Hotel was closed except for the bar and the roof garden, the management very kindly agreed to let me have an apartment there until the hotel opened, and there I have been for six weeks in reasonable comfort while I have looked for a house. In this search I am faced with the alternatives of palaces of 50 rooms and medium palaces of 25 rooms and one bath, or modern apartments outside of which a million taxis practice imitations of hot trumpets throughout the night.

Egypt is nothing if not hospitable. While the so-called "season" has not yet opened here, life is one continual round of cocktail parties, dinners and dances. I doubt if I have averaged more than one free night a week and when you realize that Embassy hours are from 8 A.M. to 2 P.M. without a break, usually work in the afternoon followed by a cocktail party and a dinner, you may understand that I practically meet myself during the night coming in after dinner and leaving for the Embassy in the morning. All this and protocol too. There are about 40 Ministers and Ambassadors in Cairo, all of whom have to make ceremonious calls on me (all of these must be returned). At these calls hospitable drinks are de rigueur. So you may see how my statistics show that during the course of those diplomatic shenanigans I have assimilated 479 cups of Turkish coffee, 84 cups of French coffee, 306 Coca-Colas, 4 cups of Arabian coffee, which will blow the top of your head off, and 76 other national drinks from Slivovitz to Vodka and Arak. All this with the known ptomaine effects of all Egyptian food leads to a constant attack of the favorite Egyptian disease known as "gippy tummy." The two biggest industries in Egypt are the Coca-Cola Company and the manufacturers of sulfasuxidine, an intestinal disinfectant.

There was some doubt when I arrived as to whether the King of Egypt would receive me, owing to his alleged violent anti-Americanism and the fact that he had refused a farewell audience to the last Ambassador, nor had any member of the Foreign Office said good-by to Ambassador "Pinky" Tuck, who was extremely popular here and who left to retire from the Diplomatic Service and accept a succulent job as a Director of the Suez Canal. But the maestro did consent to receive me, and eight large bright red Cadillacs drove up to the Embassy to take me and my staff, resplendent in morning coats, silk hats and gloves, together with all my military staff, which is a large one, to the Palace. There was tremendous cheering along the streets on the road to the Palace, chiefly, I think, for the red Cadillacs, although I bowed and raised my hat like a returning Channel swimmer coming up Broadway. At the Palace I had to go through the usual routine of bowing three times as I entered the King's presence and then shaking hands with him. But I had a lucky break. As I was asked to introduce my staff, the King spoke to the first arrival, Jefferson Patterson, my Counselor, and said, "The American Ambassador made a mistake. He called me 'Your Highness' and he should have called me 'Your Majesty.'" This gave me an opportunity to make a wisecrack to the effect that "Your Majesty, if that is the only mistake which I make in Egypt I shall be very happy." To my great relief, the King laughed like a schoolboy and told the story all over Cairo.

In any event, the goings on were quickly over. Nobody fell down as we all had to back out of his imperial presence, and all hands returned safely to the Embassy to put their silk hats and Sears Roebuck morning coats back into the moth balls. Royal presentations are few and far between. Male figures have a way of changing in a forward-looking manner, and some of the clothes that my staff dug up—not to mention my own—should be in the Smithsonian. In any event, the following week I was received by His Majesty in private audience. He is almost like an American sophomore, although somewhat over-weight, with a small blond mustache, but he is nobody's fool, speaks a variety of languages with great fluency, has a pretty keen knowledge of world conditions and a good deal of strength despite the fact that he has never been out of Egypt except for about six months at an English school. He is said to know full well how precarious his position is and how open the season for kings has been the last few years; he is reported to have originated the bon mot that after a few years there would be only five kings left: the King of England and the Kings of Diamonds, Clubs, Hearts and Spades. In any event, we talked almost entirely about Palestine.

In Egypt, Palestine is topic number one; there aren't very many other topics here except the Suez Canal, hatred of England, and the price of cotton. With the King, as with all Ministers of the Government, I have opened the subject of Palestine at once and with few preliminaries, stating that there was no use discussing other topics on the agenda so long as the Palestine question remained unsettled. This I believe is true.

Most of you thoroughly understand the Palestine problem and the hatred of the Arab nations, Egypt, Transjordan, Iraq, Palestine, Lebanon, Syria and Saudi Arabia, the seven Arab sisters, combined in the powerful Arab League, with a fixed determination never to recognize Israel and to push the Jewish terrorists and invaders, as they call them, into the sea. This is not a new goings on. If you will blow the dust off the top of that old family Bible in the library and read the first chapter of the Book of Exodus, you will read as follows:

"8. Now there arose up a new king over Egypt, which knew not Joseph.

9. And he said unto his people, Behold, the people of the children of Israel are more and mightier than we:

10. Come on, let us deal wisely [*sic*] with them; lest they multiply, and it come to pass, that, when there falleth out any war, they join also unto our enemies, and fight against us, and so get them up out of the land.

11. Therefore they did set over them taskmasters to afflict them with their burdens. And they built for Pharaoh treasure cities, Pithom and Raamses.

12. But the more they afflicted them, the more they multiplied and grew. And they were grieved because of the children of Israel.

13. And the Egyptians made the children of Israel to serve with rigour:

14. And they made their lives bitter with hard bondage, in morter, and in brick, and in all manner of service in the field: all their service, wherein they made them serve, *was* with rigour."

My cultural historians here tell me that Joseph lived about 1,350 years before Christ, so, roughly speaking, there has been a Palestine question for the last 3,300 years. The Jews, of course, claim an historic heritage to Palestine and the Arab viewpoint can perhaps be best illustrated by a story told me by Norman Armour, a distinguished Assistant Secretary of State, who has just retired. Mr. Armour said that at dinner one night he sat next to Prince Faisal of Saudi Arabia, who opened the conversation by saying that the Arabs were about to move into southern Spain and live there. Armour was somewhat taken aback and laughingly said, "Have you told Franco about it?" Prince Faisal said, "Certainly not. We lived there 2,000 years ago and there is no reason why we should not move back in. That is the theory on which you are backing Palestine."

During my first month here came the publication of the famous Bernadotte Report, and the statement of Secretary Marshall that this report would represent the Palestine policy of the United States. My duty became to "sell" the report, and its implications, to the Egyptian Government, and I shall not bore you with the warm reception which I have received from all Egyptians here who blame our Government and that of Great Britain for the present impasse; who are completely incapable of arguing wisely or with restraint on the matter, and who shout to high Heaven that they will never rest until the last Jew is driven into the sea. You will, no doubt, shed a tear for the plight of the American Ambassador faced with the cries of the Arabs "We will never accept partition" and the cries of the Jews "We will never accept the Bernadotte Plan."

I have no desire to add to the mountain of written and printed history and controversy that has grown out of Palestine. I have tried to take the position with the Arabs that I had no desire to argue with them about the past or about their theories of right and justice. I have tried to tell them that we are facing a *fait accompli* in the existence of the Israeli State, and whether the Arabs like it or not it is here to stay; that the Arabs can never progress and advance culturally or economically until they have peace, and that a fair and honest settlement will be of great benefit to the Arab States when it comes, hard as it is to face. What I try to say to my Jewish friends in the United States I can perhaps best illustrate by the following quotations from a letter which I wrote last week to a very distinguished Zionist in New York.

"I have no quarrel with you over the concern of American Jewry about the plight of their co-religionists abroad nor can I dispute your statement as to the variations in American policy and the policies of the United Nations over the past few months nor do I question your phrase that 'Anything can happen at the present session of the United Nations.' My supreme convictions only extend to two ideas: one, that if there is some small and

*Above*—The commissioner of the American Red Cross for the Pacific Ocean Areas holds a meeting of his Executive Committee outside a Red Cross hut in the New Hebrides Islands. *Below*—The author, center left, as American Red Cross commissioner talking with the island commander of Iwo Jima, atop Suribachi at the exact spot where a few days before the famous photograph of the Marines raising the flag had been taken

*Above*—Secretary Marshall gives the newly appointed ambassador final instructions. *Below*—Entering the Presidential Palace in Warsaw, Poland, for the presentation of credentials, after saluting the troops on the right. The staff of the American Embassy is in the background

reasonable compromise on both sides in this matter, it can be solved with the Bernadotte Plan as a structural beginning and, secondly, that no nation or group of nations ever won a war or ever will win a war.

"I do not think that I can wisely enter into a long argument with you or with your associates as to the relative advantage to Israel of the various partition schemes. I do believe firmly, however, that the Bernadotte geographical outline for the new Jewish State is wiser and more advantageous for Israel than any other plan which has been presented. The exchange of the desert area of the Negeb for the Galilee territory together with the creation of a far more workable and viable State seems to me to far outweigh any disadvantages in the program. And as a Christian with some knowledge of the veneration in which Jerusalem is held by Jews, Moslems, and Christians alike and with the historical knowledge of the wars that it has caused the world over many centuries, I cannot but believe that it is best for everyone that it should be internationalized.

"It is difficult, even impossible, for you amid the comforts and the pleasurable excitements of New York to visualize the human suffering that the present dispute is causing. There are almost as many Arab refugees wandering homeless through the Arab States unfed, unclothed, and without even a blanket against the oncoming bitterness of winter as there are Jews in Palestine. They are beginning to die and will continue to die as winter comes. There isn't a great deal of difference to a suffering human being between death by cold in the Syrian mountains and death in a German or Polish concentration camp. On the other hand, countless Jews in Arab countries are being persecuted and killed, and every day that this struggle continues makes the possibility of reconciliation less. Surely some way can be found to end this horror.

"And now perhaps I am making an appeal to self-interest rather than to reason when I tell you that our best political students here feel that every day Zionism is losing world sympathy because of violence and intransigeance while every day the Arabs are gaining support because of a refugee situation which is currently more heart-rending than that of Europe's Jews. They

think that the humanitarian considerations which won American
support for Zionism is now militant for the Arab and against
the Jews, who many feel have created a new half million of displaced persons, 80 per cent women and children. Mass deaths
of Arabs this winter will turn the world's heart against whoever
leaves this problem unsettled and will particularly swing the
United States' opinion. The United States is famous for thinking
with its heart. It has little patience with nationalism as such and
has supported Israel chiefly because it has been touched by the
plight of Jewish refugees and disgusted by Nazi nationalist
cruelty and callousness. What then as America begins to feel
jolted by the violence of Israel's nationalism and touched by the
plight of thousands of starving refugees? The Iowa farmer and
the Missouri gas station man don't care a damn whether Arabs
or Jews have Palestine but they do care a lot about starving
children.

"Taking the Bernadotte Plan as a basis and realizing that Jews
and Arabs alike are unanimously crying: 'We will never accept
it,' cannot some clearly stated workable boundaries be proposed
by the Israel Government which would be supported by the
Jews of America and which would show enough compromise
and will for peace that it would not need political jockeyings
and overstatements for trading sake? As it is, with all the hullabaloo and political speeches on both sides, it seems almost hopeless to determine where truth and fairness lie. Surely, having
created the long wished for Jewish State and Homeland, you
must not risk the adverse judgments of the world, the loss of all
you have gained, if the United Nations with your honest help
can find the solution. Surely no one can take the responsibility
in these days when we all struggle for peace in continuing a
war, which, if I read the first chapter of Exodus right, has been
going on since the days of Joseph in Egypt, if a fair and peaceful
solution can be found.

"You tell me how a compromise solution can be found and, if
it is possible, I will devote every resource that I have towards
its conclusions but I am certainly completely impotent against
the cries of both sides: 'We will have none of it.' I would not
urge the Bernadotte Plan on you if I did not wholeheartedly

and completely believe in it. I know perfectly well if you were the sole arbiter for the Arab States we could solve this problem in a day but we are not. You and your associates are crusaders for Zionism. I am merely a crusader for peace and, unfortunately, living in an atmosphere where not one American that I know in the entire Arab world but believes that the Arabs are right and the Jews are wrong. I may have become a little prejudiced, but I do not think so. I really believe that I have been honest and judicial in looking at it all from the points of view of Zionism, the Moslem world, and world peace in urging you to accept $\frac{9}{10}$ of a loaf, if you care to look at it that way, rather than no bread.

"Knowing you and the public-spirited men who are part of your Zionist movement as I do, I must know that you are Americans first and Zionists second. At the moment, unfortunately, the solution of the Palestine problem is overshadowed by the great problem of Communism and the crisis in Berlin. You have only to look at the map to realize that every hour that the Palestine problem is unsolved is an hour of advantage to Communism and to Russia. I do not go along with the rising hue and cry of the Arabs that Palestine is a creature of Communism, but I do believe that the vulnerability of the terrorists and other motley groups in Palestine, which always exist and attend upon the accouchement of a new nation, together with Israel's need for arms, makes Israel a danger spot so long as it is fighting for its life. You will not interpret these comments, I know, as a statement in any way that Zionism and Communism go hand in hand but merely, I hope, as a sketch of the dangers which exist in the situation so long as settlement is delayed."

In any event I believe my best diplomacy is the fact that I have really spent the greater part of my time here in Cairo in attempting to obtain money and supplies, and to organize the work, for relief of the homeless Arabs who have been displaced by the fighting in Palestine. I have tried to convince the Arab Governments once again that the first interest of the United States is in the welfare of humanity rather than in politics. Judging from the publicity I have received, I have made some progress, but, of course, I am still violently attacked in the Egyptian press for my statements that I believe in the American policy of a reasonable and workable partition for Palestine.

Last week with the Military and Civil Air Attachés, correspondents of the Associated Press, the United Press, and the New York Times, I flew up to Syria and Lebanon and spent three days driving all over these countries to visit refugee camps. I hope that many of the pictures which we took showing the utter misery of these people have by this time been published in the United States and, in any event, I know that I have had some influence in my constant pressure on the United States Government and private philanthropies to come to their aid. As I may paraphrase other statements I have made, there is no ideology in the mind of a starving baby and it cares much more for a piece of bread than for all of Zionism or the Moslem world.

After Beirut and Damascus, deep in the Syrian mountains, I had planned to go to Amman in Transjordan and thence to Jerusalem and its near-by refugee camps, but on the day we were to start south from Damascus the fighting broke out again and we sadly wended our way back to Cairo by way of Cyprus, to escape the raiding planes of Egyptians and Jews in the Negeb. If peace reigns for a while, I plan to try it again.

As I write all this, we all sit here as you do, I know, under the deep shadow of the situation in Berlin, well knowing that the little problems of the Near East of Arabs and Jews seem small in the minds of the world outside as compared with the possibilities that lie in the Berlin blockade. We have good daily news service and news broadcasts from both the Voice of America and the BBC and we read the last reports at eleven o'clock at night and the morning papers at seven, hoping against hope that there will come some good news out of this troubled and embattled world.

I firmly believe that the Palestine question could be settled in a few days if the Russo-American question were settled.

No good news has come so far, so the day starts with disappointment and as the Embassy begins to come to life at eight o'clock in the morning I am soon immersed in countless cables and dispatches from Washington, London, Paris and the Arab countries. There is the usual quota of visitors from the oil world and from American manufacturers bringing in their little wet hands for me to hold because Palestine and the lack of American dollars in Egypt has completely stopped the wheels of Egyptian-American trade.

Egypt is a very wealthy country but it has no dollars and about its only way to get dollars, unless it asks for a large American loan, which it has not done, is through the sale of its long staple cotton. However, the United States has a tariff quota on long staple cotton and while at the earnest behests of the State Department it was considerably increased for the current year, it is still not sufficiently large to take care of much more than 10 per cent of the Egyptian long staple crop, which represents about 70 per cent of the exports of Egypt. The cotton year starts on September 20, I think, and this year the Egyptians learned quite a bit about the integrity of their Russian friends. It seems that the Government here sold a tremendous amount of long staple cotton to Russia, under an agreement that it would not be resold outside of Russia, and then kept the full amount of their United States quota to sell in America for dollars. Now, as the story goes, a number of ships appeared outside of New York harbor on the evening before the cotton quota year opened on September 20. By noon the next day the Egyptian cotton quota was filled but, unfortunately, most of it was the cotton which the Russians had purchased from Egypt, and the Egyptian cargoes, which were a little on the late side, had to wend their way with loud lamentations, back to the Nile.

On oil—while Egypt is substantially self-sufficient with its small oil fields—the great fairyland of Near East oil lies to the east of us, in Iran, Iraq, Saudi Arabia and Kuwait, a small sheikdom lying at the borderland of Saudi Arabia, Iraq and Iran. Here lies an oil reserve probably greater than all the oil reserves of North and South America put together and controlled generally by the British, American, French and Dutch with the American interests probably in the ascendant, and represented by Standard of California, the Texas Company, Standard of New Jersey, Socony-Vacuum, and Gulf. These great fields are now in general shut off from pipeline distribution to the Mediterranean due to the war disturbances here, and even the construction of the great projected 30-inch pipelines from the fields to the shores of the eastern Mediterranean has slowed up or been abandoned.

All this adds to the tremendous prosperity of the Suez Canal. I have driven along the Canal from Suez to Port Said, stopping off for the night at Fayid to visit the British Army Headquarters under the leadership of the charming and efficient Sir John Crocker. Through the Canal daily go a long line of merchant ships and tankers, and you may realize something of its tremendous current prosperity if you read the Canal tariffs and know that the Canal tolls for a loaded tanker amount to approximately $15,000 and the tolls for the return of the empty tanker amount to about $7,500. Thus, the cost of the transporting of roughly 100,000 barrels of oil around through the Red Sea and the Canal, from the Persian Gulf, amounts in tolls alone to about 23 cents a barrel and brings the total cost to an estimated 50 cents a barrel. When it is realized that the cost of pipeline delivery to the same eastern Mediterranean ports, if the pipeline is ever completed, would amount to about 15 cents a barrel, the tremendous economic value of the pipeline can be understood.

Here, then, where Africa, Europe and Asia meet, and where the Arab world lies astride the Anglo-American lifelines, the Suez Canal and the proposed pipelines, lies also the great world reserve of petroleum. If you will cast your eyes a little farther north on the map you will see a tip of Soviet Russia pressing down from the north between the Black Sea and the Caspian and bordering on the extreme north of Iran. *Here is the danger spot, here the possibility—a lightning dash by the Russian armies to cut off the Western world from the oil fields and possibly even attempt the Canal itself.*

This letter might go on indefinitely, but perhaps I have brought you enough gloom for the moment. I could write indefinitely of the peculiar position of Transjordan in the Arab picture, the astonishing family relationships of the rulers of the Near East, the jealousies and the thousand cross-currents which agitate the waters of a settlement. In the meantime, the United States and England have vacillated for months in their decisions here as has the United Nations. Truces come and go, but perhaps this is the darkest hour, for during the last week we have been subjected every night here in Cairo to blackouts and the terrific rattle and roar of anti-aircraft fire. Whether these alarms and excursions are for practice or for politics, or whether they represent real defense, we do not know. Sufficient it is to be subjected to this war of nerves and to find the Embassy roof covered with ack-ack fragments in the morning.

The sun is out, the birds are singing in the palm trees, the Nile flows gently to the sea; every prospect pleases and only man is vile.

*Sincerely yours,*
STANTON GRIFFIS

## THE FOREIGN SERVICE
## OF THE
## UNITED STATES OF AMERICA

AMERICAN EMBASSY
*Cairo, Egypt, March 7, 1949*

*Dear Joe:*

The last time I wrote you one of these letters was at Halloween last year. It was a mistake. Little did I know what the pixies had in store for me at that time and that I would shortly afterwards rejoice in the far-flung title of "Director of the United Nations Relief for Palestine Refugees." Throughout most of the alphabetical era in Washington and since that time I have been able to sidestep most of the letter omelets but now I am just UNRPR to you.

I suppose that a fish sometimes vaguely wonders how he got in the ocean or an elephant in the forest and I have frequently said to myself, "How in the world did I get into this job?" but I am afraid that I know the answer. I talked too much. I'll tell you a great truth, if you will keep it a secret, and that is if anyone becomes too vocal about a job that should be done someone inevitably says "Well, you do it" and that, my children, is how I became grocer boy for 750,000 starving and ill-smelling Arabs. It all goes back to my arrival in Cairo last August, when I realized the really terrible plight of the Arab hordes which had left Palestine and its gunfire and terror and had scattered throughout the Arab world to live as nomads under the most appalling conditions and dependent for food and shelter on the generosity of the world. I shouted the need of help from the housetops. I wrote and cabled to whoever would listen to me, obtained temporary help from the American Red Cross, and continued to shout.

In November, without warning, came the usual terse "Come soonest" Marshallian telegram ordering me to Paris and Washington. Forty-eight hours later I was sitting in meetings of the American Delegation to the United Nations in Paris listening to the clear, concise directives of Marshall, the brilliantly legalistic comments of Jessup, the clarity of Rusk, the incisive suggestions of Ben Cohen, the somewhat florid declarations of Dulles, and the almost dreamy idealism of Eleanor Roosevelt. Lew Douglas had come over from London for the meeting and, as usual, increased my admiration for the soft brilliance of his Persian mind. Over the whole group, however, stood the Olympian figure of the Secretary of State who has now left us. Maybe I am a hero worshiper. Of George Marshall I certainly am. We shall not see his like again.

Having been aborted by the American Delegation of all my facts, fancies and opinions regarding Palestine and the refugees, I took off after two days in Paris for Washington.

I have lost track of the number of times I have flown the ocean. It must be between forty and fifty, I imagine, but this flight was plain horror Number One. On time at Shannon from Paris, we were diverted after a couple of hours, because of head winds, to the Azores, and I had visions of a happy stopover in Bermuda, but we were diverted again to Newfoundland and my little advertised flight of fifteen hours from Paris to New York turned out to be a full thirty-one hours in the air.

And so to Washington. There, the Big Boss asked me if I would take over the whole job of Palestine relief, taking leave in the meantime as Ambassador to Egypt. You who read this may belong to the forty-eight per cent of the people of the United States who seemed to prefer Dewey, but Truman is to me a really great man and I am frank to say that there is little he could ask me to do that I would not do, even though I thought he was a little unfair to the bitches of America in his comments on Drew Pearson. So the answer was, "Boss, if you want me to do this job, I will do it but on one condition, that is, that I will go back by ship and not fly." He said, "Of course, you can. Take all the time you want." There followed hectic conferences in the State Department, loud cries of "Hurry, Hurry" from Trygve Lie and his associates meeting in Paris. And so we compromised—I flew back. This time a perfect trip in a perfect plane, to sleep all the way in a comfortable berth; fifteen hours to Paris came true.

There is one remark of the President which sticks in my mind. As I left his desk, he walked with me to the door and I said, "Mr. President, I am going a long way away. Don't forget me." His response was "Don't worry. I never forget my friends and I never remember my enemies." Maybe there was a little double talk in the second part of this comment.

Back in Paris, I found myself in the center ring of the greatest show on earth. Don't give a thought to Barnum and Bailey if you have a chance to see the United Nations at work. How anything good comes out of this fabulous Tower of Babel, vaudeville show and twenty-four-hour debating society, God only knows, but come it does and more will come. Through all the backings and fillings, decrees on Palestine, Indonesia and way stations, to which no one pays the slightest attention, with commissions, sub-commissions, committees piled on ad hoc committees, partition plans and one thing or another has come at last a gleam of hope of peace in the Near East. Maybe it is due in the last analysis to the genius and dogged determination of a young American Negro named Ralph Bunche, who for six weeks held the Egyptians and the Jews together around the table in Rhodes. Perhaps it is due to the desperate desire of all men for peace. But somehow it has come out of the crowded womb of the United Nations.

I was glad to get away from Paris, albeit loaded with directives, financial instructions and whatnot, and get to Geneva to make my contracts for the refugee work with the three operating agencies, the League of Red Cross Societies, the International Committee of the Red Cross, and the American Quakers, to each of whom were allotted geographical parts of Palestine and the surrounding countries. In Geneva, where the Swiss milk their cows with their left hands, and all tourists with their right, which is stronger, I was ensconced in a great modernistic office about the size of Madison Square Garden in the almost deserted Palais des Nations, home of the ill-fated League of Nations. We had everything but heat and most of the time it felt as though one of the glaciers from the near-by Alps ran directly down our corridor. The ghost of Woodrow Wilson must have shivered as it made its trips through the deserted halls. In any event, with my budgets and contracts prepared, my Near East staff recruited and the fogs of Switzerland clearing for a day, I flew to Nice, Rome and Cairo, arriving the day before Christmas to plunge into the job.

I shall not bore you with much of the story. I have two jobs, one to shake the tambourine for international contributions, and the other, as I said before, to play grocer boy for Arab refugees. I am charged with raising $32,000,000, which as it comes in I am spending for food, tents, blankets and medical supplies for the distributing agencies. I have an elemental job and that is to keep these refugees alive, sheltered, and in reasonable health until Allah or the United Nations settles their future and the question of their absorption back into their homeland and/or into other Arab nations. I buy and distribute for them each month some 7,500 tons of flour, about a thousand tons of pulses (dried vegetables to you), and thousands of other tons of dates, sugar, edible oils and such other delicacies as we receive as gifts in kind from foreign nations. The Arabs will not eat the ordinary American flour, so I must perforce create an organization to mix it with barley or with corn. Most of them have never heard of canned fish, of which I receive hundreds of tons from the Scandinavian nations, so I must work out a trade of fish for sugar or wheat (cable me if you can use any nice canned herring). I receive choice tidbits of tons of canned meat, which is anathema to the Arabs for fear it contains pork. I have gifts of French francs, Swiss francs, Swedish kroner, Dutch guilders, Indian rupees, English pounds, Egyptian pounds, Syrian pounds, Palestinian pounds and a few other oddities. It is just one damn thing after another.

My hair is gone and my accountant's hair has turned gray. What is a herring in Oslo worth in Chinese dollars for delivery in Port Said? You compute it.

I have offices in Lake Success, Geneva, Cairo, Port Said and Beirut, but my actual office is where I hang up my hat. I have made four swings around the Arab world and I shall not try to tell you of the life in small Arab cities. It might disturb your sleep. Ah— the joys of the Philadelphia Hotel at Amman, Transjordan, with that bathroom way down the hall, not difficult to find if one merely follows one's Jimmy Durante but always occupied when you get there, those delightful beds which you occupy with some 50,000 other inhabitants whose presence does not become known until the lights are out, the wonderful central heating which brings the temperature up to at least 40 by late afternoon. That food so like the Colony. Heigh ho, humaday, it is all in the spirit of adventure.

But I did have one very pleasant evening in Transjordan when I dined with King Abdullah at his winter palace about halfway between Jericho and Amman. I was told by Wells Stabler, our Chargé d'Affaires, that we would arrive at six, that promptly at six-thirty the King would leave for a few minutes for his prayers to Mecca, that we would dine at seven and that the King would disappear immediately after dinner for exactly fifteen minutes (nobody knows why), and that shortly after his reappearance we could make our adieu with the usual amenities. Everything went exactly as described. We had a very plain wholesome dinner about as simple and tasteless as one used to get at the White House in the Roosevelt regime. His Majesty left and returned on schedule but throughout was charming, brilliant and entertaining, entirely through an interpreter.

Abdullah is, of course, far and away the most brilliant, the most ambitious and the ablest of all the Near East rulers, and I will miss my guess if he does not come out of the present mess with a tremendous territorial acquisition for Transjordan. We left Amman promptly at eight-thirty, I wearing the King's personal headdress of the Arab Legion, which he presented to me together with his photograph. I personally wouldn't give fifty cents for all of Transjordan but Abdullah is wise and smart. He is 68, but if he lives, watch him!*

On the drive back to Amman, with a royal guard of honor in a jeep with machine guns, I told Stabler I would like to send His Majesty a gift and asked if he knew anything he wanted. Stabler replied, "There is one thing he desperately wants and that is a wire voice recorder" which you may know under the name of Dicta-phone. I asked Stabler why he wanted this and he said, "Well, the other night he was dining with King —— of —— and made a deal at dinner time. After dinner the two Kings got into a brawl and Abdullah entirely denied his agreement, whereupon King —— clapped his hands and played back to Abdullah everything that had been said during the dinner. I guess Abdullah wants to try this game himself." Anyway, I telegraphed New York and had the machine sent to him, and when the Conciliation Commis-sion came through here the other day and told me they had dined with Abdullah, I asked them if they had seen the machine. They said they hadn't, so I assume it now rests peacefully under His Majesty's dinner table.

My refugee constituents extend in a wide crescent from Gaza and the Negeb on the south to north Lebanon and Aleppo near the Turkish-Syrian borders on the north. No man knows the exact number, for efforts to take a real census are confused by migra-tions and by the fact that wandering Bedouins and locals, scenting the prospect of a free meal, are apt to join the camps. Furthermore, most of them are named Abdul or Ahmed, and as, to the untutored Western eye, they all look alike, it is extremely difficult to sort them out. There are, however, approximately 100,000 in the Lebanon and another 100,000 each in Syria and Transjordan. There are from 225,000 to 300,000 in eastern Arab-held Palestine and something under a quarter of a million concentrated in the Gaza District still held by the Egyptian Army. Gaza is, of course, the locale of the Samson and Delilah story but it is a pretty tragic-looking place now. I haven't seen De Mille around for any location shots and I have been unable to locate Delilah or any very tasty modern counterpart.

Our main problem is not supplies of food but distribution of it.

*Abdullah was assassinated in Jerusalem shortly after this was written.

It is impossible to go through the Jewish lines from Lebanon in the north or from Port Said in the south to reach the refugees of East Palestine and Transjordan. Hence in the north we must purchase and deliver most of our supplies in Beirut for shipment by truck over the mountains to Damascus, thence to Amman in Transjordan and back into the Jericho District. The Gaza problem is relatively simple, for the Egyptian Government delivers food from Port Said to Gaza warehouses for distribution by the Quakers, but in the north, where the mountain pass between Beirut and Damascus frequently is closed by snow for days at a time, the problem is a tough one. The problem of dates we are able to solve by trucking them into all camps direct from Iraq. As the winter passes and the warm weather begins, our medical problems will develop and the ever-present danger of hot weather epidemics will be with us. However, we are preparing hospitals, storing medical supplies and, in general, making pretty extensive preparations for this danger.

On my return from one of the Arab swings (I have traveled so much and gone so hard for the last two months that I have no recollection of dates and little places), I did have one interesting day for I decided to take a short vacation and visit the Upper Nile and go fishing in the Red Sea. We flew in the Military Attaché's plane to Luxor and for an hour circled the Valley of the Kings, the temples, the tombs, the monuments of ancient Egypt. I have seen so much of archeology around Cairo that I had no great ambition to tramp around more ruins, and I see one every day at shaving time, so we cruised leisurely in the air at a low level, looking at these wonders of the world, including the Temple of Karnak and King Tut's tomb, which I assume is now occupied by the Republican Party. Dewey is, I believe, in the National Museum at Cairo. Then to land at Luxor with the exquisite beauty of the Nile and the hills beyond at our feet. In the air at three we flew to Hurghada on the Red Sea for our fishing. Here lies one of the many oil towns of the Near East without a sprig of green vegetation for hundreds of miles; fresh water even has to be brought in by boat from Suez—a scene of utter desolation. The good God puts oil in strange places. Yet I was received by the Military Governor with great honors. All of the troops, I think twenty, were lined up to give me a smart salute and we were taken on a tour which included a biological laboratory and an art exhibition by the school children. Ah, the joys of adventure. I made the mistake of breaking out a couple of bottles of scotch for dinner, with the result that the local grandees remained until the small hours of the morning. As for the fishing, we could hardly stand up against the wind off the Red Sea let alone embark in a fishing boat. But we had excellent Seattle canned salmon for dinner. We took off from the desert (without a sign of a landing field) early the next morning for the relative comforts of Cairo.

As I have pointed out, we see glimmers of light and rays of hope for peace in the Near East following the Egyptian-Jewish armistice, after months of Egyptian cries that "We will never recognize Israel let alone negotiate with the Jews." At last they have been lured around a table and as I write this, Jewish negotiations with Lebanon and Transjordan are going on. Out of it may come a semblance of peace, and the wounds of the badly defeated Egyptians may be healed with the years. Touring Tel Aviv and Jewish-held Jerusalem, it is not difficult to see why the crusading, organized and hard-working Jews have been able to defy the whole Arab world with its laziness, its corruption, its dreamy philosophies, and its fantastic mixture of great wealth and hideous poverty. Tel Aviv and Jewish-held new Jerusalem constitute a land of milk and honey, of organization, of modernism; that contrasts sharply with the Arab cities of approximately the same size and particularly with Old Jerusalem held by the Arabs and the site of the holy places of three out of the four great world religions.

"In my book," it is certainly a mistake for the Christian tourist to visit Old Jerusalem. The Via Dolorosa, along which Christ was supposed to have carried His cross, is a horror of filthy, stinking Arab shops, little improved, I think, as to sanitation, ptomaine or literacy during the past 2,000 years. The Church of the Holy Sepulchre and Calvary are beset with commercialism and dirt and I am still sufficiently naïve to want to keep my childhood illusions about Jerusalem. I will take a De Mille picture or a Sunday school colored picture of the old days rather than see it as it really is. On the other hand, while, of course, the Jewish wailing wall is deserted, the Moslem mosques are clean and well kept. I devoutly hope that some day some great world organization such as Lawrence Langner has visualized will make it their work to restore Old Jerusalem to a semblance of beauty. Call it what you will, or be of what religion you may, the beautiful illusion is better to create faith than the stinking reality which is the Via Dolorosa today. Langner's idea would be a modern drive of the smelly money changers from the temple.

There are a thousand different opinions as to what has caused all the difficulties out here and much of the unrest throughout the world today, but I think I have the elements of explanation. Assuming that the basic battle between Communism and Democracy would have eventuated in any event, one must realize that way back about the time of and following the First World War, we created with Woodrow Wilson the idea of the determination of small nations, the right of all small nations to govern themselves with freedom and democracy. We probably overlooked the fact that nations which have been governed by other great and larger nations cannot in an hour, a year or even perhaps in a generation, be given their freedom and their self-determination without political chaos. We say to ourselves that the Colonies were able to do it in 1776, but I do not see any Washingtons, Jeffersons, or Adamses around these parts. I am not referring now to the age-old quarrel between Jews and Arabs, but I am referring to the political strife in Egypt, Syria, Lebanon, Iraq, and the other Arab nations, in India and Pakistan, in Indonesia and Indo-China, wherever nations have been suddenly cast adrift from the yoke of a strong ruler and must necessarily go through the birth pains of democracy. Too much speed is expected before this process can be completed. And in this very delay, and in the turmoil which accompanies it, is the fertile soil for the seeds of Communist infiltration, which will promise all things to all men. So the United States as the burden bearer of the world must be patient, watchful and cautious to see that these backward nations are given a helping and encouraging hand as they take their places in the sun, lest they fail to solve their own internal problems and thereby fall victims to the philosophies of the Kremlin.

In this specific problem of the Near East I earnestly hope that when the bitterness and enmities die down, the Jews and the Arabs will trade together, that the Jews will be reasonable in their territorial aspirations, and that the Arabs will forget for all time their fanatical leanings towards "Holy War." The three great problems of the Conciliation Commission here are: (1) the settlement of borders; (2) the solution of the refugee problem; and (3) the internationalization of Jerusalem. I believe that the borders problem can be settled. I believe that with any reasonably judicial view by the Jews and the Arab States and with peace itself the refugee problem can be settled; and that the internationalization of Jerusalem is of vital importance to prevent wars which have been going on since the days of the Crusaders.

As I have been writing this letter, I have received orders from the United Nations to return to the United States early in April to report on the whole refugee situation, so I am off on the long but pleasant trek again. And as I write this, I have news of Jim Forrestal's resignation as Secretary of National Defense. This is indeed an unhappy day for the nation for certainly he has done one of the finest jobs in the history of American Government. With the loss of my three good friends in Washington, Mr. Marshall, Bob Lovett and Jim Forrestal, I begin to feel like the boy on the burning deck.

*Sincerely yours,*
STANTON GRIFFIS

The message from Trygve Lie telling me to return to Flushing Meadows and report on my stewardship as Director of the relief work fell on happy and receptive ears. I was completely discouraged, and felt myself entirely impotent so long as the Arabs and the Jews maintained their intransigent attitude toward refugees. The Arabs refused to take care of their own, and the Jews with equal determination and already overwhelmed with their burden of immigrants, refused to permit the return of their former Palestine citizens. The light went out when Ralph Bunche, who had concluded his work at Rhodes, returned to the United States.

My feeling that the problem was at least temporarily in-soluble so long as it remained political and not humanitarian has been mirrored through the past four years by the appoint-ment and resignation of commissions of all sorts, conciliation commissions, relief and work commissions, and commissions of every hue for tackling the problem of the refugees. I earnestly believe that the refugees themselves are in a worse situation than they were when, with high hopes and optimism, I tackled the problem in the autumn of 1948. Probably they are no worse off physically, nor worse off as to supplies, food, and shelter, for untold millions have been spent by the United States and other nations on their behalf, but the degenerative process through years of being wards of the United Nations, and of having their dreams of returning to the Palestine home-land shattered and their will to work destroyed, has brought the inevitable results.

As I turned my face toward New York, I had no intention whatever of returning to the Near East. My year of uncertain diet and constant traveling in depressing circumstances had taken its toll. While the Egyptian armies had moved safely back to Cairo, another army of parasites from the canals of the Nile had moved into my lower plumbing; and the sand-storms and glaring sun of the desert had brought about an eye condition necessitating an operation, which was performed shortly by my old friend and tennis opponent Dr. Algernon Reese.

Flying across North Africa, we dropped low to look at the battlefields where once the pride of the Italian Army had been destroyed, and where Rommel, the desert scourge, had been thrown back almost at the gates of Alexandria. The rainless desert still showed the tracks and counter-tracks of countless tanks, and here and there disabled and deserted machines of war lay on the sands. I was en route to Rome, still passing the hat for my refugee fund, and hoping to obtain a small contribution from the Italian Government, and perhaps something from the Vatican, although its own organizations had done yeoman work with the refugees.

From De Gasperi I was able to wangle 100,000 yards of cotton cloth greatly needed for Arab clothing, but while, as I expected, I was not able to obtain a contribution from the Vatican, I received something far richer in an audience with His Holiness the Pope. Finishing my discussion with the Vatican Secretary of State, I was told that the Holy Father wished to see me, and was given a parchment telling me of a prospective audience with him at eleven-thirty that morning. Never have I had a richer intellectual and spiritual hour. His Holiness not only knew the details of my friendship for the Vatican in Poland, where I occasionally acted as secret messenger and mailman for the letters to the Holy See from the high Catholic dignitaries fighting for their very lives in Poland, but he knew as well every detail of the work of the Refugee Relief Commission. His erudition, his knowledge of languages, but above all the great spiritual qualities that he emanated, left a deep and lasting impression upon me. I have met many kings and princes, both temporal and of the church; I have hobnobbed with presidents and dictators, but in my life will stand out forever, the memory of the thrilling audience with Pope Pius XII.

Returning to the State Department and the President, I had high hopes of going to France. I had been twice refused the English post and was now reluctant to seek it because of my friendship for Jim Bruce, then in Argentina, who felt that he was in line for the job. My talk with the great white father in the White House was charming, but France was not to be, and probably properly so, as Dave Bruce was doing a magnificent job there. The President wanted me to go to Argentina, but barring the two highest posts, France and England, I did not want to continue in the Diplomatic Service. After the White House interview I returned to the State Department and dictated the following letter to the President.

*April 5, 1949*

*My dear Mr. President:*

Confirming our talk yesterday, I again want to express my appreciation to you for your expression of confidence in suggesting that I accept the high post which you offered me. However, my mind is quite clear that the time has come under the circumstances for me to step back into private life.

The rule of "three strikes and out" is a good baseball rule and I am always happy to accept your decisions as the national arbiter. After two strikes on London and one on Paris I am content to go back to the dugout. I have no feeling of "kill the umpire" and only one of understanding and appreciation of the almost countless hard decisions which you have to constantly make.

You may rest assured that I have been profoundly appreciative of your confidence in me and extremely proud of the opportunities which I have had to serve under you.

The State Department boys seem to feel that I should stick with the refugee work until the full appropriation is safely through Congress, which should be within the next few weeks, and this will give me time also to arrange my successor with Mr. Trygve Lie. Accordingly, I will appreciate it if you will accept my resignation as Ambassador to Egypt, as of, say, May 15 or June 1.

Enclosed is a letter for public consumption, if it should seem necessary for use.

*Affectionately yours,*
STANTON GRIFFIS

*President Harry S. Truman*
*The White House*

I returned to New York, made my pessimistic report to the United Nations, and went tuna-fishing in Bimini in June with Gene Tunney, Bernard Gimbel, Archie Gray, Sidney Rheinstein and Mike Lerner, permanent president of the Bimini Tuna, Gin Rummy, and Fourth Helping Club. A new member, Jack La Gorce, master mind of the National Geographic Society, has but recently been elected. I returned for one month to Geneva to renew the relief contracts with the Red Crosses and the Quakers, and thought that for good and all I was back in private life.

## CHAPTER THIRTEEN

### UNCLE SAM'S CABIN IN
### ARGENTINA (with little Eva)

It was midsummer in 1949 when I returned from my negotiations in Geneva, ostensibly winding up my work as the
director of the Palestine relief activities, although nominally
I remained in charge until September. The prospect of a return to private life was entrancing, but unentrancing was the
prospect of a trip to the Ophthalmological Institute at Medical Center for a long-delayed eye operation. There is no reason that I should fail to share the great human desire to tell
about my operation, even as I am reminded of the ancient
cartoon of the two eunuchs sitting together as one inquires,
"Have I ever told you about my operation?" It comes to
my mind more vividly because I have just returned from a
few days in Palm Beach, where to my great financial detri-
ment I played bridge daily with Webster the cartoonist, who
gives the nation its morning laughter with Mr. Milquetoast
and his hatred of canasta. Webby, who looks like a combination of an old English sheep dog and a deeply spiritual prince
of the church, whom all men love and whose drawings are
dipped in a mixture of acid and honey, has for years reduced
my income tax through his bridge acumen. Now he fears an
eye operation, and to cheer him a bit I played one of the
eunuchs with him and told him about mine.

It was midday when I was given a couple of pills, someone

pricked either side of my eye with a needle, and I was wheeled into the operating room. I had seen nothing but white-robed attendants and no doctors, and after what I thought was a reasonable wait I burst out in bitterness, saying, "Where is that damn doctor Reese?" A voice from faraway answered me, "I am right behind you," and from an equal distance I said, "When are you going to start cutting?" Through the fog I heard him answer, "I am almost through." Again through a long sleep but with a good deal of venom at the delay, I said, "When are you going to start stitching?" and back through the fog rolled the voice, "I am just putting in the last stitch." So fear will remain as long as hospitals and the necessity for operations exist, but so long as man is made for suffering there must be a prayer of thanksgiving to the thousands of men living and dead who have developed the great science of anesthesia and the greater art of surgery.

The eyes returned to normal and I became ambassador to Argentina—but not as a direct result. I became ambassador to Argentina not very much on my own power, but chiefly because my ancient crony Jim Bruce, who had been occupying the post for two years, was anxious to quit and get back to Washington, where he could keep closer touch on the political pulse. His problem, in order to obtain his own release, was to provide a substitute acceptable to the President. Like an old fire horse I answered the ringing of the bell. In any event, a tour of duty with Perón and his ubiquitous wife Evita, seemed exciting and interesting, and I had never been to South America except during the few hours of my trip back from Lisbon in 1943. I sailed for Buenos Aires in late October with the usual pomp and circumstance, having counseled at great length with Nelson Rockefeller, the master of the good-neighbor policy in South America, and with Spruille Braden, the American ambassador in office when Perón came to power. To him I observed, "I may stay longer in Argentina than you did, but I will never be as famous there." In that prediction I was certainly correct.

The transition from the living quarters which I had occupied in Egypt for a year to the great Embassy in Buenos Aires was startling. In Cairo, chiefly on account of the facts that the American Government owned no ambassador's residence there, and that I had been engaged almost continually in other countries on refugee work, I lived in a four-room apartment in the Semiramis Hotel. The correspondent of the New York *Times*, upon the arrival of the new ambassador, Jefferson Caffery, from Paris, had made the statement that, "The spectacle of United States ambassadors who live out of a suitcase is beginning to rub the nerves of Cairo society the wrong way." All this from a country completely without social consciousness and with a haut monde of the wealthy pashas and the diplomatic corps, but with millions of starving fellahin.

In Buenos Aires, however, the United States did own an ambassador's house. So far as I know it is the largest and grandest of any of the United States Embassy residences in the world, with great marble hallways and reception rooms, almost a city block of gardens, a tennis court, and garages. I suspect that the past few ambassadors had not been athletes, because the tennis court needed remodeling, which I did. In contrast to the *Times* story of my suitcase life in Cairo was a note in *Time* magazine that, on entering the Buenos Aires residence for the first time, I said as I contemplated the towering two-story Embassy entrance hall, "I was once chairman of the board of Madison Square Garden, I feel right at home here." It was a fine old palace of marble and granite, with ample space for entertaining all of the socially minded Argentines and visiting Americans. Knowing in advance what the social problem would be, I had arranged for the appointment of Angier Biddle Duke, now the United States ambassador to El Salvador, to accompany me to Argentina as second secretary. He and Mrs. Duke took the social burdens from my shoulders, as they did later in Madrid. One of my first statements (recalling Jimmy Walker's description of himself as the "night mayor" of New York) was that the State Department should have two ambassadors in every country, a day ambassador and a night ambassador. The man does not live who can properly be both.

In every country a newly arrived United States ambassador is supposed to give a reception for the local press. At my first press reception in Buenos Aires I achieved the reputation of drinking a special liver-proof, nonintoxicating liquor. *Vea y Lea*, a Buenos Aires magazine, meticulously described the first reception: "The impeccable butlers appeared with a field bar, and the hands that were warm after shaking those of Mr. Griffis became cold while gripping the glasses. This reporter tried to grab a passing glass but was warned by the butler, 'this is the Ambassador's glass'; a confidante whispers in our ear that Mr. Griffis brought from Washington a special brand of whiskey, heavy with salt to make it liver-proof." In confessional let me say that experience has taught me that almost everyone who is a scotcher prefers soda, whereas I am a plain-water boy. The butler was instructed to bring me scotch with plain water.

While I may have been popular and successful with the Argentine journalists, and later with the same genre of writers in Spain, I think it was in Buenos Aires that I first realized that the policy which I adopted on the general approach of a United States diplomat to dictators, notably with Perón, and later with Franco, could never be popular in the United States. It would only bring anathema on my head and all my works. It culminated in a New York headline: "The State Department's favorite toadier to dictators."

I received my first lesson promptly. On the evening before my presentation of credentials to Perón, in the pink palace on November 17, I tried to think of a gesture that might bring his interest and personal regard. I had carried in my pocket for many years, in fact, since the famous gold withdrawal of President Roosevelt, a lucky twenty-dollar gold piece. I decided that it would be fun to give it to Perón and tell him that it had always been lucky for me, and that I hoped that it would bring good luck and good will in our relationships. After the usual proceedings, in which I was received by Perón in resplendent white uniform and blue sash, I retired to the conference room with him and Foreign Minister Hipolito Jesus Paz. After the usual desultory conversation of the occasion I gave Perón the gold piece, with a few words of the good-luck theme. As we emerged to the great reception room, crowded with photographers and motion-picture boys, Perón held up the gold piece and laughingly said: "This is the first American gold I have ever received." Some reporter who must, in my mind, be forever linked with Ananias stated that I immediately made the rejoinder, "Don't worry, Mr. President, there is plenty more where this came from." The story was a pure fabrication but it was widely repeated in the American press, with an added starter in one paper, "The report did not state whether or not the new American Ambassador kissed the dictator."

Obviously, Perón was not popular in the United States, and he was peculiarly unpopular with the American press because of his dictatorial relationship with the Argentine press. Yet I had firmly in my mind the results of the efforts of Ambassador Braden in 1944 to prevent Perón's election and interfere with the internal affairs of the nation. For right or for wrong, Braden's policy and efforts created a Peronista political slogan which has continued even to the present day: "Do you want Braden or Perón?" It made the United States "the colossus of the North," the villain of the piece, whenever an Argentine election was proposed.

Rightly or wrongly, I decided to proceed with the policy of attempting to attract flies with honey and not with vinegar.

I tried to make friends with the great dictator and his powerful wife, and thus I hoped to achieve the fulfillment of American wishes and American policy despite the constant attacks on me by the American press, which apparently felt that I should devote the major part of my time to an attempt to force Perón to give complete freedom to the Argentine press.

Later from Spain, facing an almost exactly similar situation, I expressed my feelings in a letter to Harry Luce, proprietor of *Life, Time,* and *Fortune,* who had continually attacked me on both my Argentine and Spanish policies. I attempted a very friendly letter, for I am very fond of Harry Luce. He is brilliant, erudite, and talented, as is his wife; she is prettier, too.

Unfortunately, I have not learned nor have been able to master the diplomatic approach to rulers to whom I have been accredited, along the lines which you apparently advocate, that is, to accomplish the desires, whether social, commercial, military or otherwise of the United States by approaching the rulers with my credentials in my left hand and cracking them in the nose with my right fist at the same time. That is a technique in which you may have been successful. I rather doubt it on the record, but I am afraid I am not sufficiently skilled along this line to meet your wishes.

Certainly I am not so stupid as not to understand that any man who desires to serve his country by entering public life should have the skin of a rhinoceros and the sensibility of an amoeba, but all of you, Roy Larsen, Dan Longwell and the many others of your staff, know me well enough to know that I am no dictator lover, that my whole life has been a reflection of my belief in the American system. My background of wealth (or lack of it) and family is almost identical with yours. I believe in free elections, a free press, freedom of conscience and assembly, and above all, I believe that these systems must be protected by a strong and dynamic United States which can help other countries to help themselves. That is why I am here.

At this moment in the history of the world, I do not feel that the United States Government in its own self-interest should attempt to create instability in countries opposed to Communism by interfering in their internal affairs. I took that position in Argentina as you know, and I am following it in Spain. Officially and publicly I neither approve nor disapprove of governments, whatever my private convictions may be. I came to Spain primarily to try to see to it that if trouble came, the United States would have Spain as a firm ally. I did not and do not feel that this can be accomplished by insults to the dictator; the harmless words of friendly greeting that I spoke to him out of courtesy have been so twisted as to discredit your country's representative in the eyes of his own people.

However, I hope that I have long since learned, like Don Quixote, that it is futile to tilt with a commercial windmill, but my job is a double-barrel one and I need your help not your attack. If I am to accomplish the job of lining up Spain on what Joe Louis called "God's side," I must develop American support for such a policy. Your magazines have gone far in trying to undo anything which I may hope to accomplish. Rightly or wrongly, I still believe I could have prevented the La Prensa denouement had I had anything but attacks in the United States.

All of the above is to try to point out to you in the middle of your busy life what I am attempting to do here, and the grave responsibilities your publications impose upon you when they persist in these attacks. Otherwise, with high regards——

In retrospect, and even during the years of service when I was accredited to dictators and being constantly attacked by the American press, I know that there are two sides to this question. The active newspaperman in constant search for news, and with a driving zeal to fix the searchlight of truth on government action, feels that freedom of the press is substantially paramount. The diplomat on the other hand, always influenced by his country's policy of noninterference in the internal affairs of a sister country, usually feels that he will do his mission more harm than good if he publicly campaigns for freedom of newspapers and commentaries in the country to which he is accredited. I so felt, and so acted, to the exasperation of my friends the American newspaper correspondents.

The situation in Argentina was constantly kept in a state of ferment by repeated acts of the Perón government, which, on one pretext or another, harassed or actually closed newspapers critical of Peronismo. There were constant rumors that these acts of attrition would be finally extended to the closing of the great independent newspaper of Buenos Aires, *La Prensa*. Its proprietor, Ganza Paz, waged a gallant fight for the life and freedom of the newspaper. A favorite weapon of the Argentine Government against opposition newspapers was the seizure of portions of the limited amounts of newsprint in the country, or the rationing of it with favoritism always to the government-controlled or government-favored periodicals. While it is true that I did not openly, publicly, or frequently defend the freedom of the press in Argentina, I many times privately interceded to assist independent papers in obtaining proper supplies of newsprint. From the day of my first talk with Perón until I finally left for the United States, I was assured by him that *La Prensa* would be permitted to continue its operation and opposition and that it would never be closed. The world knows the final and tragic end of this problem.

Let it not be said, however, that I was entirely alone in my feeling of what the policy of an American ambassador should be when assigned to a dictatorship government. I have been forever grateful to Bill Henry, who wrote in the Los Angeles *Times*, under the heading "Man for Job":

This quality of putting first things first is not one for which our government has been recently famous, but most people back here think another example of that sort of selection is found in the appointment of Stanton Griffis as Ambassador to Spain. Griffis is a cheerful cynic with great aplomb and a complete understanding that an ambassador is not an apostle whose mission is to convert wicked dictators to our way of life, but rather a salesman whose job is to get the best possible relations, and being a gregarious cuss who is full of disarming ways, he will doubtless do as he did in Argentina, establish himself as a likable, friendly chap who will be able to get results for the United States without sacrificing any principles.

While he was in the Middle East he suddenly had wished on him the thankless job of feeding one million displaced Arabs who had been shoved out of Palestine. It didn't occur to him to take sides in the fearfully touchy Jewish-Arab question, or to fret over the rights or wrongs of the complex problems of the Middle East —his job was to feed Arabs, so he fed them. If this sort of thing continues, the United States may get a practical rather than a political government.

My second diplomatic duty was to call on the dictator's wife, the beautiful Evita. This I did accompanied by my counselor of Embassy, Lester Mallory. We were received at the Perón town residence, which appeared rather bare except for a series of violently colored paintings of the dictatoress, usually in the French fashions of the day and ablaze with jewels. Far from discussing diplomacy or world relationships, we talked of poodles, as her small black favorite, Tambour, frolicked with his mistress. Making conversation, I inquired if the dog had a wife, and was told that there was no wife good enough for him in Argentina but that his mistress greatly desired his marriage to a silver poodle. To carry out the tradition of Yankee go-get-it enterprise, I returned to the Embassy and telephoned my secretary in New York, giving her specifications of a proposed wife to carry on the Perón dog dynasty. Within three days there arrived in Buenos Aires, the princess apparent in the form of a young silver miniature named Sylvia, who was duly presented to Evita. Her parting thanks carried a note of political logrolling. She told me that now that I had found a wife for Tambour she would have to find me a wife "from among the *descamisados*—no oligarch." The followers of Peronismo were widely known as the *descamisados* or "shirtless ones." Evita's rage at and hatred of the landed gentry had led to her describing them always as oligarchs. Although, unfortunately, I have no recent news of the development of the dynasty started by Tambour and Sylvia, it is my guess that it has developed along usual doggish lines and might perhaps be expected to flourish longer than the dynasty of their human master and mistress.

The dog story was not received in the United States with unalloyed pleasure in all quarters. From one correspondent I received the following little billet-doux: "A few nights ago at Madison Square Garden one brute nearly killed another to the amusement of about ten thousand degenerates, sadists and morons, and I thought how sad you must have been in not having been there. I send you my sympathy. To satisfy our curiosity, I am asking Mr. Acheson if to be a prize-fight fan or promoter or to give a French poodle adds to the prestige of a diplomat of your quality, I just wonder what people in other lands think of our peculiar representative."

Following the poodle incident, there came an immediate invitation from the ruling lady to take a trip with her around Buenos Aires to visit the many installations of her famous charity, La Fundation Social. These personally conducted tours of the great lady have been celebrated in song and story by so many visitors to Argentina that I shall not attempt to repeat them here, but like most other commentators I gathered the impression that a great many of the operations were pretty phoney—particularly the children's village, which looked more like a collection of Hollywood sets without any actors. I have never believed that the poor children of Argentina have much opportunity to use it. However, to drive through the streets of Buenos Aires with Señora Perón was a real adventure, as at every stopping point crowds of people forced their way around the car, throwing in envelopes and letters which invariably carried some hard-luck story. But it is to her everlasting credit as a good publicist, if not a great philanthropist, that every one of these appeals was answered —usually through a personal summons to visit her in her office at the Ministry of Labor, where she daily handed out largesse in the form of peso notes. It can be said with absolute truth that no one in Argentina worked harder than Evita Perón.

For good or for evil, she was a violent and tireless crusader for Peronismo, and often was quoted as saying that were it not for the softening influences of her husband she would have been even more constantly on the soap box, intellectually scratching and biting at every form of wealth or special privilege. Through the years Evita did not soften toward the oligarchs nor did the gentry soften in their hatred of Evita, and all that she represented. Many a good man and true, including Jim Bruce and me, attempted social gestures to bring a few of the leaders of old Argentina into the same drawing room with Evita, but without success. The oligarchs would absolutely refuse to enter the Embassy if they thought there was any possibility that Perón, his wife, or even any of his ministers would be present.

The weeks rushed on and the Argentine springtime, which is our autumn, made the city aglow with the masses of blue flowers that cover its trees. I ordered hundreds of new rose-bushes for the great garden in the rear of the residence, and criticized my gardener for using a north slope for them, before I realized that in this new country the sun shines from the north. The tennis court was completed, on which I ended my tennis days forever, as I tore an arm muscle while engaged in violent combat with Dr. and Mrs. Robin Adair, who were vacationing in Argentina. For the blazing summer, which started at about our Christmas time, the Dukes and I rented a small quinta with a swimming pool in the country, and here we usually spent our week ends. The polo season had come and gone, with the Americans defeated by the hard-riding, hard-hitting Argentine teams; but the horse races were perennial, and on literally thousands of tennis courts in and about Buenos Aires the citizenry pursued their favorite game.

In February came the great event of the season: the visit to Buenos Aires of Assistant Secretary of State Edward G. Miller. Eddie Miller was and is the perfection of a diplomat for Latin-American relationships, born with a silver spoon full of Spanish verbs in his mouth, educated in the Latin countries of the West Indian Islands, and trained in a great New York law firm. He immediately captured the hearts and affections of the Argentinos, although, never perhaps, quite to the extent of leading them down the road of the American ideal of freedom.

Perón is a notoriously early riser and worker, usually starting operations in his office at the Casa Rosada before six-thirty in the morning. An American diplomat's habits are not always the same, and as a result of this there arose one night one of those amusing incidents that sometimes develop from a linguistic cross-purpose. I had never realized that Perón knew any English words at all, and as we completed a conference one evening long after ten I heard Perón say to Miller, "Shall we resume in the morning at seven?" I jokingly said to Eddie in English, "Tell him to make it four and we won't have to go to bed at all," but Perón understood me and laughingly said, "All right you lazy Yankees, let's make it nine o'clock"; which we did. This jestful yarn probably bears out the truth of the story about the time Perón's secretary called Ambassador Bruce for an appointment and said that the dictator would like to see him "tomorrow at seven." Bruce arrived on the minute of seven in the evening to find that Perón had long since left for the day and that he was exactly twelve hours late for his appointment.

With Miller, I proceeded to Rio de Janeiro for a gathering of all the United States ambassadors to South America. I renewed old acquaintance with Ambassador Herschel Johnson of Brazil, whom I had known so well in Sweden; with

The ambassador presenting his credentials to El Caudillo, Francisco Franco. At the right, Martin Artajo, Spanish Minister of Foreign Affairs

The ambassador consults with the Secretary of State

The President of Argentina holds the gold piece given him by the newly arrived ambassador

In conference with Evita Perón, who is holding her favorite poodle, Tambour

Willard Beaulac of Colombia—now promoted to Cuba; and with Walter Donnelly of Venezuela, who is now serving us in Germany. Amid the unbelievable scenery of Rio and its harbor, we carried on long and somewhat fruitless conferences, fruitless I think, for all of South America was unhappy and disgruntled at the fact that there was no Marshall Plan for South America nor any in view. To be sure, loans were being made to individual countries and for special purposes by the Export-Import Bank, but our government and its representatives had built up the dream of the good-neighbor policy to the point where every Latin country felt that it should be Good Neighbor Number One and favored with unlimited American grants and loans. I felt so strongly that the conference had accomplished little or nothing, and that any statement of results would only be apt to open old wounds, that I strongly opposed the issuance of the usual "we discussed and considered at great length the mutual problems existing between our government and those of the South American governments, et cetera," but I was unanimously overruled and the statement was issued for what it was worth.

However, one great compensation for the days spent in the heat of Rio came through a visit of George Kennan to Buenos Aires as my guest. I do not know the words to properly describe the brilliant and scholarly statecraft of this slender dynamic man, who shortly after his visit gave up his State Department work to study and write for a year at Princeton, and who now by the grace of God, and the wisdom of Mr. Truman and the Department, represents us as ambassador to Moscow. George Kennan may accomplish little as United States ambassador in Russia, but one thing can be certain, he will accomplish more than any other United States citizen could. As we sat in our quiet and beautiful garden in Buenos Aires, I learned much from my long conversations with him, and I can only pray with other Americans that more men like George Kennan will join our Department of State.

Mr. Kennan's visit fortunately coincided with that of General Hoyt Vandenberg, Chief of Staff for Air, who flew down upon us in his great bird of a Constellation on an air tour of South America.

During my duty in Argentina, and with the seeming good will that we thought was being developed through the visit of Eddie Miller, it at least seemed apparent that there was a great deal of progress in solving the many difficulties encountered by American business firms in Perón's country. There were the constant difficulties of the American packing houses such as Armour, Swift, and Wilson, known in Latin parlance as *frigorificos;* the long unsettled problems of the proposed expropriation of the properties of the American and Foreign Power Company; the stagnancy of the American motion-picture industry, which was denied the right to bring pictures into the Argentine; and the ever-present problem of withdrawing dollar profits and royalties acquired in pesos by American manufacturers and importers. The constantly declining peso greatly added to all these problems. However, there seemed some gleam of hope on the horizon at that time, sufficient that, upon his return to Washington, Eddie Miller wrote me an extremely amusing letter which said in general, "I told the Secretary that we were really having a United States-Argentine honeymoon, but I was unable to answer his very pointed question, 'Which is the bride and which is the groom?'" The answer would be simple today.

No real progress had been made or was being made, although with the rising prices of wool—which, as well as beef for England, always constitutes one of Argentina's main exports—the Argentine was gradually beginning to pay off part of the something over two hundred million dollar defaulted acceptances due American companies. However, the United States Government, through the Department of Agriculture, constantly stood firm on its refusal to permit the export of

Argentine beef to the United States, on account of the dreaded hoof-and-mouth disease, although the Argentinos always regarded this careful attitude of our government as discriminatory, excuseful, and unrealistic. In the meantime, the important contract with Britain for frozen meat had expired and the Argentinos and the British had been unable to agree upon a renewal. Always the situation was complicated by the iniquitous operations of the great government purchasing firm I.N.I., which bought substantially all farm products for export at unrealistic prices and which had its fingers in all industrial pies. The government's agreement to subsidize the packers to the extent of meeting their losses, and to give them a reasonable operating profit, had not been implemented and I understand still remains in status quo today. The oil companies were constantly exasperated with the tactics of the Argentinos, and Ultramar, one of the two great American oil entities operating in Argentina, has within the past few months given up the ghost and sold out to the Argentine Government. Fortunately, the motion-picture impasse has been finally adjudicated.

Following such industrial hopes as there were, and in an attempt at least to correct the situation to the extent of paying off the Argentine's past due bank indebtedness to the American manufacturers, I flew to New York on March 20, accompanied by Ramon Cereijo, the Minister of Industry and one of the chief cabinet supporters of the Perón administration. There, joined by Eddie Miller and the Argentine ambassador, we negotiated long and arduously with the Export-Import Bank. The Argentinos talked in terms of hundreds of millions, but the bank was loath to make any sizable loan whatever although many millions had gone into Brazil, a situation not without pain to the proud Argentine spirits. The mountain finally heaved and gave forth a mouse in the form of $125,000,000 credit to be used entirely in paying off the defaulted bank promises to American companies, with no new money whatever for agricultural machinery or the various heavy goods which the Argentine so desperately needed. Negotiations with a group of New York banks were aided and abetted by the genius of Sosthenes Behn, chairman of the board of International Telephone and Telegraph Company. I. T. and T. had already extended some credit to Argentina but the new negotiations failed on account of the requirement of the banks that one hundred per cent coverage of the loan be deposited in gold. This the Argentines refused to accept, and the net result of these long negotiations was that substantially not a dollar of new American money went into Argentina. Probably the decision of the American bankers in the whole negotiations was a correct one, but it is hard to say what might have happened had we made any successful effort to solve the Argentine's financial plight.

Every ambassador knows that neither loans nor lack of loans to a sister country will be a guiding factor in good relationship if there is not a happy trade between the two nations, a trade flow that is profitable and favorable for both sides. The United States has never been able to buy friendship through loans, nor can it disregard the old and worn adage that the best way to lose a friend is to lend him money.

When I first went to Argentina I preached and hammered this theory that real friendship between countries must be founded upon the exchange of trade, good trade in which both countries make a profit. I believed then and now that to create a flow of trade between two countries and to keep it flowing is far more important than all of the good-neighbor talk in the world. But there exists a basic barrier to trade relations between the United States and Argentina. Almost all of our other South American neighbors are producers of copper, oil, coffee, cocoa, tin, or of some other basic commodity that can be sold for dollars. This is true in Argentina in a very small way, for excepting wool and quebracho, the basic element of tanning solution, she has little which the

United States needs. She has substantially no mineral wealth and produces only about half of her domestic oil requirements, and her great crop of beef is shut off from the United States as I have already noted by the Department of Agriculture's mandate on the hoof-and-mouth disease. The agricultural economies of the United States and Argentina are surprisingly similar. We produce an excess of wheat and corn, as does Argentina, and it is extremely difficult for various reasons for Argentina to compete in our markets with these commodities. The American farm bloc looks after its own.

There exists then in Argentina a basic need for dollars with which to carry on American trade and purchase our goods in competition with her long-time customer, England. One must recognize another recently created bloc as well as the similarity of our economies. Look back through the post-war history of our southern neighbor. Argentina came out of the war rich in dollars and sterling, garnered through her semi-neutral, semi-Axis position. With little understanding of the developments of the future, Argentina made a historic error in disposing of her great stocks of exchange. First the nation paid off substantially all of its internal debts and, excepting the Export-Import loan, it is the only country in South America today, with the exception of Venezuela, that has no external funded debt. It purchased the English-owned railroads; it purchased the shipping lines and all forms of airlines and transportation; it hoped to depend, as always, upon the conversion of sterling. The United States must assume some responsibility for its many statements that it would hold sterling convertible by loans to Britain. But these hopes failed and Argentina found herself deeply in dollar debt, through the guaranty of payments to American manufacturers.

With the shutting off of sterling convertibility Argentina has never been able to recover her postwar position in foreign exchange. She still has possible exports to the United States of wool, hides, canned corned beef, and quebracho, but the dollar gain is a drop in the bucket compared with the need for all types of American manufactured projects. Now with the decline in Argentina's exportable surpluses of agricultural products, the future of trade relationships between the United States and Argentina is bleak. Perhaps Argentina is learning the primal lesson of government ownerships. Trades of government jobs for political votes, as England may ultimately understand, spell only two words—red ink.

In this great country, so susceptible to agricultural development that a tractor-drawn plow could turn a straight furrow for five hundred miles in deep soil, endowed with almost every type of climate from the sub-tropical north to the windy pampas of the southern sheep country, and with plentiful man power, both the agricultural and the industrial situation has become steadily worse. The peso has fallen to new lows against the dollar as the Perón administration has kept an iron-fist control of both industry and agriculture, exacting almost unlimited invisible taxes on its purchase and export of agricultural goods.

Returning to Argentina in June, I encountered another one of the strange quixotic gestures of the dictator. In accordance with its hopes for hemispheric solidarity, the State Department greatly desired to persuade Argentina to sign the Rio Pact. Somewhat along the lines of a South American NATO, it had been drafted as an offensive and defensive agreement prepared for mutual aid by all of the Latin countries in case any were attacked. Not even the charming blandishments of Jim Bruce had been able to persuade Argentina to sign the pact, and all of my efforts with Perón had been in vain. One day, following our return from Washington, however, Cereijo told me that Perón was very much pleased with our work in the North and wanted to see me. With Foreign Minister Paz we started our usual exchange of jests, Perón leading off with "You are too good to be an American Ambassador, I'm going to persuade you to become an Argentino and work as an Argentine ambassador." I answered, "Mr. President, I think that you are going to get an opportunity within the next two or three weeks, because if you don't sign the Rio Pact, I'm going to be fired and I will be looking for a job." Perón said, "Well, I really wouldn't want to see you fired, the Rio Pact will be signed within two weeks." And it was. Perhaps his happiness over the Washington results were based on the fact that, as he had repeatedly stated in political speeches, he would cut off his right hand before he would sign a request for an American loan. For that reason we had been very careful to label the Export-Import Bank loan a credit.

One of my good friends in the Argentine was Hipolito Jesus Paz, the young Minister of Foreign Affairs, who had suddenly emerged to power just before my arrival. His very beautiful wife was an artist of quality and frequently went on painting expeditions with Margaret Duke of our embassy. Paz was the son of a distinguished Argentine lawyer. Because he wanted to write and his bride wanted to paint, he had picked out the Balearic Islands for a future home. Having a slight acquaintance with Perón, he had made an appointment with the President to request the humble position of Argentine consul in Majorca, so that he might make his home among the beautiful scenes of the island that had sheltered George Sand and Chopin.

His meeting with Perón had strange results, for after a three-hour conversation Paz emerged from Perón's office as the new Minister of Foreign Affairs. Young, able, scholarly, and aggressive, he made a fine record during his tenure of office, and he later became ambassador to the United States. Regretfully, however, he was strictly of the machine and never disobeyed orders to think as Perón thought.

On the great and glorious Fourth of July came an event of which I had high hopes but which I think sealed the doom of my constant efforts to create United States good will for Argentina. It was the arrival of a Pan American stratocruiser with a great pilgrimage of American journalistic brains, chaperoned by Juan Trippe, president of Pan American. The visitors included a cross section of American journalism. There was Helen Reid of the New York *Herald Tribune*, General Adler of the New York *Times*, Barry Faris of International News, Bill Hearst and Dick Berlin of the Hearst chain, Norman Chandler of the Los Angeles *Times*, Gardner and Fleur Cowles of the Cowles magazines, Tex Moore of Time, Incorporated, Dan Mahoney of the Miami *Daily News*, Jack Wheeler of the North American Newspaper Alliance, Bob Smith of the Los Angeles *Daily News*, Amon Carter of the Fort Worth *Star-Telegram*, Francis Murphy of the Hartford *Times*, Elliott Bell of McGraw-Hill, George Healy (my old OWI boss) of the New Orleans *Times-Picayune*, and finally Jimmy Stahlman of the Nashville *Banner*. They were almost all old friends of mine, through whom I was supposed to introduce and interpret Perón and Peronismo to the United States.

There was a great round of entertainment, culminating with the spectacle of Evita christening the great plane Friendship with a bottle of Argentine champagne. But the high note of the visit was a long press conference arranged for the visitors to meet and question Perón; this took place around the great cabinet table with its countless microphones in the Casa Rosada.

The questioning was ungloved, and Perón answered every question thrown at him with ease and vigor, but not, I fear, with complete truth. He declared unequivocally that there was freedom of the press in Argentina, and that it would remain; that he would never close *La Prensa*, and he called attention to the fact that its circulation had almost doubled during his administration. He declared that there was complete freedom of radio in the Argentine, which was notoriously untrue, and that the United States should not make loans to South American countries because such a policy would cause the Latin to stop work.

Evita's line was as usual—she was only a humble worker in the field of Peronismo, but to her dying day she would work and support the great doctrines of the great man. Unfortunately, I fear, as we say in the theatre, "the show did not click." Two of the master showmen of the world had failed to hold the critics or obtain good reviews. Certainly as the reports appeared in the United States, they were a little on the poisonous side.

The journalists came and went along with many other delegations. One was a large group from the Associated Women's Clubs of Texas; they were insistent on meeting Perón and an audience was accordingly arranged. One of these rather buxom ladies spoke some Spanish, which she used to make a general comparison of Texas and Argentina, all, I may say, to the great disadvantage of Argentina. Through it all Perón was very polite—until the leader of the group suddenly said in English to her fellow visitors, "All right girls, let's go," and without warning, the entire delegation closed around Perón and burst into the strains of "The Eyes of Texas Are upon You." I had never seen the dictator look frightened before, but he was quite uncertain what it was all about and looked anxiously at his guards lurking behind the screens. Nevertheless he sat it out and finally bowed out the delegation with a translated assurance that the eyes of Texas would be fully satisfied in watching his administration befriend the *descamisados*.

Late in September, I returned again to the United States, to make a speech before the Investment Bankers' Association in which I attempted to explain the difficulties of understanding the differences between the United States and Argentina. I did not attempt to explain Perón's famous and often discussed "third position," which he describes as a middle ground between Communism and capitalism; I did not attempt to explain it because I don't understand it nor does anyone else, including Perón. I had become a dispenser of apologies for the Argentinos and for their government, which was in every way a change of feeling and sentiment since the early days of my mission. I made the statement, which I believed then and believe now, that the Argentinos were far from ready in their present stage of development to understand and practice true democracy with all its attendant freedoms as we have it in the United States. The statement brought mixed reactions in Buenos Aires. *La Prensa* felt that "for the Ambassador to express doubts regarding Argentine readiness for democracy raises another doubt whether the person who expressed himself in that way has sufficient knowledge of the recent past of Argentina." This may be so. Another newspaper, *La Epoca*, stated that it agreed "with the Ambassador that Argentina is not prepared for democracy . . . he has emphasized a notorious truth and expressed a very clear thought." That, too, may be true.

I did not return to Argentina, but as I remained in the United States I bitterly watched the development of the various Peronista trends, which had become more and more marked, and more and more violent, during my last weeks in Buenos Aires. The world is fully familiar now with the final and closing history of *La Prensa* as a free instrument of expression of opinion. It went the way of all freedoms in the southern republic. I watched with sadness as Perón and his lady, through one pretext or another, violated every promise and agreement they had made with the American ambassador regarding this great newspaper. I watched them throw to the winds every atom of the good will that ambassadors have attempted to build up between our nation and theirs during the many years. Coincidentally and unhappily, I watched, too, the rapid and fearsome decline of their industries and their agriculture; the decline in the peso and the constantly shrinking output of their cattle and wheatlands returned them to an economic low point of years ago.

I read and listened to the almost incoherent mouthings of Perón and Evita as they again decided to remain as heads of the country's political machine. With death and degradation they destroyed every effort of political manifestation against them. Perhaps I best expressed the disastrous failure of my efforts when later talking in Madrid to Sir John Balfour, who had been my British colleague in Buenos Aires. When the Spaniards awarded me the great Cross of Charles III, I told Sir John at a dinner next evening that I felt that the Spanish were a little parsimonious in giving me only one cross; both he and I remembered the many times in Argentina when Perón had given us the double cross.

Today Juan Perón rules Argentina alone, for the frail body of Evita ceased its struggle for life in late July of 1952. Even before I left Argentina the mark of blood weakness or deficiency was upon her, and although she struggled many months thereafter in work and political effort, she was at last laid low, presumably by the most terrible and all-consuming disease of mankind.

Evita Perón represented one of the most astounding paradoxes in social and political history. Without any economic knowledge whatever, or understanding of the lifeblood of a modern state, she embarked on a Robin Hood crusade of taking from the rich to give to the poor, with the result that she has probably, at least for a long time to come, destroyed both rich and poor in her beloved country. Her political philosophy and policies were elemental, that is, to grant substantially every wage demand of labor, both in industry and on the farms, although taking away from each raise a sufficient percentage to build up an enormous chain of charities and philanthropic enterprises, which, however, were subject to no audit nor to national knowledge. The results were as simple as the policy itself; the industries were unable to make profits on account of the fantastic wages which they were forced to pay, and with the news of these wage increases, the gauchos swept into the cities from the pampas and the landowner was unable to produce his wheat or fatten his cattle. From a country exporting hundreds of millions of bushels of wheat and hundreds of thousands of tons of frozen beef to England, Argentina has changed into a country that is hardly able to support itself or satisfy its own consumption of bread and beef. Yet, I have very little doubt of the integrity of Evita Perón's belief in herself and her philosophies. A little knowledge, especially in the hands of a beautiful, driving, and ambitious woman, is indeed a very dangerous thing.

What may be the future of Argentina's destinies following the death of its great mistress, no man can tell. Knowing Evita to have been by far the most radical of the two leaders, it would seem logical to assume that Perón may turn swiftly to the right. It would seem that some kind of extremely radical change would be necessary to prevent not only national bankruptcy, but indeed revolution.

During the current American political campaign there has been much talk of captives, each party charging the nominee of the other with being a captive of this or that organization. Probably the most gruesome form of captive in the world today is Evita Perón's body, held in the headquarters of the famous Argentine CGT (Confederación General de Trabajo) to whose welfare she devoted her life and her powerful political energy. It is reported that the body will be preserved and super-embalmed for exhibition, somewhat along the lines of the great crypt that holds the body of Lenin in Moscow, but Evita's body will remain the property of the CGT, and if real strife comes in Argentina it will be between the army and the CGT, with the labor confederation massed ideologically and perhaps actually around the wasted and waxed remains of its leader.

In Connecticut, upon my return, both Brien McMahon

and Bill Benton were up for re-election to the United States
Senate. The President suggested that I stay awhile in my
State, helping along with the campaign, and after the election
come in and have a talk with him about the future. This I
proceeded to do. My efforts, particularly for McMahon,
brought down upon me the animus and anathema of Bill Hearst
and the Hearst newspapers, for they had campaigned continually and constantly against him. The Hearst newspapers
advanced the astounding theory that a United States ambassador had no right whatever to engage in local campaigns,
and attempted to invoke the Hatch Act and to obtain Senate
action in the matter.

## CHAPTER FOURTEEN

## CASTLES IN SPAIN

I cannot write about Spain without telling the story of its poverty and degradation, its lack of freedoms, its religious intolerance, its dictatorship heading a bumbling and sprawling bureaucracy of government, its primitive methods of business and agriculture, and its eternal spirit of mañana. Yet at the same time there must shine through the story my deep affection and love for the country and its people; even for most of the men who operate its government, and my respect for the head of the state, General Francisco Franco.

It is a chore indeed, and would take a better writer than I will ever be to give it a semblance of logic, but there it is, and I must perforce try to write it in the way that I have just described it, for certainly my diplomatic mission there gave me the greatest happiness of any year which I have ever spent outside of the United States. I accomplished more, lived more, and certainly found greater happiness than in any other diplomatic mission which has been mine.

After the Connecticut elections, as the President had suggested, I dropped in at Washington to talk with him for the first time in two months. Meanwhile I had been hearing reports from the Secretary of State, through Eddie Miller, that after all these years we were about to reverse our policy on Spain and send an ambassador there. I had been told that

I had been selected to take the job. Before I saw the President I tried very hard to persuade Eddie Miller to go to Spain. He would have been an ideal ambassador in every possible way. However, Eddie, owing to financial and family reasons, did not feel that he was ready to go to the field, and he worked on me to accept the post.

It was alluring to a degree. I had long been at odds with the State Department's policy on Spain, and had decided that I should be flattered and happy to take the ambassadorship if the President asked me to do so. In the meantime the President had made the announcement at a press conference that it would be a long time before we sent an ambassador to Spain, so I regarded the whole matter with doubtful eyes. However, the President did ask me to go, and I told him that I would be delighted if I could have a few weeks of vacation in Florida first. He said, "That's great and exactly what I want. I don't want you to go for the present—so soon after what I said a few weeks ago. I have been a little overruled and worn down by the Department."

It was at that meeting that I had a strong inkling of the trials and tribulations which were to be mine in Spain, for there was and remains a deep conflict between the viewpoint of the Spanish on religious toleration and that of the President. Mr. Truman, as everyone knows, is a deeply religious man, a Baptist, and a little bit of what people have called a hard-shell Baptist. He showed great feeling in discussing the religious problems in Spain as he said to me, "I do not know what your religion is, I do not even know if you have any, but I am a Baptist and I believe that in any country man should be permitted to worship his God in his own way. The situation in Spain is intolerable. Do you know that a Baptist who dies in Spain must even be buried in the middle of the night?"

Unfortunately, the knowledge which I had picked up in Spain during my visit there in 1943 had not included a study of religious bigotry, and I had no historical information as to

269

the truth or accuracy of his statement. However, I told him if he felt so strongly about the matter it would be one of my first efforts in Madrid to encourage religious tolerance, and that he could count on me to do it if it were possible. I left Washington for Florida, and did not return until my nomination went to the Senate in January 1951.

Now I greatly detest what I call three-day historians, that species of writer or commentator who visits a country for a few days and then proceeds to write or broadcast a dogmatic and usually completely inaccurate story of its history and its current religious, political, and war viewpoints. I have had many of these gentry visit me in every country, and their method is universal. After reading some books and a magazine article, they arrive in the nation's capital, put up at the best hotel, and proceed as far as possible to drain the officers of the United States Information and Educational Service, the ambassador, and the members of the embassy of their knowledge and opinions on the passing show.

It sometimes takes a very, very long time in a country to have any real understanding of its aspirations, its beliefs, its traditions, qualities, and nuances, and even an all-wise ambassador who has formulated an opinion is not able to transmit it with accuracy in a fifteen-minute interview. But the stories go forth, very frequently to the intense embarrassment of the embassy officers, who are often called to the Foreign Office to explain statements that the writer claims were made. One of the chief classes of offenders in this matter includes the Senators and Congressmen who roam the earth when Congress is not in session, and frequently when it is, often acting as newspaper correspondents and frequently making radio speeches from the country that they are currently visiting. They are able, within twenty-four or forty-eight hours of arrival, to transmit a great mass of misinformation to the world.

So with my compliments to three-day historians, I am going

to be one myself. When I was traveling in Europe in 1942 and 1943 for the Office of Strategic Services, and had spent only a few weeks in Spain, I followed the plan of writing General Donovan the results and observations of my tour of study and consultation with all types of men. That was about nine years ago, but the clock has not moved forward with speed in Spain. The comments I made then in one of my letters fit so nearly the conditions that I found when I arrived in Spain as ambassador that I am going to include one of the letters.

The letter to which I refer is dated February 9, 1943, and reads in part as follows:

Franco's theory of operation is simple. Internally he has come to power through being the victorious general of the Revolution, and this power he holds by playing against one another the four chief social and political factors—the Monarchists, the Falangists, the Army, and the Church. Though the people may starve, so long as the Army is well fed he holds the trump card, and the electorate— if there were one—would vote for him on the old Woodrow Wilson theory, "He has kept us out of war," for it is war above all things that the Spanish individual close to the remembrance of the terrible days of the Revolution desires to avoid.

Externally smiling on the Allied Government and their representatives, and far from unmindful of the tremendous amounts of pounds and dollars being poured into the country by pre-emptive buying of Spanish products, he continually throws sops to Germany by frequent transmission of special envoys to the Fuehrer, by an ironclad censorship which translates every Spanish news article in favor of the Axis effort, and by a publicity campaign— far beyond the real importance of the subject—dramatizes the famous Blue Division recruited from Spain and fighting with the Germans against Russia. This division of probably less than twenty thousand men at any time is popularly supposed to balance the number of men which Germany sent into the Spanish Revolution to help Franco, but with constant newspaper campaigns to raise funds and presents for its members, by almost daily publicity of its activities, by demonstrations to its returning officers and men, and by the flamboyance of its uniform, its importance is terrifically magnified throughout Spain.

The keynote of every Francista and real or pseudo government utterance in Spain today is an unswerving hatred of Russia and things Bolshevistic, finding its genesis in Franco's rise to power against the help of the Russians to his enemies. The almost unanimous viewpoint and writings of American journalists too, opposing Franco during the Revolution, are far from forgotten and the tremendous German influence in all departments of the government is extremely real. Any favorable news whatever in connection with the Allied efforts is immediately smothered in all Spanish newspapers, and every British and American propaganda effort has a desperate swim against the tide.

Only recently, under the influence of Salazar and no doubt American and British advances in North Africa, has there been the slightest apparent weakening in this regard of the Spanish government or of the Spanish press. I have already referred to the recall of the former German Ambassador following the formation of the Iberian bloc and the arrival of von Moltke, the new German Ambassador, who recently came to Madrid with a great blare of trumpets and who, in the words of the British Ambassador in Madrid, arrived with "an iron fist" which, also in the words of the Ambassador, "will fail."

The Monarchists and the Capitalists in Spain are, of course, satisfied with the status quo and all pro-Axis pressure in Spain today emanates from the Falangista Party. Yet, all in all, there may be a slight trend today towards the improvement of Spanish relations towards the Allies. The straws in the wind seem to be the dismissal of pro-Axis foreign minister Suner and the elevation of Jordana, the development of the Iberian bloc, the apparent integrity and fearlessness of Jordana, the decline of German credit in Spain, the increasing dependence of Spain on American and British supplies, and the importance to Spain of its rising dollar and sterling balances. However, Franco, who is almost Russian in his stubborn, suspicious, peasant mind, although apparently personally honest and completely all out for Spain, is the unpredictable X in the political mathematics.

It is, I believe, in the economic and not the political situation where the real danger of a complete upheaval in Spain lies. The nation today represents the picture of a few people—largely bankers, speculators and government officials—making tremendous amounts of money out of Allied buying and black-market operations of all sorts. While the great mass of the people are beaten and bewildered by an almost daily rise in the cost of living, while the country is strictly rationed and supposedly held in the grip of price fixing for substantially all foodstuffs and commodities, while there is a fixed rate of exchange and in theory no other rate is permitted, while economic rules of every sort are promulgated, actually not the slightest attention is paid to any of these laws or regulations. It is said by all and sundry that not even the lowliest peasant can keep body and soul together under the rations allotted him, either because they are insufficient per se or because the food covered by his ration card is completely unobtainable at the official prices. The same bread which sells per unit for one and one half pesetas on ration sells for fifteen pesetas in the black market. Sugar sells in the black market for 28 pesetas a kilo or approximately $1.50 per pound at the official rate of exchange. Meat at 30 pesetas per kilo, flour at 12½, and butter at 50 pesetas, represent some of the recent black-market quotations. While lorry gasoline is for sale officially at two pesetas per liter, and pleasure gasoline at five pesetas, the established practice on the road is to buy gas at around ten pesetas per liter on the plea that you will produce your coupons next week and the difference between the price charged and the official price will be refunded. That is a bourne to which no traveler returns. A frequent result of this kind of situation is that in times of temporary gasoline shortages, taxi drivers purchase their gas rations at official prices, resell them at much higher prices, and live quietly at home with their taxis in the garage. The same general practice is apt to apply to the licensed owners of gasoline fishing boats. One of the laws consistently disregarded is that which provides that no taxi or car can drive outside of its city without official permission.

No one knows better than the government officials and perhaps no one talks more than the government officials regarding the flourishing condition of the black market, and it is the general and cynically accepted opinion in Spain that the market is allowed to flourish chiefly because the government officials themselves are profiting through its transactions.

Of course, the entire Diplomatic Corps is openly or secretly engaged in black money operations. As I have pointed out, it is obvious that with the Lisbon market for pesetas at around twenty-one to the dollar and with the official rate in Spain at around ten, no one who can add two and two together is willing to pay the official rate, and accordingly Lisbon is one of the chief beneficiaries of the Spanish money situation. The temptation to a foreign government official charged with buying any goods, and who is not under financial control, is obvious. The buyer of ten thousand pesetas' worth of goods who represents that his purchase was made at official rates can, without undue difficulty, obtain his pesetas at half the official rate and make a personal profit of fifty per cent.

With the complete dislocation of world currency, it is difficult in the ordinarily accepted economic terms to estimate the value of the peseta. The Lisbon market, as I have stated, is widely erratic, but at the present time is between 20 to 21 pesetas to the dollar. Various bankers and economists differ widely on their own estimates of what it is really worth in buying power of commodities. I have heard British bankers in Madrid estimate it is worth 18 pesetas to the dollar. Walzer, the head of the United States Commercial Company in Spain, estimates it as worth 25 to the dollar. Frank Schoonmacher, who has made a very careful study of the matter and has had a wide experience in Spain for years, believes that the peseta is worth between 2 ½ and 2 ¾ ¢ and backs up this opinion by a careful study of pre-war and present wine prices which have been virtually unaffected by war influence such as pre-emptive buying, et cetera.

As I have pointed out, such buying by separate or combined Allied purchasing agencies has a marked influence on the economic fabric of Spain today. In the battle for wolfram the price has been pushed to at least ten times the world market, and the price of olive oil and a number of other commodities to a percentage somewhat less astronomical. The Allies buy sheepskins, textiles, woolen goods of all sorts, olives, olive oil, cork, and various commodities. Germany buys wolfram, skins, iron, pyrites, lead, iron ore, et cetera, in exchange for coal, machinery, pharmaceuticals, et cetera, but it is estimated by the Allied purchasers that she will not be able to meet more than twenty-five per cent of her commercial treaty agreements during the current year. Apparently the credits given to Germany by Suner of upward of three hundred million marks are not being increased, but on the other hand through Allied buying, Spain is reported to have built up a dollar balance of around eight million dollars and a sterling balance net of British credits of approximately a million and a half pounds.

Where all this strange action and counter-action of economic influences in Spain will lead is difficult to determine. It is something new in a world pattern but certain it is that the inflation spiral in Spain is increasing in pace. The rumbling of an economically bewildered peasantry is heard from one end of the country to the other, and again I repeat that barring a political or military disturbance from an unexpected quarter the upheaval in Spain and the final inescapable pressure on the Franco government will come from an unbearable economic situation rather than from the many conflicting political influences in Spain, though it will of course be influenced and urged by rising political aspirations and by the tremendous population which remains inimicable to Franco, whether they are quiescent and at large or, as is frequently reported, part of the population of several hundred thousand former enemies held in prison.

In this theory I am not entirely at one with the American and British ambassadors who believe that the entire question in Spain is a military one depending solely on when, as, and if Hitler either feels that he has the manpower or it is to his final interests to march into Spain. Sir Samuel Hoare feels that the danger of the inflationary spiral is great, but that so long as the army is fed and controlled all will be well. He does not believe that Germany has anywhere near sufficient manpower today to risk an invasion and the defense of Spain.

There is little difference of opinion in high sources, as there is in Sweden, as to whether or not Spain would attempt to defend herself against an invasion. While, as I pointed out, the entire population is still war weary and violently opposed to any military entanglements except their gesture against Russia, there is a universal feeling that Spain would defend itself in any eventuality.

While Spain has substantially no air force or navy, she has a war-hardened army of probably 350,000 men under arms and most of these are probably good fighting men, for that is a Spanish characteristic. But it is the general belief that the corruption of the government and the influence of the years since the Revolution have softened the officers to a point that at least in the beginning the army would have little or no leadership. Caldwell, the manager of the Telephone Company, who has been in Spain for many years, has no doubt whatever that Spain would fight viciously against any aggressor, and his knowledge is backed by his close contact with the War Office through the manufacture by his technicians of many war materials for the Spanish Government.

From the point of view of the scope and effect of Allied propaganda in Spain, our situation could hardly be worse. Any of the Spanish daily newspapers might easily have been printed in Berlin so far as the integrity or accuracy of their news is concerned. Unquestionably encouraged by Franco's strategy, probably highly subsidized by the German Government and, in the opinion of the Allied Governments in Spain, steadily falling in circulation, the Spanish newspapers nevertheless represent practically a division of Dr. Goebbels' Ministry of Propaganda. Any news favorable to the Allied cause is usually diluted or misinterpreted and even the actual Allied communiqués buried as far inside the newspaper as possible. All Russian advances are characterized as part of brilliant German strategy, although in recent weeks the explanation of the North African and Russian situation has called for violent journalistic contortions.

The British Ministry of Information boys, while long in the field, do not seem to have made much of a dent in the situation and are apparently badly torn by internal Embassy strife. Our own OWI boys have but recently gotten started.

However, they are under-staffed, have substantially no available help or manpower, and their efforts and those of the British must be contrasted with a long-developed, highly organized German organization controlling the press and the censorship, entirely unscrupulous in its use of funds in a country always highly susceptible to these methods, and operating a tremendous mailing list and propaganda contacts throughout the nation. In addition to this, the German Government has rented and operates two large stores in the center of Madrid on the Grande Via, under the name of "Alemania" and "Turista" respectively, in which large crowds congregate daily to read frequent mimeographed war bulletins, handed out in quantities and highly colored, to look at pictures of German victories and to absorb great quantities of freely offered German propaganda. We, on the other hand, are just beginning to circulate a few pamphlet pieces of propaganda . . . of the last two, one was suppressed by the censor on account of its violent personal attacks on Hitler and the other, devoted largely to the magnificent design and efficiency of the aircraft carrier Hornet, became obsolete before its arrival on account of the destruction of the Hornet.

These comments are given as facts, not as criticisms, for the Germans are longer established, nearer, and have all the great advantages of tremendous pro-German feeling while our boys are new in the field, have little help, and of necessity are slow in getting started. They are however, I believe, able and efficient, and given proper backing should be of great help in Spain.

The situation as to American and English books, magazines and newspapers in Spain is extremely bad. Substantially no books, newspapers or magazines in English have been permitted in Spain since 1936. A survey of the bookstores in Spain reveals a few ancient Tauchnitz books of about 1930 and '31, and substantially the only available books in English in the entire country are to be found in the tiny lending libraries operated in connection with the British and American Embassies. No English or American newspapers can be purchased anywhere and the American in Spain, except for the daily mimeographed sheets of radio and State Department news, is as completely cut off as the traveler to the head waters of the Congo.

In the three neutral countries of Sweden, Spain and Portugal, the absolute and basic determination of every government and popular thought, trend and decision, is based today not on who is going to win the war, not on what will be the best alliance to fulfill nationalistic hopes and aspirations, not on what economic help and trade relations can be established, but overwhelmingly on the question of what is Russia shooting for and what is Russia going to do.

We can baby and pet Sweden till the cows come home. We can let her grow fat and prosperous at our expense by pouring millions of tons of materials into the heart of the German war effort against us. And we can do every unconscionable thing in the fantastic hope that Sweden will be a friendly power when, as, and if we invade Norway, but it will avail us nothing as long as Sweden feels that her ultimate enemy is Russia. And when we have done all these things and Sweden fears that Russia may sweep through Finland to face her on Finland's west coast, she will still come into the war on the side of Germany and not on the side of the Allies.

In Spain we can buy Spanish oranges at five hundred dollars a dozen and we can fight Germany by any economic, psychological, or propaganda warfare, or by any method from gangster to kid-glove diplomacy, and we will still find that the guiding spirit of Spain is a fear of Bolshevism and a hatred of all things Russian, and that in the last analysis anything that is pro-Russian is anti-Spanish.

In Portugal you can have an English alliance extending back for hundreds of years, an ostensible predisposition towards England and its Allies, and a deep admiration for America. You can still be assured that if you scratch the surface of the suave friendship and the economic balance of Salazar, you will find underneath an almost fanatical anti-Russian.

The neutral world in Europe, confused as it may be in its ideas as to who will win the war, still thinks that when the war is concluded Mr. Stalin will sit at the head of the table and say, "Well, what did you boys do in 1941 and 1942? What victories did you win while I was carrying the burden of Germany, and what the hell are you here for anyway in Europe? Now go home and be good boys and let me have what I want—it's really none of your business!"

All of which leads me to say that unless this situation is changed and changed speedily, unless in some way we can break down the Russian suspicion and reserve, either through intelligent representation in Russia or otherwise, and unless we can by some fortuitous effort force Russia into some kind of a real declaration of its war aims, we are making a lot of false motions and doing a lot of useless work in the neutral countries. I do not know *how* this can be accomplished. I only know that it must be accomplished some way.

Probably the most astute political observer in England today is Beaverbrook, and after talking about it privately for four months he has suddenly come out with his attack in the House of Lords on the English failure to really help Russia. What he has up his sleeve I do not know, but I feel confident that he would echo the feeling which I have just expressed to you.

I had a long talk with Dave Bruce on this matter last night and I am going to try to persuade him to talk at length to Beaverbrook, who knows more about and understands more of the Russian situation, I think, than anyone here. In the meantime, I commend these thoughts to you in Washington.

From the vantage point of an embassy year spent in Spain, eight or nine years after these paragraphs were written, they still seem to me to express with reasonable accuracy the business and governmental situation which existed in the Peninsula at that time and which still exists. Certainly the analysis of the political judgment of Russia, held by many of the countries of Western Europe, gave something of a fair prophecy of affairs today. The diplomats of the West still try to peer nervously through the thick walls of the Kremlin and determine the convolutions of the Russian mind; even our own American lives are tortured and governed by the moves in Moscow. Stalin has at last said, in effect, what my prediction made it clear that he might say.

It is unfortunate for the writer on the current Spanish scene to have substantially no books of reference, for few worthy books have been written in English concerning either the years of the Civil War or the postwar period under Franco. There are plenty of books on the history of the ancient days when Spain dominated the world, and up to the time when she became a third-rate power through the Spanish-American War. But concerning recent years, few indeed are the books which are historically sound, and are not written with the pens of prejudice for or against Franco. There are two that are worth reading. *War Mission in Spain,* by our own ambassador, Carlton Hayes, has all of the extrovert and disinterested viewpoint that a true historian commands. It is a far cry from the publication of Sir Samuel Hoare, now Lord Templewood, the British ambassador of the war days, who, in his volume titled *Complacent Dictator,* rather flamboyantly invites the reader to believe that he won the war singlehanded, particularly in Spain. One would judge from its reading that there is no United States Embassy in Spain, nor any United States army or navy. Yet it does have an interesting appendix, which includes Winston Churchill's answer to Franco when, following the war, the Spanish dictator through the Duke of Alba held out a feather of the dove of peace to England, suggesting that bygones be bygones. The British Premier said in part:

I would let your Excellency fall into serious error if I did not remove from your mind the idea that His Majesty's Government would be ready to consider any block of powers based on hostility to our Russian allies, or an assumed need of defense against them. His Majesty's Government policy is firmly based on the Anglo-Soviet Treaty of 1942, and considers permanent Anglo-Russian collaboration within the framework of the future world organization as essential, not only for our own interests but also the future peace and prosperity of Europe as a whole.

Possibly these sentences prove that no one should ever put pen to paper.

It was against this backdrop in 1946, under strong Russian influence during the waning days of the United States-Russian honeymoon, that the United Nations self-righteously decreed that the major powers should withdraw their ambassadors from Spain, believing no doubt that this diplomatic spanking would bring the Spaniards to their senses and result in the overthrow of Franco. Actually it rallied the Spanish people to their ruler, who they felt had been unjustly attacked by other nations. Britain immediately withdrew its ambassador, and our own Norman Armour, who for a few months had succeeded Ambassador Hayes, left for a new post. It was almost five years before this unhappy error in diplomacy was rectified and I was sent to Madrid as the first ambassador to represent the United States there since 1946. Even then the move was dictated to some extent by the feeling of many U.S. military students that the circle of defense against Russia to the West should be completed to include Spain. It was bitterly assailed by labor unions, by anti-Catholics, and by many others, including those who were still influenced by the misleading and romantic stories published by American novelists who fought with the International Brigade against Franco during the Civil War. But my nomination was confirmed in the Senate, and I departed for Spain on the great liner *Independence* on her maiden voyage, early in February 1951. It is an interesting coincidence that Washington Irving when he traveled to Spain in 1832 as American minister sailed the Atlantic on a sloop called *The Independence*.

I had planned to disembark at Gibraltar and drive to Madrid, but finding that I had opened an old Spanish sore in their prejudice against the English for the theft of Gibraltar, I was importuned to land on Spanish soil at Cadiz. Unfortunately, the *Independence* was unable to make the landing on account of her great draft, and the Spanish Government went to the lengths of dredging a new channel in Cadiz harbor so that the great ship could land its incoming ambassador directly in Spain.

The line had invited the mayor and the civil and military governors at Cadiz on board to lunch with me, along with a few friends who turned out to be substantially the population of the town. I doubt if the American Export Line made any money on the voyage. In any event, it was a magnificent welcome. The chief officers of the Madrid Embassy, which had functioned through the years under Paul Culbertson as chargé d'affaires, came down from Madrid to meet me, and at mid-afternoon I was off for Seville, where I spent my first night in Spain.

The next day I traveled the route of Don Quixote with Angie Duke, who had flown over and who called himself my Sancho Panza. There were few windmills left in Spain at which a modern Quixote might tilt, but plenty remained in the United States in the persons of American critics of our new Spanish policy. That night we stayed at 5 Ramon de la Cruz, the house that had been occupied by the American counselors because the great rented palace of war days had been given up.

My first callers were, of course, the Baron de los Torres, Minister of Protocol, and the head of the American section of the Foreign Office, the Marques de Prat, who enjoys the nickname "Perico." He is suave, gracious, and a brilliant linguist, a diplomat of the old school, and I was destined to see much of him during the coming months. Almost immediately he escorted me to make my first call on the Minister of Foreign Affairs, Señor Martin Artajo, who was breaking all historic records in having held his portfolio during the many years since the death of Jordana, the last wartime foreign minister. He was a wise, astute, and hard-working head of his Ministry, though influenced in every action by his former position as head of Acción Católica, the great lay organization of Spanish Catholics. Artajo spoke no English and my elemental Spanish was hideous, but the perfect English of De Prat bridged me over this and many another linguistic impasse. Artajo told me that I would be received by the Caudillo within the next week.

In the meantime I established myself with the Spaniards by attending the first available bullfight, at which I had the company of the Duke de Primo de Rivera, who had just been appointed the new Spanish ambassador to England. As I came into the ring, the solid mass of Spanish spectators rose and cheered, acclaiming a new era and an American ambassador who was willing to attend an exhibition of their national sport.

Some additional publicity eventuated when one of the bulls in a mighty effort to escape his tormentors jumped the barrier and landed almost at my feet. Spanish newspapers and their contemporaries all over Europe published a remarkable photograph taken by some agile cameraman that showed the bull in mid-air jumping toward me, and was captioned "The Spanish Bull Calls on the New American Ambassador." For attending bullfights I received the bouquets of the Spanish press, which expressed delight that I was an *aficionado*, and from the American press a flood of remonstrance that I should, as American ambassador, sink so low as to view this horrid and cruel sport.

Now that I have left Spain I can say confidentially that bullfights do not greatly exhilarate me and that I went largely for good-neighbor purposes. My lack of interest does not derive from any feeling of cruelty to the animals, for at least they have their twenty minutes of glory before a great audience, while the bull that appears as steak on your tables has only a few minutes as he plods up the slaughterhouse runway to be hit on the head and prepared for his transmigration into beef. But the utter sameness of the ritual and the well-known fact a bull has little chance against his human enemies spell merely a tiresome proceeding for me. I suspect and confess that my hope was frequently that the matador would be hurt. Perhaps it is the same psychology that leads great crowds to prize fights in the United States.

The day of my presentation of credentials and my meeting with Franco was set for March first at noon. Three magnificent red and gold eighteenth-century coaches, each drawn by six horses, appeared in front of 5 Ramon de la Cruz, accompanied by more than two hundred of the picturesque Moorish guards of the Franco household, dressed in their native costumes and carrying lances, and with their horses' hoofs embellished with gold and silver. Never, I think in the history of Spain, had there been a more picturesque procession through the streets to the mighty Oriente Palace. The emotional and sentimental Madrileños were keenly aware of the history-making advent of a new United States ambassador to Spain after five years. The mighty procession, in which I occupied the leading coach with the Minister of Protocol, with my senior officers and military attachés occupying the two following coaches, all preceded and followed by horseman guards, progressed at snail's pace through the center of Madrid to the courtyard of the palace. There we paused while the military band played the national anthems of the two countries.

Up the stairs of the mighty palace, all of us arrayed in full evening clothes at noontide, accompanied by the officers of the royal household, we proceeded to the presentation room where Franco and his Minister of State Artajo stood to receive us. The ceremony was brief. The dictator and the ambassador shook hands, and we proceeded to the usual small conference room for an exchange of pleasantries and compliments which meant nothing to either of us. Back then to the rooms and stairways of the palace, with flashlights popping like star shells. Flanked on either side by Moors presenting their spears, we went out to the courtyard and the procession returned to Ramon de la Cruz through the same shouting and well-wishing crowds of the Spanish people. I was at last a fully accredited ambassador to Spain, the Spanish press was ecstatic, and that section of the American press that opposed the appointment of an ambassador to Spain was cynical and bitter.

Two days after the great ceremony, there arrived in Madrid the new ambassador of His Britannic Majesty, Sir John Balfour, with whom I had served and formed a great friendship the year before in Argentina. Jock Balfour is a great citizen and a great diplomat. Complete and peculiar are his advantages as a linguist; serving through most of the war in a German prison camp, he had taken advantage of the fact that his cellmates changed frequently and came from many different countries. His years as a prisoner were spent in learning the languages of these men, and as a result he is fluent in all languages ranging from Russian to Chinese dialects. Socially charming, and being not only able, but willing, to do a comic Scottish song or an imitation of Hitler at the drop of a hat at any party, he was also a fine diplomat of the old school of the British Foreign Office.

My affection and admiration for him and for his wife, Frances, are unbounded, and I went out of my way to meet him at the Madrid station when he arrived in Spain. His appointment as ambassador to Spain was an almost untenable one owing to the extreme bitterness that existed between the Spanish and English governments. Spain had been constantly heaped with abuse in speeches in the British House of Commons; and the ghost of the British ownership of Gibraltar within Spanish borders for a period of a hundred and fifty years was inevitably trotted out when Britain or any of its works was mentioned. But Jock Balfour knew no fear, and expressed himself as being an ambassador in the doghouse. I wanted to express to the Spanish people my deep affection for England and all its works by meeting the new ambassador in Madrid. The photographers and newspapers did not fail to make note at great length of this gesture, and I think with political effect. While England has laid down a large part of her empire and the United States has taken up the burden with none of the advantages, I feel now, as always, that the safety of the world depends much upon the friendship and back-to-back relationship of England and the United States.

It speedily became apparent that from the American viewpoint the two great areas of disagreement between Spain and the United States concerned labor and religious freedom, or as Al Smith put it "The right of every man to walk with his God in his own way." From the Spanish point of view the results of the McCarran Act, which aimed at Communists, nevertheless provided in effect that anyone who had been a member of a totalitarian party, or had been employed by one in any country, should be denied a visa for entrance into the

United States. It so happens that Senator McCarran, an ardent Catholic, has been for many years the great friend of Spain in the United States Senate, and it was certainly not within his vision that the act which he fathered and fostered should per se make it impossible for any affiliate of the Spanish Government or any member of the Falange Party in Spain to obtain a visa. In Spain it was substantially impossible for any one of working age to obtain employment and rations without affiliation with the Falange; even its Monarchists are frequently tied in some way to the party, and the difficulties arising from the McCarran Act extended from diplomats to ordinary tourists. The resulting heartbreaks and difficulties consumed, I should say, more than a majority of my time and substantially all of the time of our consular service in Madrid. The arduous provisions of the McCarran Act have been lightened somewhat, but the resulting scar on the pride of the Spanish body politic will remain for a long time.

Beyond this there existed the problem of American loans to Spain. While Congress late in 1950 had voted a loan of $62,-500,000 to Spain, the Export-Import Bank, which was charged with the administration of the loan, put such barriers and conditions on it that not until my departure in January 1952 were the purposes and distribution of the loan fully determined and in operation.

Meanwhile the United States Government had granted loans of hundreds of millions of dollars to Tito. The logical Spanish mind was totally unable to understand why, with our financial policy to stop the spread of Communism in Europe, we could make loans to the Yugoslavian dictator, an avowed Communist, and deny loans to the Spanish Government, which had been the enemy of Communism for a period of many years and which remained violently anti-Communistic. I must confess that I am completely unable to understand this policy myself and have many times so expressed myself to the State Department and to my Senate and House friends.

There existed also the question of the United States' desire to arm Spain against the common enemy Russia, or to establish bases in Spain as part of the defense of Western Europe. All of this, of course, became part of the problem of Spain becoming a member of NATO.

There was also the fact that Spain was the only country in Western Europe outside of the Russian zone which still went through the archaic practice of demanding visas from American visitors. Last but not least in the Spanish mind was the question of the right of American newspaper correspondents to live in a hospitable country and to write violent attacks against its government and interfere with its domestic problems. This last problem came to a head shortly after my arrival; the Spanish Government declared Sam Pope Brewer, the correspondent of the New York *Times*, persona non grata, and took up his *carnet* of residence in Spain.

Shortly after the presentation of my credentials, I asked through the Foreign Ministry for an audience with the Caudillo and was received by him in El Pardo. I felt that it was better to mince no words. From what I had seen of him, I felt that he might be willing to speak to me with frankness and integrity. Accordingly, in my talk with him I plunged immediately into the question of religious freedom in Spain. I told him fully of the President's feeling, of his instructions to me as to his hopes and wishes, and of the intensity of his own and other Americans' pronouncements on the matter. After a long discussion in which Franco declared that freedom already existed, he nevertheless promised that he would issue a manifesto to the civil governors of every province in Spain, instructing them to see to it that there was no infringement of the right of worship, the right of burial, or the right of assembly for any religious sect so long as they kept the peace and obeyed the law. Feeling greatly encouraged, I returned to the Embassy and advised not only the President but the Department as well of the results of our talk. I included the military aspects of our conversation, which had brought statements from the dictator that Spain did not desire to become a member of NATO, but would welcome a bilateral agreement with the United States whereby Spain would be bound to any and all of the obligations of NATO membership if, as, and when she received proper military aid from the United States, co-ordinated with her long-time Iberian agreements with Portugal.

However, carrying out the instructions even of a dictator on the question of religious freedom is not so simple as it seems. Catholic Spain with its population of perhaps twenty-eight million people has, I believe, less than ten thousand practicing Protestants. At the maximum Protestants make up less than one tenth of one per cent of the population. The stern religious history of Spain through the Inquisition to the present day is well known, which makes it one thing to issue orders to the civil governors that there shall be freedom of religion, but another thing to force upon the small towns and villages an order, even of a dictator, which violates the beliefs and principles of the clergy down to the village priest who has never been beyond the confines of his village. To him a Protestant is some special emissary of the devil, who has been sent to his village or town to torment him.

A Protestant minister may apply for the right to build and operate a chapel, which he must do under the law, but the civil governor is harassed on one side by the orders of his Caudillo and on the other side by the solid mass of public opinion. The result probably is that the request for a chapel is simply left unanswered for months and years. If the request is approved the military governor, who represents an entirely different autocracy from the civil governor, may plant soldiers around the chapel for the intimidation of the faithful Protestants. Protestant cemeteries are few and far between, and it is obvious that Catholic authorities will not permit Protestants to be buried in what they regard as sacred ground.

Other complications arise from the unquestioned fact that a

number of the Protestant leaders in Spain are renegade Catholics, and certainly not of the quality characterizing even the lowliest of the Protestant clergy in the United States. There are political aspects of the matter as well, arising from the reported action of certain of the Spanish Protestant clergy during the Civil War. The essence of the difficulty arises from the church itself, not from the government, of Spain.

Nevertheless, I appointed two or three officers of the Embassy to spend substantially all their time in studying the situation of Protestantism in Spain. While we did arrange for the opening of a number of chapels that had been denied existence for years past and while we listened to complaints from Protestants in many towns and wrote innumerable unanswered notes to the Foreign Office on the whole situation, I cannot but believe that we failed in our efforts to create freedom of religion in Spain as we understand it in the United States, and I am a bit doubtful that it will be so created in our time.

Apparently, however, the Protestant clergy in Spain who were in communication with the President had indicated to him that our campaign was more of a success than I thought it to be, as President Truman wrote me on April 19, 1951, as follows:

*Dear Stan:*

I read your confidential communication of the 5th with more interest than anything I've read in a long time.

You are really making progress on this religious situation in Spain. Keep up the good work. Eventually we will improve not only our relations and the situation in Spain, but it will have its effect on the whole of South America.

*Sincerely yours,*
*Harry S. Truman*

*Honorable Stanton Griffis*
*American Embassy*
*Madrid, Spain*

About six weeks after the presentation of my credentials to Franco, I was confronted with the unhappy case concerning

Sam Pope Brewer of the New York *Times*. I had come to Spain with no affection for Brewer, and in fact was personally extremely bitter at him for attacking my efforts in the Near East as director of the Palestine relief work, and for publishing statements regarding our food purchases in Syria and Lebanon that I believed to be untrue. I had pleaded with Arthur Sulzberger, the proprietor of the New York *Times*, to send a man to Spain to replace Brewer before my arrival, in order that I might have a fair chance in my efforts. Sulzberger had refused to do this, perhaps properly, saying that any such action would affect the morale of all his correspondents in foreign countries, who perhaps would feel that an American ambassador might sway their destinies. He did promise me that he would instruct Brewer to give me a run for my money in Spain.

During my tenancy Brewer had been meticulously fair, and I greatly regretted that on my shoulders came the responsibility of deciding a course of action. Accordingly, I wired the Department that, as they knew, I was highly prejudiced in the Brewer case and should debar myself from participation in it, but nevertheless would meticulously follow any orders in the matter. Their response was that as freedom of the press and the right of any American correspondent to call the plays as he saw them is engrained in the American mind as a basic freedom, I should make every representation to the Spanish Government that might lead to the cancellation of the Brewer ban. This I did, and to the best of my ability. I harassed Martin Artajo, the Foreign Minister, in frequent and consecutive conferences, and the day came shortly when he called me to his office and said, "Purely as a personal tribute to the American Ambassador, Spain will renew the Brewer *carnet* and he can remain in Spain." I so wired the Department and was immediately instructed that the United States could not accept the action of the Spanish Government as a personal tribute, but that it must be done on the basis of the principle of the freedom of the press. It seemed impossible to me to deny the

Spanish Government a face-saving gesture. I wired the Department that the Brewer case was closed, and it was.

Not the least of my more pleasant troubles in Spain was its social life, for it is a very happy, social, and hospitable country. Its people are always smiling and gregarious. A peasant may be underfed and overworked, but give him a guitar and a flamenco partner and he will dance all night. It may be said, too, that this characteristic extends from the peasant to the Monarchists, the moneyed and social mentors of Spain. But Spain is a country where you have dinner tomorrow. The cocktail hours, the bane and horror of all diplomatic life, are from eight-thirty to ten-thirty, and dinner invitations are ordinarily for eleven, which means the soup course at quarter to twelve and a pleasant game of canasta starting at about two in the morning.

I couldn't take it, and formed a defensive and offensive alliance with my good friend the Duke of Alba, whose Cordon Bleu dinners were scheduled for exactly nine-thirty. Alba is one of the great in Spain. He was for a long time the Spanish ambassador to England; he is the recognized leader of the Monarchists in his country and possesses one of the great private collections of Hispanic art. It was his lady ancestor who was painted with and without by Goya, and despite the recent histories, he claims that though she may have sinned with everyone else in Madrid, it was not so with Goya. Our campaign for earlier dinners in Spain made little progress. I found that after returning to my house at 3:00 or 4:00 A.M. it was difficult to operate successfully an Embassy which opened at eight in the morning, and gradually I spread the news that I did not accept dinner invitations. This shortened my social and business hours but no doubt lengthened my life. I am willing to confess that my propaganda toward complete religious freedom in Spain and for changing the Spanish dinner hour were equally unsuccessful ventures.

On May eighth, celebrating the annual meeting of the

American Chamber of Commerce in Spain, I made a speech in Barcelona in which I attempted to clarify the American policy in Spain, saying in part:

"These policies provide for a dual purpose, to the ends that loans to Spain and to Spanish interests should be for the purpose of making substantial contributions to the Spanish economy, towards making Spain self-supporting and at the same time contributing to a United States policy for the creation of a healthier world economy. There has been, as you probably know, some difference of opinion between Spain and the United States in the interpretation of this policy, which is directed towards lasting contributions for the benefit of the Spanish people as a whole, and therefore to a large extent excluding the use of loan funds for expendable goods. However, at the earnest plea of the Spanish Government, exceptions to this policy have been made as to cotton, fertilizers and wheat; these, especially wheat, are regarded by our government as non-recurring items, with the earnest hope that the gap between springtime and the harvesting of the crop this year will be successfully bridged and that the new crop will be as bounteous as the beauty of the fields through which I have driven would indicate.

"Another aspect of this policy should be made clear. The government of the United States has stood, since its inception almost two hundred years ago, as the champion of private enterprise. Our government believes, nurtures and defends the belief that personal enterprise, personal initiative, is the great keystone to economic development. Economic nationalism has made little progress in the United States.

"In Spain we realize fully that the use of funds provided by the United States cannot be devoted solely to the needs of private enterprise on account of the vast development of nationally controlled properties; we realize that government-owned railroads and other enterprises require aid if there is to be a well-balanced economy here. But our theory is merely that so far as it is economically sound, we should favor private enterprises, and it must be observed that our study of the situation turns us towards the agricultural enterprises of Spain; the necessity of making its people independent of the outside world as far as their food supply is concerned is of primary importance.

"While I cannot accurately forecast the precise development of the United States policy with regard to Spain, the most recent statements on Spain made by my chief, the Secretary of State Mr. Acheson, give us a clear indication of the general direction of the United States policy in relation to this country. Speaking before a Senate committee in February, he said, 'The importance of the association of Spain and the defense of Western Europe I think is clear, I think it is also clear that the relations with this country, and I hope of the other countries with Spain, are now entering a new phase.'

"However, assistance of this character is not a one-way street; there is great co-operation and many forms of it that we desire to ask of Spain. In the economic field we are hopeful that many of the restrictions now applied to American business operations can be ameliorated or removed. We hope that American corporations may be encouraged to make investments in Spain through permission to obtain larger interests in Spanish companies than is now allowed; we believe that the economy of Spain and its dollar shortage can be greatly aided by a campaign to bring American tourists here to this country of charm and beauty and hospitality."

The reference in the speech to private enterprise somewhat disturbed the Spanish Government, but brought cheer to the many engaged in private operations and certainly to the American companies. In the meantime, rumors and counter-rumors were sweeping the Spanish cities concerning plans and proposals arising in the United States for increased financial aid to Spain along with a military arrangement that would tie in directly or indirectly with the NATO defense of the West. Franco and his people were fully aware of the antagonism both of France and of England to any proposals that would include Spain in NATO. The age-old hatred of Spain by and of its neighbors had lasted certainly since England seized Gibraltar and Napoleon swept through the Peninsula. Speeches by British and French politicians were continually outraging the

Spaniards, and it was obviously necessary for Franco and his ministers to take the position about NATO that any candidate for a good club, who knew that he would be overwhelmingly blackballed, must take. Of course, it would be "I do not want to join the club." But they were anxious and hopeful for some kind of a military bilateral pact with the United States and were acutely aware that their military resources could not be effectively built up and maintained without the contribution of economic aid.

Their needs were so basic that a story was popular in Spain at the time of a conversation between a Russian and a Frenchman that was close to being true. "How long in case of war would it take the Russian Army to reach the Pyrenees through France?" asks the Russian. "Three days," replies the Frenchman. "How long would it take them to cross the Pyrenees?" "One week." "How long would it take the Russian Army to get from the Pyrenees to Madrid?" "Six months." "Why?" asks the Russian. "On account of the roads."

In the Embassy we waited impatiently for a final determination of policy by the Pentagon and the State Department, and it was with delight, but substantially no warning, that I received the news that Admiral Sherman, one of the Joint Chiefs of Staff, would arrive in Madrid about the middle of July to confer with Franco. The meeting at the Pardo was historic. The Marques de Prat interpreted for the Caudillo's discussion with Admiral Sherman and the American ambassador. To Sherman's carefully phrased questions as to whether or not the Spanish Government would be willing to negotiate the American use of Spanish naval and air bases and to his questions concerning Franco's probable policy in case of war, the Caudillo answered directly and without reserve.

He would of course be willing to negotiate, but pointed out that it would be of little use to grant the privileges asked by the Americans unless there was parallel economic assistance sufficient to make the air bases and harbors efficient. He out-

lined Spain's historic opposition to Russia, and repeated unequivocally the statements which he had made to me four
months earlier, that while Spain did not desire to be a member
of NATO she would be willing with proper American assistance to take upon herself all of the responsibilities of a NATO
nation in case of attack. He added that there would be no question of a properly armed Spanish army's refusal to fight north
of the Pyrenees, or anywhere else, if the occasion demanded.
His only reservation seemed to be the normal one that the use
of the bases and the harbors would be at all times regarded as
the use of Spanish property, and would remain in Spanish
ownership after any war.

As a thousand new rumors swept the capital and the international press, Admiral Sherman and I returned to the city to
phrase our respective dispatches. The next day we attended the
Caudillo's historic annual dinner that always precedes Franco's
departure to his native Galicia, and the migration of the government and the diplomatic corps to San Sebastian, in escape
from the hot Spanish summer. It was in San Sebastian three
days later that I received the tragic news of Admiral Sherman's death in line of duty at Naples. It was a crushing blow
to us all.

Through August and the dismal weather of the north coast,
we eagerly awaited the arrival of the military and economic
missions which had been promised the Spanish Government as
the result of Admiral Sherman's visit. I snatched a week of
vacation to cruise the Mediterranean to the Balearic Islands on
the princely yacht of Charlie Wrightsman and Bob Young,
returning to Madrid in time to meet the Pentagon group under
the leadership of General Spry and the representatives of the
Economic Co-operation Administration, headed by Professor
Sydney C. Sufrin, of Syracuse University. Both of these
groups were efficient and exhaustive in their studies. The military group, in constant and friendly co-operation with the
Spanish general staff, completed their voluminous reports by

the middle of November. But it was close to Christmas before the economic studies on every aspect of Spanish industry and commerce were dispatched to Washington for perusal.

The intervening time was open season for Congressmen and Congressional committees, all of whom, of course, desired to talk personally to Franco. It is a salutary thing that more and more Congressmen desire to see and study Europe first-hand, but it is sometimes a bit wearing on the local ambassador to accompany them and hear the same questions and answers over and over again. After about the tenth Congressional-Franco conference—during which I heard the repeated questions: Does Spain desire to join NATO? Does Spain wish a bilateral arrangement with the United States? Does Spain wish economic aid? What is Spain's attitude toward Russia? What is Spain's attitude toward freedom of the press and freedom of religion?—there finally developed a bit of by-play between the dictator and the ambassador. He would glance at me with a near wink when he answered an oft-repeated question with oft-repeated explanation.

In the meantime I was asked by every Congressman and visiting newspaperman if American aid to Spain was not in reality direct aid to Franco and the support of Franco. There was only one answer to this question, and that was unequivocally yes. Franco was Spain. Read his history and the history of Spain from any point of view for the past seventeen years and you must come to this inevitable conclusion.

Referring back to the letter and the analysis I made in 1943, one can, I think, say that during the intervening years the Falange has lost some power, compared with the Monarchists and the Church, with the army holding its own. There is a little change for the better in the black-market situation, but the peseta, in company with almost all world currencies, has gone up to an outside market value of from 45 to 52 to the dollar, as against 20 to 21 then. The condition of the peasantry is little worse and little better than it was in '43, or indeed than it was under the republic or under the monarchy. Political prisoners have greatly dwindled.

Certainly I cannot, nor will I, defend dictators nor dictatorship. But I believe that almost every important business and thinking man in Spain today would be horrified if he felt that Franco would die tomorrow. Most of all, the Monarchists would shake with fear if they felt that their cries for the return of Don Juan were by some trick of fate to be answered and he were to come back suddenly.

Franco is an avowed Monarchist. He has arranged for a succession in case of his death, to the end that a regency will select a king who must be a Spaniard, thirty years of age, a Catholic, and of royal blood. At the moment, of course, the leading pretender is Don Juan, the son of Alfonso XIII, who lives quietly in Lisbon, who is occasionally in contact with Franco, and whose two sons are being educated in San Sebastian by the Franco government. The leading Monarchists of Spain visit him as part of his court every few months, and speak of him as "the King."

However, the definition provided in the regency law might be read to include the Carlist pretender and might even be stretched to include young Prince Otto of Austria. The stage is set, therefore, by Franco for a return to the monarchy when the curtain falls on his reign. But I believe strongly that there will be no descent of the curtain until he dies or he himself feels too feeble to carry on. As he constantly hunts and fishes in the most rugged country, and I have seen him display for several consecutive hours at a time almost super-human mental and physical control, I do not believe that there is any imminence of his physical degeneration. I have watched him stand on a dais, in heavy uniform, never moving a muscle or changing his stance during almost three hours as more than two thousand grandees, officers, diplomats, and government servants filed past him, clicking their heels and bowing.

From an economic point of view, it must be realized that

Spain is intrinsically a poverty-stricken country with an average per capita income of about $160. Probably less than fifty per cent of its land is arable, even under the most satisfactory weather conditions, which in the Iberian Peninsula are undependable to say the least. For a decade Spain has not been able to raise sufficient wheat to feed its constantly and feverishly growing population. For years it purchased its necessary surplus on the cuff from Argentina, until even Perón, a great friend of Spain, decided that a little cash was needed. This year and last, with abundant rains, Spain has come very near to its goal of self-support in wheat, the deficit having been made up in part by the American loan. It is possible that with the additional economic aid promised from the United States, with new supplies of fertilizer, and new shipments of agricultural machinery she may once again be able to feed her people.

Yet here we must face the interrelation of religion and economics. Spain is one of the most outstandingly Catholic nations in the world, and its religion teaches that there must be no human interference with the natural biologic developments of mankind. Yet it is hard to believe that even an ardent churchman in Spain today would not admit its present overpopulation or view with alarm its prospective population. I have maintained always that Catholicism is the most potent and the most violent enemy of Communism. But sometimes in arguments with my Catholic friends I express the paradoxical belief that through some of its doctrines the Catholic Church is one of the great friends of Communism, for an excess of population always breeds human misery and Communism fattens and fosters on the misery of the masses. So in Spain, with its arid fields, and its cities and villages teeming with ever-increasing numbers of people, the economists must recognize that the troubles of today may not vanish tomorrow even with the friendly help of the United States.

With all the other troubles and burdens of Western Europe, certainly we cannot afford today or tomorrow any political upheaval in Spain. I know no man in Spain today who could take up the torch if Franco dropped it, nor do I believe that the return of the monarchy would improve conditions in the slightest. Wishful thinking it may be, but I do believe that if Franco is able to raise his people above the starvation line, he will begin to give them more freedom—religious freedom, if the tenets of the church will permit, freedom of the press— which is already beginning to show here and there in the Spanish newspapers—some freedom of assembly, and some freedom of public speech. Although every Spaniard comments loud and long in the cafés and in his home of the iniquities of the government, he is not allowed to express those opinions in general assembly. As strikes are illegal and prohibited in Spain, the lack of freedom of labor completes the totalitarian circle.

The thinking Spaniard will tell you that conditions were no better and probably little worse in the pre-Franco days. While he may express deep hatred of Franco, and invariably will in the manifold cases where members of his family were killed or imprisoned during the Revolution and the Civil War, he will nevertheless grudgingly agree that following the country's own internecine war the dictator kept Spain out of the Allied-Axis jaws of World War II. With consummate statesmanship, although perhaps along double-faced lines, and with the German Army just across the Pyrenees, begging for the opportunity to take Gibraltar and close the Mediterranean, Franco, nevertheless, for whatever reason, stood firm and would not permit the march of the German Army across his country. In his conferences with Hitler he is said to have been the only man who so thoroughly exhausted Hitler in argument that the number one Nazi fled back to Berlin. "He kept us out of war," is a powerful argument in any country. My own personal guess is that in an open election for a president of Spain today Franco would be elected, and would probably remain a dictator. One other development there would certainly be in an open election: the sudden emergence of some twenty or thirty political parties, no one of which would control over ten or fifteen per cent of the Cortes; accordingly, the possibility of operating a successful government would be even more remote than in the present situation of rising and falling governments in France. Repeating again that the political and economic situations of any nation are inextricably woven together, the student of the current Spanish scene must realize that whatever maintenance of, or improvement in, the already low Spanish standard of living exists, was accomplished by the dictator; it was done without outside aid of any sort or description except perhaps the small credit sales of wheat made by Argentina.

From 1945 until 1952 the United States has been engaged in pouring literally hundreds of millions, even thousands of millions of dollars into England, France, Italy, and the smaller nations of Western Europe in general aid programs and finally through the Marshall Plan. Of this aid Spain received not a dollar, nor did she receive any dollar of American loans until late in the year 1951. Yet she existed. She remained non-Communistic and she remained strongly anti-Communistic. This perhaps is no mean record. It may be argued by the critics of the Spanish Government that Spain had none of the suffering, the rigors, and the destruction of the great war; true enough, but immediately prior to World War II, Spain emerged from its own horrible Civil War, in which more than a million Spaniards were killed, hundreds of thousands disabled, and millions in property destroyed.

I am not a trained economist, nor an economic optimist, nor would I call Professor Sufrin of Syracuse, who made the Spanish report for the Economic Co-operation Administration, an outstanding optimist. But the monumental report which was the fruit of his work and that of his many associates has this to say of the Spanish economy in its first two summary paragraphs:

The National Product of Spain, in gross or per capita terms, is low because of the scanty natural resources of the nation and the paucity of its investment fund in relation to its population. However, the National Product of Spain may be raised appreciably by small injections of investment and technical assistance because of the general under-utilization of Spanish resources, natural and industrial. This is not to say that Spain's per capita national income can be made to approach that of France or even that of Italy. It is to say that Spain's per capita income can be raised by as much as 6% to 8% per year for at least two or three years with moderate outside assistance. Since there is somewhat more than a small inflation in Spain, industry has no lack of pesetas; the lack is in foreign exchange.

The population problem of Spain is a pressing one. The 28 million inhabitants of Spain require more food, shelter, and clothing than they presently get, but more important, the population growth of about 3,000 per week can only be supported by an increase in national income. If the national income grows only equally with the population, Spain will continue as an unstable or at least potentially unstable area, from the political and social viewpoint. With the rest of the Western World bettering its per capita income position, *any* Government of Spain must face the challenge. Furthermore, not only must jobs be found for the younger generation, but a chance for advancement and for social recognition must be secured. For better or worse, we are living in an era in which social circulation is increasing its tempo. From the long-range point of view, Spain cannot continue as a stable State unless it, too, provides opportunities for its people. In spite of censorship, the press, radio, motion pictures, and the limited foreign travel and tourism, Spain is not sealed from the rest of the world. The changes in the Western World will affect Spain regardless of the official philosophy of the Regime.

During my year in Spain, talking with innumerable Congressmen, itinerant writers, and plain American tourists, I preached unceasingly the wisdom of American military and economic aid to Spain, and perhaps used too much effort in glossing over its faults in order better to paint its virtues. I have perhaps done this again in this chapter. But I have already pointed out that I firmly believe that, at the present moment in the world's crisis, most American aid to other countries should be given almost solely for the purpose of directly or indirectly aiding and protecting the United States now or in the future.

It seems to me to be the essence of stupidity from the point of view of statecraft to permit England and France, hereditary enemies of Spain, to dictate a foreign or military policy which leaves the great manpower of the Iberian bastion unaided, unequipped and untrained. Are we so proud that we are not willing to permit the fighting Communist-haters of Spain to lay down their lives to protect us against Russian aggression? Are we so stupid as to leave a broken link in the chain of defense around Russia to the West? Are we so filled with prejudice against Franco and dictatorship that we are going to make our statecraft and our military philosophy one of prejudice and not of intelligence? With the example of aid to Tito in mind, this can hardly be the case, and I do not believe it will be.

From an economic point of view, aid to Spain is the greatest bargain in Europe today; costs of labor and materials throughout the country may at present run approximately one third of similar costs in England, France, and the United States. Even with the probably inflationary results of the presence of American troops and technicians in Spain, the military studies have indicated that the cost would still be about fifty per cent of that of other nations. So far as its ancient and honorable pride will permit, Spain holds out the hand of friendship and hope to the United States. We cannot afford to disregard it.

The autumn social season began, and once again the happy hermit lot of an American ambassador was clear—every American visiting abroad usually expects to be entertained at, or at the least invited to, a cocktail party at the Embassy. The American tourist in 1951 was beginning to realize something of the beauties of Spain, as the French had long since realized its opportunities in low prices. It may be that I did no great service to the Spaniards in later arranging with them to discontinue requiring visas for the entrance of American tourists, for now a good hotel reservation in Spain during the winter season, and particularly during Semana Santa and the Feria in Seville, is worth a king's ransom. With the aid of flamenco dancers and diplomatic scotch we were able each week to run through three or four hundred VIP American visitors with their corresponding Spanish local counterparts in the Embassy.

I had long since moved from Ramon de la Cruz on account of its small size, and with the Dukes had rented the ancestral palace of a Spanish prince, filled with masterpieces of Velasquez and other Spanish artists. It also had a beautiful garden. Unfortunately, I did not remain long enough to see the completion of the great new Embassy and office building now rising on the Castellana, but I did have the happy opportunity of supervising its plans; for the first time in American diplomatic housing, so far as I know, an Embassy will be divided into two separate entities: one for the ambassador's public life, his dinners and entertainments; and one for his private life. This residence will adjoin a massive office building of eight stories, a motion-picture theatre, and a general office housing all the staff, including the military attachés with their respective organizations, the consulate division; and the other Embassy departments which are now scattered all over Madrid.

One of my most pleasant and successful jobs about this time was the development of a campaign for the construction of a modern British-American hospital in Madrid, to replace the shabby and outworn apartment that had been used as a makeshift five-bed nursing home for so long. Joining with the British, we beat the bushes for contributions of every kind, British, American, and Spanish. Through the kindness of the Allied Reparation Commission, we obtained as a gift the broken-down property of the old German Hospital, which had passed into Allied hands at the close of the war. Before we could negotiate its sale, the Spanish Government gave us the assistance of promising its direct purchase. The Ministry of Education, which is charged with the administration of University City, offered us a long leasehold upon a plot very close to the medical college, which we accepted with great pleasure. All American companies operating in Spain, as indeed the British companies, were importuned for contributions, and I laughingly called these requests a sort of high-grade blackmail when they were addressed to my business friends in the States. Tourists were sand-bagged for contributions, and thousands of letters sent to other Americans, British, and Spaniards brought great results, surprising results I may say from our Spanish friends. As I write this chapter plans for the hospital are being drawn with a building fund of close to eight million pesetas.

As the winter came and I realized that all of the preliminary job in Madrid that I had been sent to do was accomplished, or nearing fruition with the shortly expected arrivals of new and instructed military and economic missions, I flew to Paris to pay my respects to Secretary Acheson. I wanted to urge speed in aid to Spain and to tell him that I felt that the first phase of the new Spanish rapprochement was over and I should step out, particularly since I was approaching my sixty-fifth birthday, a date on which I had for many years planned to retire definitely and finally. As the weeks wore on I heard nothing from the Secretary regarding a replacement, and just before Christmas I wrote directly to the President as follows:

AMERICAN EMBASSY
*Madrid, Spain, December 17, 1951*

*Dear Mr. President:*

The beginning of the New Year will, I hope, mark three milestones in my life: First, the end of ten years of almost uninterrupted service in government; second, my near approach to my sixty-fifth birthday; and third, if you will permit, my retirement as United States Ambassador to Spain.

It is difficult to end my long and happy connection with the Department of State under two great friends and distinguished secretaries: General Marshall and Dean Acheson, and, I must add, with countless other faithful and unselfish servants of the Department. It is impossible to feel that I am severing connections with you.

You have honored me with four important ambassadorial posts, i.e., Poland, Egypt, Argentina, and finally, Spain. You have given me every possible aid, comfort, and co-operation. You have and will have always my deep admiration and respect, and my great personal affection. Yet, after ten years in government, the call back to private life is very strong, and I have much to do in the years to come.

This letter, therefore, signifies my resignation as your Ambassador to Spain to take effect at your earliest convenience.

It closes with the old Spanish expression "Dios guarde a V. E. muchos años"—"May God keep Your Excellency many years."

*Sincerely yours,*

STANTON GRIFFIS

*The President*
*The White House*
*Washington, D. C.*

The President and the Secretary, busy with many world matters, did not get around to acknowledging the letter or permitting my resignation for some weeks; but rumors spread in Madrid, and when the letter was finally published I found that in the Spanish mind my use of the expression which terminates so many important Spanish communications, *Dios guarde a V. E. muchos años*, was a diplomatic ten-strike, and the sentimental Spanish took me closer to their hearts on account of it.

It was an astonishing coincidence that the Paris post, which I had so often wanted and hoped for, suddenly became available about this time through the transfer of Ambassador Bruce to Washington to become Under-Secretary of State. However, diplomatic posts of any sort tempted me no longer; I had firmly made my decision and I stuck to it.

During the weeks previous to my resignation, I had kept the Spanish Foreign Office fully informed of my plans, and when the announcement of the resignation was received they understood my motives perfectly. Yet they were extremely kindly in their regrets, and, astonishing as it may seem, I received several hundred letters from unknown Spaniards thanking me for my efforts to draw the United States and Spain closer together, and for my attempts to understand the Spanish scene.

At a farewell meeting with Franco, we reviewed all of the efforts and results of the past year, and mutually hoped that the incoming commissions would tie our two countries more closely together. The Caudillo told me that the Spanish had gone to great lengths to find a decoration for me which would be outstanding; that I would be awarded the Knight of the Cross of Charles III, and would be the fourth American to receive it and the only one since 1918 and the days of Alfonso. Needless to say, I was extremely flattered, and felt that I looked extremely decorated and decorative when the evening before my departure the Foreign Minister gave a tremendous dinner in my honor and I was able unofficially to wear the great Cross.

Perhaps it is not generally known that active American ambassadors are not permitted to receive orders of foreign governments, and I could only technically and temporarily receive this order until like MacArthur's old soldiers I just faded away. The regulation which I have described is certainly not without merit, and I have no regrets that even a long-time American ambassador may look nude as compared with his military attachés who are ablaze with stars, crosses, and medals. I have no regrets either that an American ambassador appearing at foreign courts and entertainments of the Diplomatic Corps looks like a female pheasant in the midst of a gathering of highly feathered males, for his associates wear every decoration, plume, cross, and gold and silver decoration that the sartorial artists of the world can design.

In any event I was never awarded that famous decoration that a potentate of a Near East State is reported to have given to a prim and New Englandish spinster social worker in his country. In all seriousness and with deep respect for her work in his country he awarded her his government's decoration, the Order of Chastity—second class.

Anxious to obtain a decision on my final return to private life, I made repeated telephone calls to Carl Humelsine, who finally brought me the news that the President would release me and that my successor would be a fine career diplomat, Lincoln MacVeagh, then ambassador to Portugal. Following my rolling-stone impulses I was anxious to call it a day. The amenities of necessary large farewell receptions and diplomatic calls were completed, and again I booked passage on the *Independence*, this time from Gibraltar, and on February 4, 1952, I was New York bound.

## CHAPTER FIFTEEN

### RETROSPECT

As I left Madrid I received news that the January snows had made the mountain roads north of Málaga impassable and that I would have to change my automobile route to Gibraltar and go by way of Seville and Algeciras. The cavalcade of cars was at the door of the residence that I had occupied at Lista 14. My secretary had brought me the last official mail, and I took a ceremonial cup of coffee with the various members of the Embassy staff who had come to bid me farewell. In the first and last cars of the procession were the stalwart guards of the Spanish Government and the city of Madrid who had looked after my welfare for many weeks, and in my galloping Ford was my faithful Swedish valet and friend, Hallin, who after many years of life abroad was overjoyed at the prospect of returning to his family in the States. With him was my almost human guard Mustapha, the police dog presented to me by the Spanish Army Dog Corps, who had guarded me well for months. He speaks English now and guards the beautiful estate of Margaret Emerson in Brookville, Long Island.

Again, as through my entire year in Madrid, the air was filled with rumors of planned attacks against my life by Communists and other violent anti-Francoists. A few days earlier I had traveled to Valencia to visit the great American fleet, and the Spanish Government had honored me by placing a soldier every kilometer on the hillsides and in the fields from Madrid to Valencia, a distance of almost two huudred and fifty miles. My right arm had become weary with saluting, and I hoped that this regal performance was over. However, as I left my residence I received news that I was again to be guarded per kilometer all the way to the Mediterranean, but my vanity wilted when Louis Nevin, the Madrid correspondent of the Associated Press, said to me, "Don't be too exhilarated about this, they did the same thing for the German ambassador during the war."

So we were off. I was going home at last, no work in sight, no headwaiters in every capital of Europe calling me "Your Excellency," and no more "Mr. Ambassador." The prospect was Elysian; I was unquestionably getting lazy in my late years, and for a good many weeks a song that Irving Berlin wrote almost thirty years ago had been running through my brain:

> *Lazy—I want to be lazy*
> *I long to be out in the sun*
> *with no work to be done*
> *under that awning*
> *they call the sky*
> *stretching and yawning*
> *and let the world go drifting by,*
> *I "wanna" peep*
> *through the deep tangled wild wood*
> *counting sheep 'til I sleep*
> *like a child would*
> *with a great big valise full of books*
> *to read where it's peaceful*
> *while I'm killing time*
> *being lazy.**

At last I was headed toward the peace of the deep-tangled wild wood, with a great big valise full of books. I planned to find a place in which to build a cottage—a place so exquisite

*Used by permission of Irving Berlin Music Corporation. Copyright 1924 Irving Berlin. Copyright renewed.

that as Bing Crosby once said, "Rand wouldn't even tell Mc-Nally about it."

We passed the thousands of saluting guards on the red earth roads to Seville and reached Algeciras, where we spent a bitter cold night, huddled around a root fire in a tiny hotel. On the next day, for the first time in my life, I was on The Rock, that fortress made famous by the Prudential Insurance Company, and which has perpetuated the age-old bitterness between England and Spain. The Governor kindly showed us around the great labyrinth of fortifications, the lairs of the carefully nurtured Barbary apes, whose history carries with it the prediction that when the apes die out the great fortress will fall. We saw the little beach where the body of Nelson had been brought ashore after the great battle at near-by Trafalgar, and we bought British woolens and French perfumes at supposedly bargain prices. With the slow Mediterranean dawn, the great ship rounded the point of a rock, the tender picked us up, the amenities of good-by were concluded, the engines turned—and I was going home. As the Spanish Coast faded in the distance, I knew only that I had left there a great happiness and affection; but no tiny regret at anything that I had done, even to the decision of leaving those shores for my own native land.

As I sat in my deck chair, reading against the light, which is always somehow peculiarly uncomfortable on ocean liners, I distressed myself not at all, either at the dictum of many doctors that all active men should be chloroformed at the age of sixty-five, or at the pronouncements of many others that no active spirit should retire at that or any other age, lest indeed through change of habit and very inertia itself his physical functions will rapidly disintegrate and he will be shortly gathered to his fathers. I think perhaps that the first dictum is probably more reasonable than the second, but I remembered the philosophy of my father who did not die, but whose body without pain or suffering simply released his great soul to its maker at the age of eighty-five, and who frequently told me that the happiest days of his life were after seventy.

I used to think that he was just whistling himself past birthdays, old age, and the cemetery, but now I am sure that he was deeply honest in his pronouncement. Writing, thinking, and studying, he always found plenty to do in his later years, and I am sure that I shall. The kaleidoscope of life around me was never more fascinating. There are a million things to do. There are a few friends and thousands of acquaintances. There are the fascinating sounds and smells of New York City and the fragrant hills of Connecticut. There is the constant rattle of that instrument of my favorite vice, the ticker, and every morning a new world-wide crisis for breakfast. There is the soul-stirring strike of a big fish as he hits your lure, and the scented waters and beaches of the tropics as they caress your body. There is always, one hopes, a roof over one's head, three meals a day, and an occasional drink. No man can have much more, except perhaps the gentleness of a woman. There was indeed this book, which had to be written. In one of his recent tomes, Morris Ernst, who crowds a hundred hours into a day, profitably battling for lost causes or running errands for Presidents, said, "No man can write an honest biography." God forbid that this volume of reminiscences might be called a biography, but believe it or not, whatever it is I have tried to make it honest. I have tried to tell the bad as well as the good, at least to the extent that it can be issued by a respectable publisher, and I hope it proves that the good God has given me the ability to laugh at myself. He knows that I have, many times, and will continue to do so. Probably indeed, I have laughed in this book not only at myself but too much at many other things that men might conceivably hold sacred. Certainly I have laughed at Communists, at kings and at dictators, and at all their works, for I believe that without laughter and without song man will perish from this earth. No one knows better than I, a bookseller, that there are plenty of serious books, and plenty of silly ones, too, and in our day and age there are far too many books written with pens dipped in mud and sewage. One can do no more than make a try at both life and writing, and from my childhood favorite, the *Rubáiyát,* I recall the quatrain:

> *The Moving Finger writes; and, having writ,*
> *Moves on: nor all your Piety nor Wit*
> *Shall lure it back to cancel half a Line.*

Of my life the moving finger has pretty well writ, and I can truthfully say that there are even very few half-lines that I would cancel, though I must confess that I would like to do it all over again.

My publishers, following a habit that must have originated with the publishers of the Gutenberg Bible, have inserted in my contract (in the usual small print, which my magnifying glass detected), a provision that they shall have an option on my next book, a cautious desire which in my mind represents the primeval spirit of American optimism.

It brings to my mind a story that was current at about the time of the financially ill-fated World's Fair in 1940, when Billy Rose was the entrepreneur of the Aquacade at Flushing Meadows. As the story goes he was approached by a somewhat seedy-looking individual who told the maestro that he was the creator of a peculiarly interesting vaudeville act, and would like to join Billy's troupe. When Rose asked him what the act was, he said that his specialty was jumping from a hundred-foot platform into a barrel of sand. The proposition deeply impressed Rose, who proceeded to prepare the necessary platform and to pour out the barrel of sand on the concrete edge of the swimming pool. The artist jumped, landed with some grace and agility in the sand, and approached Rose for further negotiations. "That's great," said Rose, "I'll give you five hundred dollars a week to do that for me twice a day." The man said, "No." Rose went to seven hundred and fifty dollars, and finally to a thousand dollars a week, with stern refusals by the seedy one. "This is ridiculous," said Rose. "You look to me as though you hadn't eaten a square meal for weeks, you simply can't afford to turn down an offer like this. It's absurd. What's wrong?" The answer from the seedy one was elemental. "I'll tell you, Mr. Rose, I never tried that before and I don't like it."

The vaudeville gentleman felt the same way about a second try. With all my laughter, with all my cynicism at the passing show, and with all my sardonic attitudes toward politicians the world over and particularly in the United States, may I finish on a serious note, with a credo in which I profoundly believe.

I have walked the earth in many countries, I have been part of many great business developments and a Jack-of-all-trades in a busy life, but I have seen enough of the world at large to compare, at least in my own terms, America's ideals with those of the rest of the world. I am proud of our democracy and freedoms, which are a beacon light in a filthy and unhappy world. And I am proud of our scientists and of our great industrial development. But God himself gave us our great national resources and perhaps from them, from our earth itself, has sprung the freedom of development that in itself created our love of freedom. I am proud of our contributions during the last two great world wars, of aid and comfort and of countless young American lives, to keep the world from a return to the dark ages. Yet perhaps that was really the emanation of our deep-rooted desire to protect not so much Europe's but our own hearth and fireside, and when the chips are counted one finds that our contribution to civilization was pretty small compared with that of the rest of the world. I am proud of the fact that there are bacon and eggs for breakfast in almost every American home, that there are two chickens in every pot and a Ford in every garage. I am proud that there is a radio in almost every home and there will shortly be a television machine to shrink distance even farther. I am proud of our great educational institutions and of our hospitals, of our social security, and the government's care of those men who risked their lives in our defense, and of our fantastic national prosperity.

I have watched all of these qualities reflected in the pleas of thousands of men, women, and children in the countries to which I was accredited, urging me to fashion a magic carpet that would carry them to our United States and away from the tyranny and hunger of their homes.

I am proud of our churches, our faith, our optimism, and our far-flung farm production, which feeds the world. I am proud of almost every aspect of this country, but deeply fearful of the responsibilities which they entail. I am proud of the freedom of our press, the right of every man to walk with his God in his own way; freedom of speech and assembly, and the freedom of individual action of any sort so long as the puritan principle of keeping the peace is maintained.

But I am most deeply proud that this beloved nation of ours has bred and is breeding a race of men who through opportunity or accident of birth, through genius, tortuous labor, ability or just plain timing, gain fortunes from the cornucopia of American opportunity but know that it is their responsibility to return to the nation a large part of what they have accumulated. I am proud to be part of a nation that can produce the Rockefeller family, who through three generations have set the world an example of philanthropy and service. Yet they are but one of many families and individuals who are so inclined. A nation that can inspire such a philosophy and turn toward the public welfare the fortunes of such men as Carnegie, the Fords, Alfred Sloane, Harkness, Paine, Lasker, and innumerable men of lesser fortune must remain always a great nation. I wish that I could say that I had seen some sign of this philosophy in other countries, but I cannot. I wish that I could seriously hope that Communistic peoples might understand America's tradition of devoting its great wealth to education, medical research, and the betterment of all our brother nations. But this millennium is far in the future. No human mind can grasp the possibilities of the Utopia that would evolve if all men realized that there is never any victory in war, no happiness in hate, no heaven except in a peaceful world.

Dear God, I am glad to be home. I guess I feel a bit like Cardinal Wolsey in Shakespeare's *Henry VIII—*

> *An old man, broken with the storms of state,*
> *Is come to lay his weary bones among ye;*
> *Give him a little earth for charity!*